STAYING ALIVE

THE DISCO INFERNO
OF THE BEE GEES
SIMON SPENCE

TO THE BARNSLEY BOYS CLUB

STAYING ALIVE
THE DISCO INFERNO
OF THE BEE GEES
SIMON SPENCE

A JAWBONE BOOK
FIRST EDITION 2017
PUBLISHED IN THE
UK AND THE USA BY
JAWBONE PRESS
3.1D UNION COURT
20–22 UNION ROAD
LONDON SW4 6JP
ENGLAND
WWW.JAWBONEPRESS.COM

ISBN 978-1-911036-27-2

EDITOR TOM SEABROOK
JACKET DESIGN MARK CASE

PRINTED IN THE CZECH REPUBLIC BY PBTISK

1 2 3 4 5 21 20 19 18 17

WITHDRAWN

CONTENTS

BARRY GIBB
WE'D LIKE TO DRESS 'STAYIN' ALIVE'
UP IN A WHITE SUIT AND GOLD CHAINS
AND SET IT ON FIRE.

ROBERT STIGWOOD
THERE'S NEVER BEEN
A MORE PERFECT MARRIAGE
OF MOVIE AND MUSIC.

PROLOGUE
NIK COHN

NIK COHN
FROM THE START I JUST FELT THAT
DISCO WAS THE MOST EXCITING
DEVELOPMENT IN 70S POP MUSIC.

BARRY GIBB TO NIK COHN
IT'S ALL YOUR BLOODY
FAULT, ISN'T IT?

He did not want to talk about it 'just now'. And he did not want his famous June 1976 magazine article reproduced here, as a prologue to this book. The 'project', Nik Cohn said, was not for him. He recalled our former meetings and said he had enjoyed them, but felt 'the subject' had long since been 'flogged to death—certainly for myself'.

The *New York Times* dubbed Cohn's celebrated article 'the monster', and all 8,500 words of it can be read on a number of free-to-access websites, not least the electronic version of *New York* magazine, where it was originally published as a cover feature under the title 'Tribal Rites Of The New Saturday Night'. Look hard enough on the internet and you can find a facsimile of the actual magazine, reproduced page by page. The sophisticated layout and the vivid James McMullan paintings that accompany Cohn's text are a reminder of the American magazine's then pre-eminent position among its rivals with a reputation as a high-class, cutting-edge cultural beacon. McMullan's paintings of disco club action take up five pages of the fourteen given over to the story, including the entire cover, and look much like a primitive storyboard for the movie that developed out of the article. Cohn's story, sold as a reportage piece ostensibly about disco culture but tightly focused on the lives of a gang of unknown teenage characters and one particular nightclub in a run-down Italian American neighbourhood of New York, Brooklyn, was, of course, the spark for the film *Saturday Night Fever*, the movie that sent The Bee Gees, John Travolta, impresario Robert Stigwood, and, indeed, Cohn himself into the stratosphere.

Cohn told me he still owned the rights to the article. He had written it when he was just thirty.

Forty years on, despite him having several best-selling books to his name, it remains his most famous work. 'In America I have always, and will always be, the guy that did *Saturday Night Fever*,' he said in 2013. 'I'll always be known for that.' The rest of his work, Cohn added, was not even 'a wart on the fanny of *Saturday Night Fever*'.

Although the movie was celebrated for its authentic representation of the period and the working-class youth culture on which it was based, for Cohn, an Irish man who had spent the best part of the past decade around Soho in London, the night-time rituals of backwater Brooklyn were something of a mystery. He had, in fact, only been resident in New York a few months when he wrote the article. In that time he'd rarely left Manhattan, the trendy centre of the city where *New York* magazine was based. 'Brooklyn was a foreign country to most *New York* magazine editors,' Cohn said.

Cohn had arrived in America with a reputation as one of the UK's best, most precocious and perceptive writers on pop culture. And anyone who had followed his work closely would have recognised in 'Tribal Rites Of The New Saturday Night' some of his familiar tropes: the overheated style of the narrative, the almost fantastical character traits of its key characters, and, above all, his breakneck commitment to the subject. They would also have wondered—considering he was by then author of a handful of hyperbolic novels that revelled in exaggerating aspects of pop culture, such as *I Am Still The Greatest Says Johnny Angelo* and *Arfur Teenage Pinball Queen*—how much in the article was real and how much Cohn had imagined to complete his beautifully sculpted mini opera of blue-collar disco life.

Cohn, however, was not widely known for his fiction, even less so in America. His cultural cache was attached to his journalism, his role in creating the idea for *Tommy* and 'Pinball Wizard' for The Who, and two celebrated music books. The first, about 50s and 60s pop and rock'n'roll icons, *Awopbopaloobop Alopbamboom*, was published in 1969. It had been ahead of its time in appraising and venerating the culture of pop and rock music and its associated acts, and it had done so in a blur of attitude with prose as fast-paced and overblown, raw and alive, as the records it described. Even now, *Awopbopaloobop Alopbamboom* is still considered one of the greatest music books ever written, regularly featuring in Top 10 lists, often at #1.

It was this book, above all, that had established Cohn as the Elvis Presley of British music journalism, a real pioneer and a heavyweight, seminal, almost mythical figure. *Awopbopaloobop* was infamously written in a Kerouac-style stream of thought, fuelled by drink and drugs, loud music and demons, in just a few weeks. Throughout much of the 60s Cohn had been untouchable in his field, his journalism never far from controversy. In 1968, for instance, he'd famously savaged The

Beatles' *White Album* in the *New York Times*, calling it 'boring almost beyond belief'.

All along, his chief concern was with weaving his own self into pop mythology. He was obsessive about it, and he created for himself a brilliant image. 'For a while, back in the 60s, he was "the kid of the moment", to use a Lillian Hellman Phrase,' writes the author Gordon Burn. Cohn was a rebel, snotty and cocksure, an upstart in the literary world and a youthful irritant in the world of newspapers and magazines. He was part of the new pop aristocracy, one of the in-crowd in London's swinging set, among those profiled, alongside figures such as Mary Quant, Twiggy, and David Bailey, in Jonathan Aitken's notorious 1967 *Young Meteors* book. The *Observer*, for which Cohn wrote regularly, described him as a 'wise guy, whizz-kid, hustler'.

Looking back, for a 2011 newspaper profile, Cohn was wonderfully self-coruscating, describing his younger self as more of an 'insufferable, arrogant little twit'. Under close scrutiny, the image fell apart. His background was bourgeois, privileged, and he'd been privately educated. His father was the historian Norman Cohn, author of cult classic *The Pursuit Of The Millennium*, and his mother was a Russian writer who had been part of the Dadaist art scene.

'I have always been fascinated by the self-inventors,' he told me when I interviewed him in the late 90s for *Stoned* and *2Stoned*, Andrew Loog Oldham's two volumes of autobiography. It was easy to see why. Cohn had a tremendous admiration for the outrageous teenage Rolling Stones manager Loog Oldham, but of all the 60s bands he was most closely associated with The Who, particularly their managers, Chris Stamp and Kit Lambert. 'I never hung out that much with the bands,' he told me. 'I found the managers to be more interesting because they were more articulate.'

Inexplicably, during the 60s, Cohn, also developed a deep-seated, long-lasting admiration for self-aggrandising American solo singer P.J. Proby, best recalled for his trouser-splitting outrages onstage. It was Proby that provided the inspiration for *I Am Still The Greatest Says Johnny Angelo*, Cohn's second novel, published in 1967 when he was just twenty-one. In it, in a sign of things to come, the line between fact and fiction is outrageously smeared. The book, which details the rise and fall of a mythic rock star transmogrified into a cult type religious leader, is best recalled for part-stimulating David Bowie to create his Ziggy Stardust character.

Cohn's long-forgotten first novel, *Market*, a collection of vignettes about street-market characters, published in 1965, had led to him being compared to the French literary giant Emile Zola, famed for his naturalist portraits of working-class life. By the 70s, he was more often being compared to Tom Wolfe, the acclaimed author and leader of America's popular New Journalism movement, which mixed literary techniques with first-hand reporting. Until Cohn, Wolfe's journalism, articles such as 'Radical Chic: That Party At Lenny's' had been the most famous work published by *New York* magazine. Cohn, however, said he hated Wolfe.

The comparisons flattered Cohn. By the time he got to New York, in 1975, his halcyon days were behind him. His 1971 follow-up to *Awopbopaloobop Alopbamboom*, a book about men's fashion movements in London entitled *Today There Are No Gentlemen*, only intermittently hit the mark and was not widely read. He had said all he could on pop, and he was feeling for a way out of music writing. For a period he had actually semi-retired to a farm in Hertfordshire to breed pigs. He was bored particularly with the 70s drift into heavy, progressive, album-orientated, rock. The 'teen dream pop' he had eulogised was dead.

'Pop went out of fashion in the 70s,' he told me. 'It was sneered at, so all the thumps and the crashes and the crescendos and the sudden diminuendos, all the sort of soap-operatic drama that a great pop record had became very much out of fashion.'

Cohn was also taking drugs. He'd started in London, a thin boy just out of his teens in the mid 60s, and an advocate for the use of cocaine. He told The Who's Pete Townshend it was the best drug that there had ever been. 'The only trouble is that it doesn't work for very long,' Townshend recalled Cohn telling him. 'He said for about a year you are going to be as good as you're ever going be,' Townshend told me. 'This was when he was only eighteen. He said, The terrible thing is that you realise from thereon it's never gonna work in quite the same way again and that you're in permanent decline from there on in.'

Townshend much admired Cohn, called him dynamic and fantastic—and for good reason. He had directly inspired Townshend to write one of The Who's biggest hits, 'Pinball Wizard'. The 1969 hit single was the centrepiece of The Who's best-selling rock opera double album of the same year, *Tommy*, which told the story of a boy rendered deaf, dumb, and blind who, after a number of livid experiences, becomes a sort of spiritual leader. Townshend had played a rough mix of the album to Cohn, who told Townshend that it was 'great' and 'a considerable achievement' but 'a bit boring'.

'Does it have to be about this God stuff?' Cohn asked Townshend. 'It's all so passé.'

'This is long before the God stuff became passé,' Townshend said.

The pair had recently been hanging out playing pinball with the teenage girl Cohn would use as the inspiration for the principle character in his 1973 novel *Arfur*, a young pinball queen lost in an *Alice In Wonderland*-type stew of bizarre characters. Cohn had become obsessed with pinball and found it analogous to pop. He often wrote about the pop characters he admired 'shooting' fat or clean lines. Townshend felt Cohn might be teasing him about the boring 'God stuff', and teased back, 'What about instead of him become a spiritual leader, a sort of pseudo rock star thing, what about if he was a pinball champion?'

'Now that would be interesting,' Cohn said.

So Townshend went away and wrote 'Pinball Wizard' (chorus: 'That deaf, dumb, and blind kid sure plays a mean pinball!') for *Tommy*, and then he wrote pinball back into the lyrics of a couple of other songs on the album to smooth out the story. It all added to the Cohn legend, and fortuitously for him, when he touched down in New York, *Tommy* was once again big news thanks to an acclaimed film version of the album, also called *Tommy*. Released in March 1975, the film was produced by Bee Gees manager Robert Stigwood and starred Roger Daltrey as Tommy (who attains spiritual enlightenment through pinball) with supporting roles for Oliver Reed, Jack Nicholson, Ann-Margret, and Elton John, among many others. Townshend had been nominated for an Oscar for the film's soundtrack, which outsold the original album, peaking at #2 in America and the UK. Cohn glowed.

On the page, however, he found he had withered. There were, of course, hot flushes of brilliance, but his clarity of thought had deserted him. His proclamations on pop began to seem foppishly irrelevant— for instance, he still maintained, as he'd once told an incredulous Townshend, that moody 50s solo Brit pop star Billy Fury was far superior to The Beatles. Cohn's sharpness had given way to a sense of befuddlement and ennui. He seemed lost. Drug use was part if it, but he had been careless in his estimations of the changes in the music industry and lazy with engaging in new scenes. As he saw it, in the new rock landscape, only accountants and cold businessmen thrived. They had driven out the outlaws and crazed wild men, the 'inspired lunatics', he most admired. Gone was the 'guts, and flash, and energy, and speed' he loved. The music business, he felt, was now 'just another industry, a matter of churning out product'.

At *New York* magazine, Cohn was billed as a Contributing Editor, tasked chiefly to write a rock column, but approaching his thirtieth birthday, he was hoping he might break into writing screenplays for films. His latest novel, the confused and convoluted *King Death*, had stiffed. In it, Cohn imagined Elvis's (real) stillborn twin brother surviving to become an assassin talent-spotted by an English impresario who organises for the assassinations to be played out on TV, making the hit man an unlikely superstar. In essence, it was another riff on Cohn's old routine—pop as religion, blind audience adulation, fake idols—except, for Cohn now, killing superseded the hit record as the ultimate in pop. He thought it was his best work at the time, but would later admit it was his worst.

There was little to suggest Cohn was about to write the magazine piece that would make his fortune. Not even the release of a second acclaimed music book, *Rock Dreams*, a lush coffee-table effort published in 1974. Although Cohn is credited as its author, the book is dominated by the photorealistic paintings of Belgian artist Guy Peellaert, whose work famously appears on album covers such as Bowie's *Diamond Dogs* and film posters such as *Taxi Driver*. The book, sold as 'rock'n'roll for your eyes', was Peellaert's visual interpretation of *Awopbopaloobop Alopbamboom*, but his colourful paintings took the pop imagery further. Peellaert's work for the book—for instance, the Stones in Nazi uniforms, partying with naked prepubescent girls, and later dressed in ladies' shiny rubber S&M wear and silk stockings and suspenders— caused a sensation and helped the book become a hit. Cohn's name was on the cover, but his written contributions were limited to short surreal bursts of text.

This was the man, then, frayed and a little unhinged, who was about to change the course of musical and celluloid history, without whom it's possible that disco would just be a dimly remembered fad.

Certainly, without Cohn there would be no Bee Gees megahits, no John Travolta superstardom, no Robert Stigwood multimillions ... and so no nostalgic polyester parties for decades ever after. Barry Gibb reportedly once said to Cohn, 'It's all your bloody fault, isn't it?'

•

By coming to New York, Cohn had hoped to connect with new youth cultures, but instead he floundered, out of touch. Then he found a man, a dancer, called Tu Sweet, and he grabbed hold. Tu Sweet, of course, wasn't his real name. His real name was Abdul Jami Allen and his father had been a jitterbug champion and an inspiration. Tu Sweet had been entranced by the moves, the loud music, and the lines of eager girls waiting to dance with his father. He started to dance himself as child in local 'shacks'—illegal clubs for blacks—down in Delaware. When his mother died, he told Cohn he'd moved to New York and spent time shining shoes. He also ran with street gangs and spent three years in prison for armed robbery, although there was also a rumour he'd killed the man who raped his sister. By the time Cohn met him, he had hit his mid-twenties, picked up his memorable nickname, and been transformed into one of the most popular dancing figures in the city, winning dance contests throughout the five boroughs. People went to see him dance on Saturday nights at disco clubs such as Leviticus and Othello.

Tu Sweet danced the bugalo, the merengue, and the funky Broadway, but he was best known as the king of the hustle, the era's most popular disco dance routine for couples. He was 'amazing, in a class of his own', Cohn said. The hustle was so popular there were myriad versions of it: the Spanish hustle, Latin hustle, New York hustle, and LA bus stop hustle, to name a few. It had a long history as a dance but had really exploded into a craze following the 1975 US #1 smash-hit disco classic

'The Hustle' by Van McCoy. It was a dance that would be made famous the world over when it featured in *Saturday Night Fever*.

This was Cohn's introduction to disco, a scene that had been happening underground in America since 1972 and had exploded into the mainstream with huge hit singles such as 'Rock The Boat' in 1973 and 'Kung Fu Fighting' and 'Rock Your Baby' in 1974. Now disco music was dominating the American charts and New York's nightlife. Cohn was a long way behind the curve. 'There'd been a hit record called "The Hustle" that suggested there was a club culture that wasn't being written up,' he said. 'I started going to clubs in Manhattan. I met this black dancer and he became my guide to the scene.'

Cohn first came across Tu Sweet when he attended a hustle dance contest in Rockland County, upstate New York. 'That was the first time I was really exposed to disco dancing,' he said, despite the fact that at the time there were popular disco dance shows on American TV such as Marty Angelo's 1975 series *Disco Step-By-Step*. The event was advertised as the 'Great American Dance Contest'; Cohn watched for hours as three hundred couples were cut down to just two, one of them led by Tu Sweet. Cohn said that ultimately Tu Sweet and his partner had to share the $1,000 first prize, even though they were clearly the best dancers. It was because Sweet was black that he had not won outright Cohn felt. A similar scene plays out in *Saturday Night Fever* but not Cohn's finished *New York* article.

The two men started to hang out together. Tu Sweet took Cohn to the Othello club in Manhattan, where he held court and they drank endless Grand Marnier-and-Cokes. Cohn wrote an article about Tu Sweet for *New York* magazine headlined 'Tu Sweet, No Sweat'. In it, Tu Sweet bragged of winning many dance contests, and of having a choice of twenty-one girls to dance with. 'They call me the black Fred Astaire, the Nureyev of the hustle,' he said. He also claimed to have worked up a whole new version of the hustle he called the 'Tu Sweet'. Cohn called him 'quite simply, the best street dancer that I'd ever seen'. But the article ended on a downbeat note: Tu Sweat was broke, his rent overdue, his best costumes in hock and his dance partner set to desert him. 'For all his talent and achievements, he owned nothing,' Cohn wrote.

It was only a one-page feature, black and white—no big deal to Cohn. He'd described Tu Sweet as floating on the dance floor, his style full of 'loops and dips, double takes, sudden freezes, ebbs and flows'. Cohn also parlayed a little light history of the hustle, as told to him by Tu Sweet, noting that it had 'started in the Barrio, then worked its way outwards to Brooklyn, Queens, the Bronx. Along the way it got simplified, cheapened and soon it was turned into hits records, great fortunes'.

For Tu Sweet the article was major publicity, pure validation. For Cohn it was the start of a connection to the present day. He found something in disco music he liked. It tended to be full of overwrought crescendos and soap opera dramatics, and it was all about the hit single, the pop sugar rush. Cohn also enjoyed going against the grain; music purists tended to look down their nose at disco as cheap and throwaway music, a beige version of R&B. The problem for Cohn was that disco had few clear charismatic, dream-inspiring superstars—certainly no one Cohn could really project anything on to.

So Cohn continued to follow Tu Sweet across the city, watching him competing in disco dance contests. 'He was dazzling,' Cohn recalled. They talked disco, and Tu Sweet gave Cohn a potted history of the music that started in gay black clubs, progressed to straight blacks and gay whites and from there to mass consumption, Latinos in the Bronx, West Indians on Staten Island and, ah, Italians in Brooklyn.

'With him we started going to gay clubs, watching the dancing there,' Cohn recalled, 'and he said, Well there are these Italian kids over in Brooklyn, you ought to take a look at them.'

Of the Italians, specifically, Tu Sweet told Cohn, 'Some of these guys have no lives, dancing's all they got.' Cohn loved the sound of this. For him, 'rock'n'roll attained its great power when have-nots went on the rampage'.

'Dancing's all they got,' Cohn repeated. 'To me it sounded like a rallying cry.' He sniffed a way in. Living to dance, dancing to escape. If disco didn't have any real stars to excite Cohn, could he make stars of the nobodies who found themselves on the dance floor?

Cohn's editor at *New York* magazine, Clay Felkner, was not impressed. He was not interested in disco, which he saw as a culturally worthless fad, even less in the people who went to dance to this music in the uncultured, blue-collar, run-down suburbs. It was not what *New York* was about. Cohn persisted, and Felkner grudgingly allowed him 'months' to 'study and absorb' the rise of a new generation of disco kids in the New York suburbs, 'specifically the young Italian men of Bay Ridge' in Brooklyn. Felkner was glad to have his misfiring British pop journalist out of the way. *New York* magazine, which Felkner co-owned, was enduring a period of tumultuous change, with Rupert Murdoch in the process of a hostile takeover of the publication that would force Felkner out of his seat as editor.

Felkner had founded *New York* in 1968 and pitched it as the younger, hipper, brasher version of the city's venerated *New Yorker* magazine. From the beginning it was a bastion of New Journalism, with high pedigree and soon-to-be-celebrated contributors. The magazine's standing grew rapidly, and it continues to maintain its position as America's best cultural periodical, selling in excess of 400,000 per issue and the winner of more National Magazine Awards than any other magazine in the country. And Cohn's disco cover story remains, and is likely to always be, the most famous article it has ever printed.

It began when Tu Sweet took Cohn to Bay Ridge on an icy

winter's night in late 1975. They were heading for a club called 2001 Odyssey, Brooklyn's hottest disco spot, which Tu Sweet had been to a few times before. He said he was accepted there even though he was black because of his smooth dance-floor moves. Cohn noted that, at the time, racial lines were always 'very strictly drawn', and there was 'no real egalitarianism about disco'. He said that at another club in Bay Ridge, Tu Sweet had started dancing with a girl and within fifteen seconds 'he was completely swarmed, knocked to the floor, kicked in the head, picked up bodily and flung out into the street'.

Tu Sweet was determined to show Cohn how the Italian boys danced at 2001 Odyssey. He had begun giving lessons, as a hustle instructor, at dance studio, and been impressed by their style.

'I remember the first night I ever saw the club,' said Cohn. 'It was the dead of winter. In those days, that whole area was a wasteland. There were automotive chop shops and nothing else except storage spaces with attack dogs. Finally, we see in the distance this small patch of red neon light. This was a biblically bitter night. And these guys were standing outside wearing those skin-tight disco shirts. One guy came over and leaned in the [car] window and threw up on my trousers. At which point I didn't think this was my night.'

A drunken brawl broke out and Cohn told the cab driver to head back to safety, to Manhattan. He did not even make it inside the club. One image of that fleeting trip stayed with him, however. He recalled a figure in flared crimson pants and tight black shirt, stood in the club's doorway, 'all grace and hunger'. Cohn said he built this figure up in his own mind as a star: 'All that passion and no place to let it loose but here, in this nowhere club, on this nothing dance floor, where no one would ever know,' he later wrote.

Cohn did eventually make it inside 2001 Odyssey. The manager of the club, Chuck Rusinak, recalled him looking 'out of place'—this 'squirrelly guy in a trench coat'—among the strutting, sexually charged young Italian men and women. 'It was a very different kind of disco dancing than in the 60s, with everyone sort of waggling themselves around and waving their arms in the air,' said Cohn. Here, the hustle was performed as more of a line dance than in a coupled fashion. 'As soon as "The Hustle" came on, everybody would line up and do pre-ordained steps,' Cohn said. 'The leader would sort of call out the claps ... the boys didn't face the girls, they faced forward in a military phalanx.'

Cohn had taken respected illustrator and artist James McMullan to the club. McMullan was a longstanding *New York* contributor who had helped define the graphic look of the magazine. His illustrations for the article would be key in persuading the underwhelmed Felkner to run the finished story.

The idea to use an artist rather than photographer to accompany Cohn's text seems to have been a reaction to the success of *Rock Dreams*. McMullan said he based his paintings on photographs he took in 2001 Odyssey but claimed fundamentally that he never met Cohn's protagonists as described in the finished article. 'I went to the club twice and moved around, taking my photos without interacting much with any of the patrons,' McMullan recalled. 'Nik took a different path through the crowds so we didn't exchange notes. I finished my paintings several weeks before Nik finished his story so I wasn't really reacting to how he saw the scene at the club.'

The most famous of the McMullan paintings was widely believed to be based on a photograph of eighteen-year-old Eugene Robinson, a $150-a-week grocery-delivery boy from Bay Ridge and a weekend disco king at 2001 Odyssey. Robinson would later claim his lifestyle was the inspiration for *Saturday Night Fever*, and when the film was released he would enjoy a brief moment in the spotlight, asked, for instance, to judge disco dancing contests at Caesars Palace in Las Vegas.

'Anybody who fancied himself as king of the disco for twenty miles around could say they told [his] story,' said Cohn, who would state in 2007 that Tu Sweet was the real inspiration behind the famed *New York* article. Tu Sweet always believed as much, and he initially flourished after *Saturday Night Fever* was released, landing a role on American TV's *Soap Factory*, the premiere disco show of the era. Tu Sweet was the only paid dancer on the weekly show. When the disco boom passed he could not shake his drug addictions, and they consumed him. Cohn heard Tu Sweet had died in prison. In fact, he is alive and well and now helps run a charity organisation in aid of the homeless in Atlanta.

The design director of *New York* magazine, Milton Glaser, was impressed by McMullan's paintings. 'Clay [Felkner] also came to see the work that day,' McMullan recalled. 'I suspect that because the art was all ready to go before Nik finished writing, it put some pressure on him to get it written. Had the paintings not already impressed Milton and Clay, I suppose it might have been easier to scuttle the whole project.' Felkner's doubts about the cultural worth of unknown Brooklyn disco kids never went away, but the feature was scheduled to run. Cohn admitted the 'pressure to produce the piece was great' and he faced an insolvable problem at the heart of it. He had failed to engage with any of the people he hoped to write about. Once inside 2001 Odyssey, he explained, he couldn't wait to get back out.

'I had a few conversations at the club and I couldn't get below the surface,' he said. 'I was out of my depth. It was completely a masculine-dominated world. Girls just kind of waited around this dance floor for male pleasures.' He found the noise levels deafening and the crush of sweaty bodies suffocating. Nor did he ever find the teen he had spotted in the club's entrance on his first visit. In fact, he would later admit that he 'didn't learn much' about the club or the Italian American kids and nothing about what disco or dancing meant to them. 'I made a lousy interviewer,' he wrote. 'I knew nothing about this world, and it showed. Quite literally, I didn't speak the language.'

So he faked it. Cohn, with typical brio, conjured up an elaborate story for the teen figure in the doorway. He went back to Bay Ridge in daylight and noted the major landmarks, went into shops, studied the people, the clothes, the gestures, the walks. He asked a fellow *New York* magazine employee, Mark Jacobson, who lived in Brooklyn, to drive him around the area. 'He wanted get a couple of street names,' said Jacobson. Then Cohn sat down and 'imagined how it would feel to burn up, all caged energies with no outlet but the dancefloor and the rituals of Saturday night'. He presented the story as fact. 'There was no excuse for it,' he later wrote. 'I knew the rules of magazine reporting, and I knew that I was breaking them. Bluntly put, I cheated.'

Cohn's title for the article was 'Another Saturday Night'. Felkner changed it to 'Tribal Rites Of The New Saturday Night'. On the magazine's contents page, the teens at the centre of the article were said to 'congregate at a disco club where, surrounded by awed, pliant girls, they surge across the dance floor like soldiers across a battlefield, churning out an endless array of dances in perfect form and formation'. The intro to the actual article, purportedly by Cohn but carrying the whiff of a circumspect Felkner, ran as follows:

Over the past few months, much of my time has been spent watching this new generation. Moving from neighborhood to neighborhood, from disco to disco, an explorer out of my depth, I have tried to learn the patterns, the old/new tribal rites. In the present article, I have focused on one club and one tight-knit group that seem to sum up the experience as a whole. Artist James McMullan also spent many hours observing this development, but his paintings, reproduced here, are less specific; although they deal with the same locations and group, they are generalized images of these Saturday night rituals. Everything described in this article is factual and was either witnessed by me or told to me directly by the people involved. Only the names of the main characters have been changed.

This intro seemed designed to cover the magazine from any claims of fraud, suggesting staff already suspected foul play. To those familiar with Cohn's work, the article does mostly seem to be a re-tread. It hums with ideals, action, imagery, and phrases he had used before to describe youth cultures, and the central character was a typical Cohn teen rebel: poor, doomed, trapped, tragic, obsessive, and imbued with a heroic dignity and beauty.

'It did seem like an amazingly dramatic story arc and the kind of "working-class" story he was already famous for,' said McMullan. It's hard now to believe how Cohn dared hope to pass off the audacious story as literal truth. 'It reads to me as obvious fiction, albeit based on observation and some knowledge of disco culture,' Cohn said. 'No way could it sneak past customs now. In the 60s and 70s, the line between fact and fiction was blurry. Many magazine writers used fictional techniques to tell supposedly factual stories … no end of liberties were taken. Few editors asked tough questions. For the most part it was a case of "don't ask, don't tell". "Tribal Rites" being fiction was never a great secret. I remember once, at the end of a long night, blurting out to a publisher that the story was made up. "You don't say," the publisher drawled. "And Liberace is gay."'

Cohn starts the article by attacking the 'smug' New York trendies in Manhattan and their devotion to the accepted youth-culture trendsetters in the nascent New York punk-rock movement—posing 'street punks', Cohn calls them. He declares their snobbish attitudes dreary and 'stuck in the 60s'. The real action, he argues, is to be found exactly where Manhattan trendies least expect it to be, in the looked-down-upon working-class New York's urban outer boroughs: 'Bronx-Brooklyn-Queens'. He goes further: anyone above twenty is 'dead' and the only life in the city is to be found in these woe-begotten boroughs, in kids aged 'sixteen to twenty' who are 'full of energy, urgency, hunger'. These kids, he writes, don't care about Bob Dylan or Ken Kesey (the focus of Tom Wolfe's acclaimed 1968 book about he hippie movement, *The Electric Kool-Aid Acid Test*) 'or any 60s hippie stuff'. They are not 'dropouts or revolutionaries'. They are, Cohn states, throwbacks to the simpler and more thrilling 50s, a time he describes as 'the golden age of Saturday Nights'. The 60s were 'fat with cash', but now times are tight again, like the 50s, full of attrition, continual pressure. 'So the new generation takes few risks,' he says. 'It goes through high school, obedient; graduates, looks for a job, saves and plans.' Then, once a week, on a Saturday night, 'they explode'.

The article's main character is eighteen-year-old Vincent, 'the very best dancer in Bay Ridge—the ultimate Face', with 'black hair, black eyes, olive skin', and 'teeth so white, so dazzling, that they always seemed fake'. He owns 'fourteen floral shirts, five suits, eight pairs of shoes, three overcoats'. The shirts are red, gold, pink, scarlet, and yellow. Vincent also owns the dance floor at 2001 Odyssey, 'the only club in Bay Ridge that matters'. People come to watch him dance. Cohn has Vincent doing the 'Bus Stop [Hustle]', the other dancers following his lead. Later, he mentions the 'Rope Hustle', performed with a partner, and the 'Odyssey Walk', the club's own style of mass hustle, for which the dancers form strict ranks. He also mentions a handful of current hip disco tracks, such as 'Baby Face' (a disco version of the twenties song by Wing & A Prayer Fife & Drum Corps), but only notes one hit act, Harold Melvin & The Blue Notes, who had recently played live at 2001 Odyssey.

Cohn traces Vincent's Saturday night ritual: how, to get himself sharp, he thinks about killing, about Al Pacino in *Scarface*, about guns and knives, imagining himself as the star of his own movie. In real life he works selling paint in a DIY shop. He can see no escape from the grind of the job. 'They've got me by the balls,' Cohn has Vincent saying. He is troubled about getting old, about 'turning twenty', Cohn writes, and about losing his position as the 'ace face' at the club. He talks vaguely of wanting to be star, of rising above the 'vast faceless blob'.

Cohn sprinkles in a little family background, too. Vincent is 'third-generation Brooklyn Italian', lives in a slum, a high-rise near the subway tracks, and, of course, like any good Italian boy, he loves his mother. His father, who beat him as a child, is in jail, and his three brothers are dead, crippled and 'lost' in Manhattan. Only Vincent stays home—home being just three rooms—to take care of his mother and two sisters. Saintly. This bedevilling backdrop is straight out of *Arfur* or *King Death*.

Cohn takes us back into Odyssey. It has taken four hours for Vincent to get ready for the night, and by now he is doused in Brut. He wears an open-necked shirt, gold jewellery, buckled Gucci loafers, and 'high black pants tight as sausage skins'. We meet his gang: four other young Italian American men, four more 'faces', who all, like Vincent, know 'how to dress and how to move, how to float, how to fly', with a pure instinct for 'rightness'. They are tough, foul-mouthed, full of contempt, and 'offhand in sex', Cohn writes. Girls are said to be for decoration and carnal impulses; they 'must obey and only speak when spoken to'. Cohn has one such female, Donna, aged nineteen, chasing an uninterested Vincent. He finally allows her a dance before taking her outside for sex in the back seat of a car, except she is not 'all right', by which Vincent means she has no contraceptive, isn't on the pill or wearing a coil. She buys condoms for the following week but Vincent ignores her. This is accurate reporting: 2001 Odyssey was known a singles club with the sex happening outside in cars. But there are other odd segues in the lengthy magazine article. There is a long segment, for instance, where Vincent and his gang seek vengeance on a suspected child molester who has approached one of their sisters. Again, such scenes have the ring of Cohn's novels about them, as does the denouement to the piece.

Disco culture is abandoned. Cohn pits Vincent's gang against other minorities—'Latins' (Puerto Ricans), Jews, and blacks—in neighbouring boroughs and throws up images of pitched battles. First a fight breaks out in the club involving Vincent's gang and then, in the street, one of them is beaten up and knifed by a gang of Puerto Ricans. The story ends not at 2001 Odyssey, which is fast losing its novelty for Vincent, but with the gang out 'hunting' for the Puerto Ricans.

Cohn was relieved to finish the article. He didn't think much of it. 'It wasn't a big deal in my writing life,' he said. Yet, like all his fictionalised heroes, real or otherwise, who only seem to be able to produce their best with their backs up against the wall, on the ropes, Cohn had triumphed. He had caught enough of disco life for the article to have cultural resonance, and the zip of his prose was back to its standout best. In his novels, the classic storyline he created for Vincent would have shot off in all directions, but the constraints of this being a supposedly respectable reporting job had kept the drama coherent and contained. He would never accept it, but this was Cohn as a heavyweight, the con making it all the more sweet a victory.

'I touched on an archetype,' he said, when asked what was the enduring appeal of the story. 'Disaffected youth is disaffected youth—that lad standing there in Nowheresville, thinking there has to be more to it than this. *Fever* is about that hunger. What was different was that previously people always became rock stars to escape. *Fever* concentrated on tiny stardom, the idea that you could satisfy that hunger on your own turf.'

When the article was published it caused a minor sensation.

Cohn, whose name was prominent on the cover of the magazine in the same size font as the title of the article, was unsure if he should be pleased. In his version of events (there is a longer, perhaps more accurate, version outlined in this book's main body), the first sign the article might have a life beyond the page came on the Monday morning *New York* hit the stands, when the woman he lived with took a message from someone keen to speak to him. She told him it was 'some guy called Rabbi Stigfeld'. It was, of course, *Tommy* film producer Robert Stigwood, whom Cohn said he knew 'quite well' and liked. (He had written a feature for *Playboy* in 1973 about another movie Stigwood had produced, *Jesus Christ Superstar*.)

Cohn visited Stigwood at his luxury apartment in New York that same day and found him 'fat with deals'. As well as The Bee Gees, the Australian-born impresario, now in his early forties, was also managing Eric Clapton and Andrew Lloyd Webber and Tim Rice, alongside running his own record label and music publishing, TV, and movie companies. On the film front, he had recently begun negotiating a three-picture deal with teen heartthrob John Travolta, with a plan to have him star in movie adaptation of stage musical *Grease*.

Stigwood told Cohn the *New York* magazine story could be turned into a film, and that Travolta would play the role of Vincent. 'He was looking for vehicles [for Travolta],' Cohn said. 'I had no instinct when I was writing the article that it was going to be anything. The whole thing was completely baffling to me. I mean, people didn't make films out of articles … films were films, magazines were magazines; sometimes books were turned into films but never magazine stories.' He recalled Stigwood buying the film rights to the story almost on the spot in a deal that would earn him close to half a million dollars in today's money. Cohn also negotiated a chance to write the screenplay for the movie and spent six weeks in Texas, in a hunter's cabin in the woods, doing just that. It was a failure, by his own admission, and Stigwood quietly removed him from the process.

From there, Cohn lost control of his creation, although he had adroitly, having seen the success of the *Tommy* soundtrack, demanded a small percentage interest in any future profits from the soundtrack to the movie. He went to the film's premiere, over a year later, in December 1977, at Mann's Chinese Theatre in Los Angeles, arriving in a limousine—one of a fleet of them stretched down Hollywood Boulevard. The film credits prominently stated the film was 'based on a story by Nik Cohn', but although Cohn thought Travolta was 'superb' he did not rate the movie, calling it hackneyed, 'a rehashed problem teenagers flick from the 50s updated with four-letter words and gang bangs'.

Propelled by a succession of American #1 singles from the soundtrack album—'How Deep Is Your Love', 'Stayin' Alive', and 'Night Fever', all by the Bee Gees—*Saturday Night Fever* became a huge success around the world. Travolta became a superstar. Disco was the hottest trend. The success of both the soundtrack and the movie was dubbed 'Fevermania'; the press began calling Cohn 'Fever man Cohn'. The high-priced double album sold in the multimillions, fast becoming the best-selling soundtrack of all time.

Large cheques started to roll in. It was estimated Cohn made over a million dollars from his cut of album sales. He felt he had not earned it; that his story was a fake and so was he. 'I was painfully aware that everything *Fever* brought me was shabbily come by,' he said. The knowledge, 'more and more, came to eat me up'. He found it 'very difficult to function'. Racked with self-doubt and rolling in cash, he had trouble writing, and was unable to finish a single paragraph for months. 'I completely lost my way and had enormous self-contempt,' he said. 'It knocked me off my trolley, and my trolley has never been the solidest base in the universe.'

His recreational drug use began to intensify and, in 1983, he was arrested at his West 76th Street Manhattan townhouse by FBI agents who linked him to the importation of four million dollars' worth of heroin and cocaine. The scandalous bust was the result of a covert operation stemming from arrest of Peter Mandok, once a lawyer for The Who, who had been picked up with over four pounds of cocaine at JFK airport. A woman was caught carrying the same weight in heroin. Fifteen others—including the notorious British earl John Jermyn and record producer Ben Brierley—were also arrested alongside Cohn, who pleaded guilty to a lesser charge in exchange for his testimony. He was indicted on drug trafficking and conspiracy, fined $5,000, and given five years probation.

Of course, Cohn would rally. In the 90s he was back writing for the *Observer* and supplied regular travelogues about America for the *Sunday Times*. He wrote more books: the whacked-out fiction of *Need* (1997), an acclaimed work of immersive reporting about Broadway called *The Heart Of The World* (1993), and *Yes We Have No*, an excursion across outsider England (1999). In 2005, he produced what may well prove to be his enduring masterpiece in book form, *Triksta: Life And Death And New Orleans Rap*. He is currently at work on an epic novel that, in typical fashion, he claims will exceed all else. He continues, however, to seem ashamed of his famous magazine article. He has called it 'contaminated', while the *New York Times* wrote he was 'queasy' about this chapter of his career and stated how he cringed whenever the subject is raised. Re-reading the article, Cohn said, 'filled him with deep, deep dread'.

●

When I discussed this book with him, Cohn told me he did not even want to clarify the facts pertaining to the varied reports on the amount Stigwood had paid him for the story or what percentage of the soundtrack he owned (and perhaps, as has been rumoured, what percentage of the movie he owned, if any). 'Write whatever you want to,' he said. 'I'm the last to care about accuracy in this context.' Cohn had long since come clean about the falsity of the story, but there remained conjecture over who he had based the character of Vincent on. He'd first publically admitted the article was made up in 1994, writing in the *Guardian*, 'My story was a fraud. I'd only recently arrived in New York. Far from being steeped in Brooklyn street life, I hardly knew the place. As for Vincent, my story's hero, he was largely inspired by a Shepherd's Bush mod that I'd known in the 60s, a one-time king of Goldhawk Road. All I'd intended was a study of teenage style.' He added that much of what he'd written was 'based on the belief that all dance fevers were interchangeable'.

From this stemmed the long-held belief that Cohn had based Vincent on Peter Meaden, the 60s most fabled teen Mod. Meaden had been The Who's first manager, convincing the band to change their name to The High Numbers and adopt a mod image. In Meaden's hip-speak, High Numbers were the leading mods. He wrote both sides of The High Numbers' 1964 single, 'Zoot Suit' and 'I'm The Face'. 'Face', the term Cohn had used to describe Vincent's gang, was another Meaden invention, used to describe leading mods. He himself was the 'Ace Face', the #1 mod—the exact term Cohn used to describe Vincent.

'He was starting to use his own private language, almost,' Pete Townshend told me, when reminiscing about Meaden's time as manager of The Who. 'I mean, the language he used about the mods has passed into kind of mythology. The word "face", the [derogatory] word "ticket", the word "number"; he was the only person I ever heard using those words. I never heard other Mods say, C'mon let's get the faces together and go out and kill some rockers. It was Peter Meaden who created the whole mythology.'

Cohn, however, would deny Meaden was the inspiration for the *Fever* character. In 1997, on the twentieth anniversary of the film, Cohn wrote a long piece for *New York* magazine, elaborating on the inspiration behind Vincent. The article played a supporting role to a cover story that updated Cohn's 1976 feature, the night taken over by a new set of tribes, called 'Saturday Night Now'. Cohn said Vincent had been part-based on archetypes he'd seen while growing in Derry, Northern Ireland, in particular a teen gang outside a coffee bar. He said he been bewitched by watching 'the leader' do tricks with a rubber snake. There was, surprisingly, no mention of Tu Sweet, with Cohn stating his main inspiration for the character had been a mod named Chris, just turned seventeen, who he'd come across in London in 1965. Cohn said he'd been impressed by Chris, who bought three suits a week and changed his shirt five times a day. Chris didn't do much, Cohn explained. He wasn't in any band; his 'stardom was inbuilt'.

This article, unlike the *Guardian* piece, created a wave of headlines in America. 'Writer admits faking *Saturday Night Fever* story' was one tabloid splash. It quickly passed. There was none of the prolonged scandal that would surround more modern examples of journalists filing fabricated stories, such as the brouhaha surrounding *New York Times* journalist Jayson Blair in 2003.

'I never pretended this was journalistically sound,' Cohn said. 'What I was schooled in was the mods, in London, in the late 60s. What struck me was the rites, the rituals, were the same [as in Brooklyn]. The sense, above all, that the rest of life may be shit, but come Friday night the weekend is here and you're king of the night.' Many simply agreed with Cohn, who said, in the *New York* piece, that it didn't matter that Vincent was made up. *Saturday Night Fever* had entered pop mythology: the flashing dance floor at 2001 Odyssey, 'Stayin' Alive', and Travolta posing in his white suit. These things had embedded themselves in the collective memory, Cohn said, until they came, for many, 'to define a whole decade'. Wasn't that real enough?

Fast forward twenty years and *Saturday Night Fever* still remains synonymous in the public imagination with the disco era. Whenever the 70s are evoked, it remains a safe bet that someone will strike the Travolta disco pose and attempt a Bee Gees-style falsetto. The long-lasting appeal of the film is undeniable. 'The figure never fades,' Cohn wrote. 'He was in Derry, and in London, and again in Bay Ridge. And he's still out there, somewhere or other, in his own neighborhood, caught in his own set of traps. Just staying alive.'

CHAPTER ONE

CHICKEN IN A BASKET

BARRY GIBB
WE ARE HAS-BEENS.
THIS IS ROCK BOTTOM.

Batley Variety Club was a long way from Brooklyn and the heat of disco fever. It was a squat, ugly, flat-roofed, cheap, boxy-looking cabaret venue on a nondescript road in the middle of a backwater wool town in dark northern England, seven miles south of the city of Leeds, in West Yorkshire. It was surrounded by slagheaps, mill chimneys blasting out smoke, and row upon row of back-to-back, tiny, redbrick terrace houses.

The Bee Gees arrived here in April 1974, booked to play the venue for an entire week of shows. The club was in terminal decline. The red velvet of the seating areas was shiny and stained. The carpet was sticky and dirty. The smell of stale cooking oil hung in the air. As soon as they caught sight of the club's façade, which at first they mistook for a factory building, they realised they could sink no lower. Now, Robin Gibb declared he would rather end the band than play the shows. Batley was also a long way from the band's 60s peak, when they'd fronted a thirty-piece orchestra at the packed Royal Albert Hall in London and tens of thousands of teens had screamed for them all across Europe and America.

The club owner, Rolls-Royce-driving Yorkshire fairground showman James Corrigan, tried to summon some of his old flamboyant charm, but the strain of his acute financial worries and crumbling marriage made him brittle and greasy. He had built the venue, a cross between a theatre and a club, from scratch on the site of a former sewerage works, and opened it in 1966, bragging of delivering a little bit of Las Vegas glamour to the lives of the men and women, mill workers and miners, from miles around—Batley was in the centre of a ring of entertainment-starved, heavily populated urban areas such as Bradford, Halifax, Huddersfield, Wakefield, and Leeds. Corrigan excelled at publicity, creating national news when he booked American jazz king Louis Armstrong for an unlikely two-week run at Batley in 1968. Armstrong had been tempted by a huge pay packet of £10,000 a week (the equivalent of £150,000 today).

The Armstrong booking put Batley on the map. Corrigan maintained a business model—the amount of booze consumed at Batley was legendary—that meant he could continue to pay high advances to attract other big stars, such as Cilla Black, Cliff Richard, Dusty Springfield, Eartha Kitt, Gracie Fields, Vera Lynn, Lulu, Morecambe & Wise, The Everly Brothers, Tommy Cooper, and Ken Dodd. At its peak in the early 70s, there had been talk of Frank Sinatra and Diana Ross playing Batley; back then, the club had boasted 300,000 members and was labelled the 'entertainment capital of the North'. Now it was dying. The audiences were dwindling, particularly during the week. Reduced staffing levels meant that on nights the club *could* attract an audience, there were long waits for drinks and food. The huge free car park, once a selling point, was often empty.

Corrigan was in the last days of a lifestyle that included owning a nearby mansion boasting an indoor swimming pool. This was where he had often entertained the huge stars he booked to perform at his club, but The Bee Gees exchanged worried glances at the prospect of an invite to eat there that evening. They had arrived at precisely the moment that Batley and Corrigan had reached breaking point. Despite having hosted acts such as Johnny Mathis, Roy Orbison, The Drifters, Neil Sedaka, Tom Jones, and Shirley Bassey over the past six months, Corrigan was losing as much as £15,000 a week. Britain was in the grips of recession. It was only a few weeks since the end of a prolonged government-declared state of emergency, when a three-day working week had been imposed in an attempt to conserve electricity during a strike by miners. As a result, 1.5 million people had been made temporarily unemployed. Inflation was running at 20 percent. The economic crisis hit Yorkshire hard. A night out at a cabaret club was a frivolity few could afford.

The club was still offering what it always had: cabaret (be it a comedian, singer, or band) with an inclusive dinner for a reasonable set price. Chicken and chips served in a basket was the iconic menu item, although scampi or cod was equally popular. Steak, Robin's twin, Maurice, noted, was now on the menu. It was a typical quip from the group's most sociable member and its loudest joker, designed as an attempt to alleviate the dark mood. Although it was only mid-afternoon, he was also, typically, drunk.

The Bee Gees' advisors had persuaded them to take the booking by pointing out they would be following a run of shows by Gilbert O'Sullivan, then a regular in the UK charts, at Batley. With their own careers in a deep slump, this appealed to their bruised egos. They also needed the money. Batley was the basis of a solid month of similar week-long engagements at cabaret venues in the north of England such as the Fiesta in nearby Sheffield, a club that had made its name by outbidding

Batley for attractions such as Kenny Rogers, Glen Campbell, and The Beach Boys, who could all still command a sizeable audience.

Even with such names attached to the venues and the amount of money they had been guaranteed, the three Gibb brothers had argued at length among themselves about doing these cabaret gigs. They had almost completed a new album that they hoped might re-launch them as a contemporary force. Many 60s bands, some more popular then The Bee Gees, had found themselves trapped in aspic on this sort of circuit. It was not how the brothers envisaged their future. Money and blind optimism had won out, but the latter was draining quickly as they set up to rehearse, while at the same time Corrigan was incongruously attempting to hoover the vast seating area that could easily accommodate up to 800 couples.

Although they struggled to accept they had been reduced to playing these sorts of clubs, in truth The Bee Gees were lucky to even be offered the gigs. When the Batley residency was announced, many locals expressed surprise the band was still going. Their career had flat-lined in Britain around 1969 and never recovered. It had been over five years since any of their albums had made the Top 40, and they had rarely played live in the UK during that period. In fact, in 1973, poor ticket sales had forced the cancellation of a planned British tour. They had also suffered the mortification of having to publicly cancel the release of an album because it was simply not good enough. It was called *A Kick In The Head Is Worth Eight In The Pants*, and it was so self-indulgent, depressing, and desperately dated that their manager, Robert Stigwood, told the press he had refused to let them release it. 'It's not worthy of you, not commercial enough,' Stigwood told the band. The truth was that the album had been rejected by their American record label, Atlantic, after a taster single had failed to ignite any interest.

'We got ourselves in a rut,' eldest brother Barry said. 'We shut the door on everybody and said we like what we're doing go away. That did us a lot of damage.' Atlantic's attitude toward the album had shocked the band. They had sold twenty-five million records between 1967 and 1972, but at that moment they had seen the end. 'The record company didn't want to know us, our management lost interest,' said Maurice. 'All of a sudden we were left alone. We didn't have a career. I was drinking a lot more.'

For UK audiences, The Bee Gees were those drippy 60s harmony-singing brothers whose hits, such as their 1967 #1 'Massachusetts' and 1968 #1 'I Gotta Get A Message To You', were difficult to dislodge from the memory. Two of their other hits had fast become standards, covered, to greater effect, by others. The schmaltzy love song 'Words' was a staple stage number for acts such as Glen Campbell, Frank Sinatra, Elvis Presley, and Roy Orbison, while the epic 'To Love Somebody' had been covered over two hundred times by notables such as Janis Joplin and Nina Simone, who took her version into the UK Top 5 in 1969. As a band, however, they had never quite escaped the suspicion they were just clever Beatles copyists. They had also, during their fame, cultivated a 'no drugs, no alcohol', anti-psychedelic image that had not dated well. 'You don't need drugs if you're happy,' Robin had said.

The band found it hard to reconcile their current status with the high-regard they had for their own worth and work. Robin, who tended to speak portentously about himself, the band, and their craft, told the press that although they were sneered at in the UK and lambasted by the press, The Bee Gees were regarded as 'an institution' in America. 'People in England don't value their art,' he said. 'I mean, there's no other group like us ... we've become very anti-press.' They could not accept that their time had gone. Their pronouncements were often ill judged. Maurice criticised glam-rock star Marc Bolan, predicting he would last 'as long as his face'. In an *NME* interview he rounded on other glam rock luminaries, David Bowie, Roxy Music, and Alice Cooper, calling the current British music scene a 'poofta's paradise'.

The real problem was they would not change. They still dressed in 60s suits, shirts, and bow-ties, and stood in front of orchestras churning out sad ballads when pop had gone hard and glam and brutal. 'We like to dress nicely onstage,' said Barry. 'It's nice to present yourself well onstage … we're not trying to change the world.' Cabaret was really all they were fit for. They were showbiz, corny, and even their big hit emotional ballads were now seen as fake and mawkish. 'Jukebox love songs, conveying genuine passion as accurately as Hollywood kisses capture the mess and tangle of real love,' wrote *Rolling Stone* magazine. Another *Rolling Stone* critic, Jim Miller, said that 'never before has a group so intensely and consciously set sail on a sea of syrup'. The influential magazine even dismissed their better work as 'original ersatz'.

Prior to playing Batley, The Bee Gees had completed a short tour of America, where the vestiges of their popularity—they had scored seven Top 20 US hits in the 60s—had not been entirely stripped away following a brief revival as a 'soft rock' act in the early 70s, although they were far away from the 'institution' Robin had bragged of. They'd been forced to 'paper' (that is, give away free tickets for) 2,000-seater venues to avoid humiliation, even in major cities such as New York, and a recent best-of album, compiling their most successful 70s material, had been a flop when it was released in America in August 1973. It had been almost two years since they'd scored a Top 20 single anywhere in the world. 'The years of nothingness,' Barry called them.

Backstage at Batley, amid the clutter of countless cabaret performances, Robin's spirits could not be lifted. He was already weak from a series of nervous breakdowns, and Batley seemed as if it would finish him off. It was worse than he ever could have imagined. His longstanding addiction to drugs—prescription pills chiefly, speed in particular—raged unabated, and he was all edge. Soft tears welled in his eyes. He would not be able to stand a month of this torture, away from his heavily pregnant wife and their young son, not yet two, and the cocoon of his large Surrey mansion in leafy South East England. Maurice was also weak: in 'the valley of depression', as he put it. He had been essentially poured into Batley. His heavily publicised marriage to Scottish star Lulu had recently ended in much acrimony, and he was hitting the bottle harder than ever. He had only just turned twenty-four but it seemed as if his life was over already. Unlike Robin, who was careful with his money, the trappings of his pop star past were disappearing fast. His sixteen-century mansion, set in five acres in Hayward's Heath, Sussex, was up for sale. To avoid paying tax he'd moved to the Isle of Man, into a terraced house next to a fish and chip shop. He said he only had £5,000 in his bank account; his blue Rolls-Royce was up for sale and often seen parked outside a local pub. 'It was rough, it was bloody cold,' he later recalled. 'But the fish and chip shop was good.'

All three brothers had been born on the Isle of Man and spent the earliest part of their childhood on the small rural island, with a population of just 80,000, situated in the Irish Sea between England and Northern Ireland. Their father, Hugh, then a jobbing drummer and bandleader, had spent almost a decade playing hotels popular with tourists in Douglas, the island's capital. Hugh and his wife, Barbara, had recently moved back to the Isle of Man after plans to open a 'superclub' in Ibiza had fallen though. Maurice, who had also briefly kept a home in Ibiza, was well known in Douglas. When he acted as a marshal at one of the island's famous TT motorcycle races, there was a crash on the section of track he was supposed to be looking after. It was close to a pub, and there were reports that someone had tipped nails onto the track. He had also been arrested for driving on a footpath, apparently drunk and decked out in an American cop's uniform. (Maurice was an avid collector of police regalia.) The incident saw him fined £80 and suspended from driving for two years.

Barry was also living on the Isle of Man with his wife and new son, just five months old. At twenty-seven, he was the group's central figure and driving force. He too was avoiding tax, and he seemed quite proud about it. 'Being born there, it helps us enormously if we live there, tax wise,' he said, complaining about the British government's recent tax increases. 'We'd rather build up our income over the years, rather than be hit the way Robin is at 83 percent. We're here but we'd like to live in England if the tax situation eases off.'

Barry, like Maurice, tried to see the funny side of being in Batley, making fun of the locals' broad Yorkshire accents and the predicament of the band. It was safe to assume, he said, that if you ended up playing here, you were 'not required anywhere else'. Unlike Maurice's, however, Barry's humour was not marked by a sense of black desperation. He was resigned to the gigs, trying hard not to make a drama of them, appreciative of the large amount of money the band were being paid to do them. 'We weren't what you'd call *current*,' he said. The fact he was handsome, groomed, and slick meant he came across confident despite the crumbling surrounds of the cabaret club. And he was stoned. That helped. His use of marijuana was legendary. 'We were known affectionately throughout the music business as Pilly [Robin], Potty [Barry], and Pissy,' said Maurice.

The new album they were working on, *Mr Natural*, saw the band strip back the overblown orchestration and overwrought ballads and move toward a funkier, more current, American band sound. It was a direction Barry hoped would convince Atlantic Records they were worth persevering with. For Batley, however, they were playing the game, with a live band augmented by a fifteen-piece orchestra, including brass section. The audience wanted to hear the old hits as they remembered them.

They intended to try out some new material from *Mr Natural*, too, but would also include a medley of old vaudeville songs such as 'Alexander's Ragtime Band'—a song popularised by The Andrews Sisters. These were the kind of crowd-pleasing songs The Bee Gees had been playing since they were children.

The three had been performing together since Maurice and Robin were six and Barry was nine. From the very beginning the pattern was set: Barry was the main man, strumming guitar and singing lead, with Maurice and Robin playing support. Hugh had spotted the potential right away and developed it, smuggling them into the clubs in Manchester, in northwest England, where they played alongside strippers to rowdy crowds of drunken men. The boys were thrilled with the attention their father was finally paying them. 'Dad couldn't show his emotions,' said Barry. 'You're probably looking for acceptance all the time and if you get that too easily you don't work for it.'

Hugh had moved the family to his hometown of Manchester in the mid 50s after work in the Isle of Man dried up. He was broke, jobless, and unhappy. It was a rough city, depressing and dark, poverty commonplace. There were slums. The scars of the war were everywhere. It was very bleak. The family was often without the cash to pay the bills or buy food to eat. Whatever the boys could earn from performing was welcome.

Hugh found it difficult to let go of his glory days and was mostly out at the clubs with pals in the evenings. Before picking up his gigs in the Isle of Man, tall, handsome, and showbiz smooth, he'd led a big band twice a night, six days a week, across the best dancehalls in the north of England and up into Scotland. Now he couldn't make anything stick. The jobs he did get—selling fridges was one—did not last long. Barbara, also born and raised in Manchester, worked as a cleaner. The brothers adored their mother, but she was driven to despair by them.

The three young Gibb brothers were old before their time: 'adults all our lives', said Maurice. They didn't like school, so they stayed away, and were almost feral. They mixed with other poor inner-city kids, staying out until midnight or later. Barry was a fighter. 'We were street kids,' he said. 'Our parents had no control over us.' The childhood incidents stacked up: Maurice was almost drowned in a river; Barry came close to death after being badly scalded by boiling water from a kettle (in the 70s, Maurice would often make light of the livid scars on Barry's chest by using them as a roadmap for a daft comedy routine); their elder sister, Lesley, was set alight in the front room and required a skin graft; Barry was knocked over by a car—twice. They broke into houses, thieved from shops and other children, and set fire to things for kicks—they loved to see advertising billboards or cars go up in flames. Robin burned down a TV-and-radio shop and a butchers. Barry went to court when he was caught stealing and narrowly escaped being sent to a juvenile correction centre.

Hugh beat his sons in an attempt to install discipline. They could, however—lucky for them—hit sweet harmonies instinctively. Instead of school, then, they spent hours practising in men's toilets, loving how the tiled walls gave an echo to the their voices. Barry said he was left 'staggered' by the sound of their three voices together. Hugh had wanted to be a star but he was now a bum. In his sons he saw a second chance. 'It was through us that he was going to make it,' Barry said.

Barbara, who loved to sing around the house, also encouraged her sons, but it was Hugh who worked up their act, playing them records endlessly—stuff by his idol Bing Crosby or Glenn Miller but particularly The Mills Brothers, a vocal quartet who'd been hugely popular since the 1930s. It was he who had put the 'Alexander's Ragtime Band' tune into the act. The Andrews Sisters were another touchstone, and the boys did their version of 'Chatanooga Choo Choo'. Hugh also taught them how to work an audience. In Manchester they played it cute and covered catchy singles of the day, such as 'Lollipop', 'Wake Up Little Susie', 'All I Have To Do Is Dream'—songs that were still part of their stage repertoire twenty years later. Hugh made sure they were pitch perfect. He would admonish them when they messed up routines.

Under a variety of names, the kiddie threesome picked up gigs at local cinemas, playing between films, and at matinees in the local theatres, sometimes begging for pennies while busking on street corners. They entered any talent contest they could. Sometimes Hugh backed them on drums. They were an instant hit and soon got their picture in the city's main newspaper with a small write-up. They money started to improve. 'We got £5 for our act,' Robin recalled. It was about more than money for Barry. The feeling of standing in front of an audience, he recalled, was 'amazing'. When the family suddenly emigrated to live in Australia in 1958, they almost immediately became one the country's most famous novelty acts. That was when the real hard work and a brutal sibling rivalry started.

●

Maurice had been drinking since breakfast and was unsteady on his feet during rehearsal in Batley. By showtime he could barely stand. The crowd predictably responded badly to the group's newer material. The club was only half-full. From the stage, the band could hear the sound of the audience eating, chewing, broad Yorkshire accents chatting loudly and drink glasses chinking. All sense of hope began to drain from Barry. 'It was the most horrible sinking feeling,' he said.

The group reprised various bits of comedy from their old routines. All three adored *The Goon Show*, Monty Python, and the Marx Brothers, and comedy had been a staple of their act during the nine years they spent in Australia. Even during the band's 60s height, they had larked about onstage and played idiots, dressing up in bird costumes or as babies, for instance, on TV shows. Maurice sleepwalked his way through his 'zany' brother shtick, imitating Robin's intense vocal stance, his hand pressed against his ear, straining for notes, and exaggerating Barry's onstage preening, a gentle send-up of his image as the group's pin-up. Barry frowned and wagged his finger at Maurice. It was embarrassing stuff. The Batley crowd was accustomed to the hard-hitting humour of acts such as black comedian Charlie Williams or the camp theatrics of Danny La Rue—pros both. Maurice pulled silly faces at the audience and yawned, looking at his watch, as Barry sang 'Words'.

Robin watched the waitresses deliver the drinks they held skilfully on trays to the many tables among the audience. He saw ruddy faces and heard shrill voices. The lights were hot. His bright blue stage jacket felt uncomfortably tight. He did not look healthy, his sickly pallor accentuating his protruding teeth and thick, long, wavy hair. It was his turn to deliver a lead vocal, on the band's maudlin 60s hit 'I Started A Joke'. He closed his eyes. Robin was not a polished showbiz performer like Barry. He had always been the oddball in the family, and onstage, when he sang, the emotions he conveyed, the frailty and despair that gave his vocal incredible depth of character and soul, seemed to come from a place of real personal anguish. It was a voice that had many admirers; a high, clear, plaintive vibrato that would be called 'one of greatest voices of all time' by Sex Pistol John Lydon. But not in Batley. 'Poof,' shouted one man. Robin heard a woman laughing loudly. It seemed to him as if now he was trapped in one of the band's own lachrymose, string-driven ballads. He shrivelled inside.

Backstage, after the show, Maurice continued drinking heavily. He'd only been separated from Lulu for about a month. They had married in 1969, and the entirety of their tempestuous relationship had been played out in the tabloids. Maurice complained bitterly about how the national papers were portraying him. He said they made him look like a 'mean miserable old bastard who treated her like shit' and 'belted her about now and again'. 'Believe you and me, she had a great right hook,' Maurice could be heard repeating to anyone willing to buy him a drink.

Many of those who knew the band well worried about Maurice's health as he wallowed in drugs, drink, and self-pity. He had a predilection for crashing cars and seemed hell-bent on self-destruction. Much of his pain was caused not by the breakup with Lulu but by his belief that he was the least significant brother in the group and always had been. Robin, at least, got to sing lead vocals on several tracks. Maurice never did. It tormented him. Although the brothers tended to share the songwriting credits (as B. R. & M. Gibb) he was weakest in that area too, rarely contributing, for instance, to the lyrics. He was not handsome, like Barry, or intense, like Robin. His amiable and naturally good-natured personality was crucial to the group dynamic, but it became twisted on booze. He was also losing the rich timbre in his voice, adversely affecting the band's three-part harmony sound. His abilities as a keyboardist, guitarist, and latterly bassist—the instruments he played onstage—were stunted. Barry had once called him 'the backbone of the group musically', but now Maurice was more or less a passenger in The Bee Gees.

Robin did not enjoy seeing Maurice drunk. He had fled back to his hotel room as soon as he left the stage. He didn't want to see anyone. He hated himself, his brothers, and every minute of the show. He was frail and gauche, sensitive, and the beer-swigging macho men of Batley were anathema to him. He didn't tend to socialise at the best of times. Alone with his thoughts, his mood spiralled downward. His despondency at having his art reduced to this was exacerbated by the fact that Batley had triggered terribly memories, reminding him of the many rough drinking clubs the Gibb brothers had been forced to play as children in Australia. It was a period in his life that he had detested and felt had robbed him of his childhood.

They had gone down under for a better life. Later, the band would intimate that their leaving Manchester was part of a deal struck so that Barry avoided being sent to the juvenile correction facility, but emigration was being actively encouraged at the time by both the British government, to reduce the high unemployment figures, and by the Australian government, which needed a supply of labour for their booming industries. There was a popular campaign running called 'Bring Out A Briton' and tens of thousands took the bait. Barbara's sister talked about it, enticed by the promise of jobs, housing, and a better lifestyle, and her cousin was already a 'Ten Pound Pom', so called because, as part of the Assisted Passage Migration Scheme, adults were charged only ten pounds for the fare from Britain to Australia, while children travelled for free. Hugh had the boys perform regularly to captive audiences during the four-week boat journey, sometimes in shows that went on past midnight.

In Australia, Hugh, like many Brits, found that the job opportunities were not as plentiful as advertised, nor was the housing as splendid. The family ended up in a tiny coastal town just north of Brisbane, the capital of Australia. Hugh tried his hand at photography and as a travelling salesman. More often he gambled. The family was broke. He had five kids now: Lesley was almost fifteen and a fourth son, Andy, was just one. Maurice and Robin, nearly nine, and Barry, who was twelve, ran wild in the sunshine. They gulped down exotic fruits such as bananas, swam in the sea, and looked for mischief and opportunities. They got a break performing at the local speedway track, where Barry flogged sodas for pennies. He was the driving force. They did their Manchester shtick on the back of a truck between races, and the crowd threw coins that they had to scramble in the dirt to collect. They could make up to three pounds a night. It was money that kept the family afloat. 'It's no secret,' said Hugh. 'They kept us going for a long time.'

The speedway track manager became the band's manager. He knew a DJ on a Brisbane radio station. It went from there. Barry told the DJ he'd already written 180 original songs. The DJ bought them a new guitar and recorded the brothers singing some of Barry's songs. He played one on his daily radio show. His name was Bill Gates. The track manager was Bill Goode. Barry Gibb. Barbara Gibb. 'Lots of B.G.s,' said Gates. The kiddie act had a new name. As soon as TV started up in Brisbane, in March 1960, the three brothers were all over it, soon with their own Friday night TV show, *The B.G.'s Half Hour*. Hugh took on the role now of manager. The TV show was his idea. He chose the songs they played, which were designed chiefly to appeal to an adult audience: ditties such as the comical 'Run Samson Run', 'My Old Man's A Dustman', and 'Does Your Chewing Gum Lose Its Flavour'.

'My father knew exactly what those audiences wanted,' said Maurice. Barbara helped dress them in matching outfits—zipper cardigans or waistcoats, smart trousers, shirts and ties. Throughout the early 60s they appeared regularly on a succession of regional variety-style TV shows. Mums and dads loved them. Aren't they cute? It taught them to be resilient, to deliver. 'You picked up your guitar, and you went on and you played and sang,' said Barry.

Hugh rehearsed them relentlessly, instructing them on how to behave onstage. 'Smile,' he would say, 'even if it hurts', and 'always leave them wanting more.' As he had in Manchester, he sometimes sat in on drums. They could now play a host of Mills Brothers tunes by rote. They went onstage to the tune Hugh had used as theme music in his heyday: 'The World Is Waiting For The Sunrise'. He booked them gigs in local pubs and clubs—the rowdy, decrepit, boozy places Robin disliked. They did anything to turn a dollar, vaudeville and pantomime included, but mostly it was months and months of nightclubs, hotels, and bars, more often than not dingy, sometimes hundreds of miles from home, as Hugh's ambitions grew. They wore Tuxedos now and Brylcreemed back their hair. The twins lied about their ages and stopped attending school when they were thirteen, despite the concerns of welfare officers. Barry had long since packed it in. They were barely literate.

It was tough and it was scary. It was every Friday night, three shows on Saturday, two on Sunday. Minimum. They would sometime be performing until 4am. 'We worked places where the men were so drunk they couldn't stand up, so they would fight sitting down,' said Maurice. They saw and heard things in the clubs, among the showgirls, rock'n'roll bands, and blue comedians, that hardened their hearts. They couldn't relate to other kids and had no friends of their own age. 'They never really made close friends with anybody outside the family,' said Barbara. 'They've always been sufficient to one another.'

Over time the group worked more and more comedy into the act. They started to include 'Puff (The Magic Dragon)' in the set but reworked it as an off-colour gag about Drag The Magic Poofter. Every time Robin sang the word 'puff', Maurice would get sprayed in the face with water. Maurice's role was to be the butt of the jokes; Robin played it cheeky, naughty, while Barry acted as the straight man, trying to keep control of his two crazy younger brothers. The song ended with Maurice kissing Robin on the cheek.

When they came offstage, Hugh avoided praising them, whatever the audience reaction, invariably picking out their faults instead. Maybe a dance routine had gone wrong, or a harmony was out of tune. 'My father never called me son or lad,' Maurice said, 'It was always, You sung flat.' He still beat them. Maurice got a belt for calling him a cunt. 'Dad used to hit us,' said Barry. 'It was a tough upbringing—but it wasn't as tough as Michael Jackson's. He told me some stories that would give you the horrors.' It was a strange touchstone for a strange family.

They eventually got a regular booking on the Gold Coast, south of Brisbane, working at the Surfer's Paradise holiday resort, playing nightly at hotels, sometimes doing as many as six shows a night. Sister Lesley also did an act, dancing with a snake. The Gold Coast was being developed at a rate, high-rise hotels flanking the wide golden beach, and many of Australia's top comedians and pop stars began to play hotels and clubs in the area. The Gibbs played here for eighteen months, honing their act until it was slick, mixing with the best entertainers in the country. Maurice and Barry loved it, craving the sound of applause, ever eager to please Hugh. Robin didn't. He would complain but it made no difference. 'I had to go and do it,' he said. Barry now, as well as Hugh, beat him when he rebelled.

●

The hurt welled up inside Robin. He called his wife, Molly. He could not endure another night at Batley. 'It was like a nightmare to him,' she said. 'Robin always hated nightclubs because of Australia.' She said she always felt 'some part of him was suffering a great deal'.

After Maurice had blacked out, Barry went back to Corrigan's mansion for an after-show drink, although he almost never drank. He entertained Corrigan and a few select guests by singing and playing guitar—the same cover versions, Beatles or Everly Brothers, he always played in such situations, songs he'd been playing since he was a kid. Tonight he threw in Elvis and Sinatra numbers, his ability to mimic other artists never failing to impress. Showbusiness was all he knew. It was his life.

'Barry decided to be famous and everybody got sucked along with him,' said Tom Kennedy, the band's longstanding road manager, who was slumped in a comfy chair that night. Barry missed his brothers when he sang. Although he was the group's leader on and offstage, referred to as 'skipper' or 'skip', and tended to dominate Maurice and Robin, he had come to rely on them, almost psychically. He put down the guitar and lit a joint. At their best, the three had written and performed almost telepathically, but now he and Robin were no longer close. (Robin had said he hated Barry 'intensely'.) Behind the beautiful smile and relaxed demeanour, Barry worried about the future. He had grown accustomed to living in grand style, but much of his capital was invested in shares in manager Stigwood's company, an opaque setup unfathomable to Barry. As long as people kept performing cover versions of his songs, he figured he would be OK for money, but he had no idea of knowing how long that would last. Certainly he could not predict that many of the songs he had already written would become today's modern standards. A lot then depended on the new album, *Mr Natural*. The future of the group was in serious doubt.

Their image was so toxic that Atlantic Records had created artwork for the album that did not feature any images of the brothers. Barry mentioned this to Corrigan, who was keen to hear the tapes of the new material Barry had brought with him. The music filled the room and a few guests got on their feet to dance to an up-tempo, disco-influenced track called 'Heavy Breathing' and the funky 'I Can't Let You Go', a first sign of the spectacular revival to come. The rest of the album in progress stank out the place. The contemporary gloss of the production and myriad musical styles on offer, from steamy soul ballads to country-rock, could not disguise the turgid nature of the songs.

Barry had written seven of the eleven tracks in collaboration with Robin—Maurice too drunk to fully contribute—and the process had been fractious. 'We'd lost the will to write great songs,' Barry said. Certainly the ability had long gone.

'Do "Words",' screeched Corrigan's wife, Barbara, who was drunk.

Barry flashed her his smile, the teeth so white and healthy, picked up his acoustic guitar, and began to softly strum. They'd soon be adding overdubs to complete the new album at Atlantic Studios in New York.

The second night in Batley was worse than the first. 'It was frightening,' Barry said. The venue was only half full again. Sometimes, even during the hits, he could see people turn away from the stage, back to their food and drink and conversation. A fight broke out in the audience during 'I Gotta Get A Message To You'. Throughout the show, Maurice walked offstage repeatedly to get a drink. His eyes were glazed and his bass playing lifeless. 'We are has-beens,' Barry thought. 'This is rock bottom.'

Backstage afterwards, Maurice was introduced to one of the club's waitresses, twenty-three-year-old Yvonne Spenceley. She told him she had been disappointed by the show. He fell for her immediately, and by Friday night he was asking her to come live with him. She was reluctant to get involved but eventually succumbed. 'The band got better as the week in Batley went on,' she said. Strangely, given the circumstances of their meeting, their relationship was to last. They would marry within a year, and were still an item when Maurice died in 2003, aged fifty-three.

From Batley the band went on to the Golden Garter cabaret club in Wythenshawe, south Manchester, the largest council housing estate in Europe, covering more than eleven square miles with a population of over 70,000. It was a rough and deprived area, full of small houses and wild kids. The club was on a shopping precinct full of gruesome-looking shops. The thick carpets and gold and crimson décor inside were badly dated. Many of the same acts that had passed through Batley also ended up at the Golden Garter. It seated 1,400 and offered the same sort of night out: cabaret and a three-course meal. On the first night there were only thirty people present to see the band. The crowd picked up as the week progressed, but if anything it made things worse. The air was thick with cigarette smoke, the drinking atmosphere pregnant with violence, the bouncers vicious. One night, a screeching woman rushed the stage to molest Barry. She was so drunk it was terrifying. Barry said it was 'like being in hell'.

People tried to commiserate. 'It must be awful for you, going from being so big and struggling now,' they'd say. Barry bumped into a musician he knew and explained The Bee Gees were playing in the city. 'Hey, I didn't know you were still together,' the musician replied. He shivered as he thought back on the incident. 'There is nothing worse on Earth than being in the pop wilderness,' he said.

Robin was inconsolable. The failure was asphyxiating. He could barely bring himself to look at Barry. He bristled when he thought back to the recording of the new album, with Barry singing lead on virtually every song. Robin had quit the band once already, at the very peak of their career, in 1969, and spent over a year trading vicious insults with Barry via the press. He was portrayed as the black sheep of the family and accused of being mentally unstable. The strains and ill feeling from that period would last a lifetime. Certainly, four years later, many of the issues that had troubled him then had still not been resolved. Manager Stigwood still favoured Barry as lead vocalist; Maurice was still sharing songwriting credits (and profits) on songs he'd had nothing to do with it. Robin was still not getting the recognition he felt he deserved. At the final show of the Golden Garter run, hostilities exploded. The three brothers had a huge fight backstage that spilled out into the street. The row threatened to get violent as the familiar rivalries played out, with Robin hurling scattergun profanities.

●

Barry had always been singled out as the talent of the family, first by Hugh, then by Stigwood. Before the band scored a recording contract, the songs he wrote had earned him a publishing deal with the Australian office of Belinda Music, a subsidiary of the acclaimed Hill & Range publishing company, which famously provided songs for Elvis Presley. It was Barry's songs that first suggested to Hugh there might be a life for his sons beyond the novelty kiddie act. On the Gold Coast he'd hustled Col Joye, a clean-cut Australian pop superstar and, suitably encouraged, moved his family five hundred miles to Joye's home city of Sydney, where all Australia's major record labels were based. Joye—on a hot run of Top 10 hits, including several #1s, and a regular on the main pop show on Australian TV, *Bandstand*—began to use the brothers as his support act and got them on the bill with him supporting Chubby Checker at Sydney Stadium, where they played to a crowd of ten thousand. The Gibb family was seduced by their proximity to Joye's fame, his glamorous lifestyle, flash cars, and the big house with swimming pool. Barbara started travelling with her sons on the road and even suggested that young Andy, now four, might join the group to add extra appeal.

Everything was all about Barry. Joye cut a version of one of his songs and included it as a B-side on a hit single. When they signed a deal with Joye's label, Festival Records, owned by Rupert Murdoch and Australia's most prestigious record company, the group was renamed Barry Gibb & The Bee Gees. The title of their debut album on Festival was *Barry Gibb & The Bee Gee's Sing And Play 14 Barry Gibb Songs*. When they appeared on *Bandstand* and other TV shows, Barry stood centre stage and sang all the lead vocals. One of the songs he had written became a regional Top 10 hit; Belinda Music suggested he had the 'greatest potential of any songwriter in Australia' and let it be known that American acts of the stature of Bobby Darin were considering recording his songs. By the time he was sixteen, Barry could boast that close to sixty of his compositions had been recorded by a variety of Australian performers, and one had even won him a 'Composer of the Year' award from an

Adelaide radio station. He was also juggling a harem of girlfriends, his sex life 'amazing'. The twins were not far behind. 'Sexually we advanced a lot quicker,' said Maurice, who claimed to have lost his virginity when he was nine. Fame, however, eluded them, and they worked the clubs. It was often grubby, squalid. Sometimes they slept in cars or lived in caravans or clocked up a remarkable twenty-one shows a day. They were often dirty and smelly. Robin lost a front tooth in a car accident; Barry shot himself in the eye with an air gun; and they all nearly died when the car Hugh was driving them in after a gig over-turned at 80mph.

They added more modern material such as 'Da Do Ron Ron', 'Please Please Me', and 'Blowin' In The Wind' to their set, modelling themselves on The Beatles, with Maurice playing guitar now, too. But Australia had watched the boys grow up on TV and would not accept them as a serious act. 'We became desperate to achieve stardom,' said Barry. There was talk of splitting the group and Barry having a solo career. Robin was by now a loose cannon, hyperactive and extrovert, a highly imaginative storyteller with an offbeat worldview and a cutting, almost cruel sense of humour. He could not accept Barry's authority over him and wanted to sing lead vocals and write songs too. His family dubbed his distinct vocal style 'the quavering Arab'.

Robin repeatedly challenged Hugh and would often end up scrapping on the floor with Barry. And he was vindicated when the first time he was allowed to sing a joint lead vocal with Barry, on a 1965 single, 'Wine And Women', it became a hit. He was determined it would be. Australia did not yet have a national chart, instead a series of regional radio station charts, and Robin had found out which shops were affiliated with Sydney's biggest Top 40 station—'about six in all', he said. He organised a small gang and the purchase of 400 copies of the single in an afternoon, and, as he predicted, 'Wine And Women' made the station's Top 20. Yet still Barry insisted he had more drive than anyone in his family. Later he would admit he felt challenged by the closeness of Robin and Maurice. 'They were twins, so they were always secretly chatting,' he said. 'I was the one that had to make sure we got paid.'

From the age of fifteen, both Robin and Maurice had got more and more involved in the songwriting process. The three brothers quickly developed a method of writing songs together where they'd imagine they were writing a hit for another group or act. 'We would sit around and say, Let's write the next Beach Boys record,' said Barry. They were fantastic mimics, adept at doing anyone from Elvis to the hit Australian folk act The Seekers. 'Wine And Women' had been a Hollies knock-off. 'We were emulating everybody,' said Barry. It was immediately apparent that Robin had a rare gift, adding a unique quality to the songs that elevated them beyond the pedestrian.

●

The fighting outside the Golden Garter stopped. Maurice was retching. He groaned, vomited, and sank to his knees before rolling onto the floor. It was dark and drunks staggered past, ignoring the once famous Bee Gee brothers. Robin had been smoking marijuana on top of the speed. It had made him confused, forgetful, and paranoid. He'd had a hit single after he left the band but urgent business issues and a sense of obligation to Stigwood and his brothers saw him abandon his solo career to join a reunited Bee Gees in 1971. It was not a pleasant or joyous reunion. 'We couldn't trust one another,' said Maurice. After an initial burst of success, their careers had stagnated. The rifts never healed, the sibling rivalries simmered, the work suffered—often they could not bear to be in the studio at the same time. 'If we hadn't been related, we would probably have not got back together,' Robin said.

Robin pushed Maurice into the back seat of the car that had finally arrived to take them back to their hotel. Barry got in the front seat. Robin stood for moment. They only had themselves to blame. Like Barry, he desperately wanted a new beginning for the band, but after two weeks in the North of England he couldn't see it. All he wanted now was for 'the old Bee Gees to go away'. Maurice had said the new album 'didn't have a positive direction', that the band 'were trashing about'. Robin thought of the Elvis pastiche, 'Lost In Your Love', and the one track he had sung lead on, the aimless 'Voices', and he knew Maurice was right. The whole album, in fact, was lifeless and clichéd. He tapped on the front passenger window, feeling tears forming. Barry looked at him quizzically and wound down the window.

'Stop being an asshole,' Barry said. 'Get in the fucking car.'

'I've had enough, Barry,' Robin replied. 'The group is finished.'

'Yeah, yeah,' said Barry. 'Just get in the car.'

'I'm not doing the Fiesta club,' Robin said. 'I'll walk back to the hotel.'

He turned his back and began to walk away, hunching his shoulders against the cold. The tears ran down his face.

'Fuck you then,' shouted Barry.

The car sped off. Maurice groaned from the back seat and vomited for a second time.

CHAPTER TWO
MIDDLED-AGED BLONDE MAN

BARRY GIBB
ROBERT IS IRREPLACEABLE.
THERE IS NO QUESTION ABOUT THAT.

At their lowest ebb, in their darkest hour, it felt as if Robert Stigwood had abandoned them. Stigwood was more than mere manager. He had signed the band within days of them stepping off the boat from Australia, launched them to almost immediate fame, and over the past seven years had superseded Hugh as their mentor. 'Father confessor, hand-holder, babysitter' was how Freddie Gershon, the chief operating officer of the Stigwood Group of Companies, described the relationship. In fact, he was more than that. He was a godfather to their children, a best friend, a muse, a benefactor, a corporate chief, as well as being the boss of their record label and head of their publishing company. 'To us he was a god,' said Robin. 'He was just an exceptional visionary who sees things other people do not see and for us he was everything, both personally and professionally.'

Robin had played the week of gigs at the Fiesta club in Sheffield under extreme duress; he had felt utterly alone and hollow, close to collapse. Maurice had also teetered on the edge, downing spirits for breakfast and drinking steadily throughout the day. Barry had admitted defeat and cancelled the final week's booking at the Bailey Club in Liverpool. Then, embittered, full of hatred for one another and lost in self-doubt, they had hurried home to lick their wounds. More than ever they needed the guidance of Stigwood, but even if he could rescue them, which seemed unlikely, multiple others of his more promising projects were demanding of his attention. 'Part of our problem,' said Maurice, 'was Stigwood had become so involved with movies and stage shows that he'd taken his eye off us and we were kind of drifting. We were left alone. All of a sudden, we didn't have a career.'

Stigwood was currently on the south cost, near Portsmouth, overseeing the shooting of a new film he was producing, *Tommy*, based on The Who's rock opera album of the same name. The film had long been in deep financial peril, with Stigwood's Robert Stigwood Organisation (RSO) at risk for the entire $3.3 million budget (around twenty million dollars in today's money). Having signed up director Ken Russell and stars such as Elton John, Oliver Reed, and Jack Nicholson, Stigwood had gambled on being able to sign distribution deals around the world for the film. It had consumed him, and over the past few weeks, he had, territory-by-territory, raised two and a half million dollars from distributors including Columbia Pictures in America by offering 50/50 deals on gross revenue.

'I don't take any nonsense from distributors,' Stigwood said. 'We buy the properties and we retain the director. If you ever go to a studio and ask them to buy you a book to produce, that's the end. The other great ploy, usually at the eleventh hour, just before the film starts rolling, is [for the studio] to try to change the terms of the deal. If they try and do that with me, I tell them to shove it. The expect you to be in some flat spin if the dollars can't be there on the due day.'

He had also raised $750,000 from Polydor for a deal for the movie soundtrack, with many of The Who's songs cut by other acts. (Elton John sang 'Pinball Wizard'.) The whole scheme had been typical Stigwood: innovative and perilous with the promise of a huge pay-off. The result was RSO now risked none of its own money for *Tommy*, owned the movie rights, and stood to take an improbable 50 percent on ticket sales. 'I'm a perfectionist,' Stigwood said. 'I'd rather not do something than not do it properly. I never do anything to be defeated.' As a businessman he was famous his take-no-prisoners toughness and willingness to take risks. He was once described as being 'as gentle as a shark with tungsten fillings and a toothache'.

Stigwood had also included Eric Clapton, the other music act he managed, in *Tommy*. It was another move typical of his approach to work; he was always looking for a synergy in his projects that could bring maximum reward. Clapton, who had found huge global fame with Cream and Blind Faith, sang a song on the soundtrack and had a minor supporting role in the movie. Clapton had been suffering from depression and heroin and alcohol addiction and had not had a significant hit since the single 'Layla' in 1972, but Stigwood was determined to re-launch him. His new single, 'I Shot The Sherriff' was picking up radio support and would soon reach US #1. The album that would follow, *461 Ocean Boulevard*, would launch him back to superstardom, selling two million copies. It would also be the first major hit for RSO Records, launched in 1973.

Stigwood also had a hit West End musical, *Jesus Christ Superstar*, and several TV projects to oversee. While the Bee Gees had sunk to the very bottom of the showbiz world, he was reaching the very peak of his creative powers with an empire stretching across all facets of the entertainment business.

Having been a success in the music business since the early 1960s, and more lately a hit in musical theatre, his first love, it was the film industry that Stigwood longed to conquer. Prior to *Tommy*, he had only produced one movie: the 1973 film version of the controversial *Jesus Christ Superstar*, which had grossed twenty-five million dollars worldwide. In an illustration of what a remarkable deal he was getting on *Tommy*, Stigwood had retained what was considered a healthy slice of profits of *Jesus Christ Superstar*: a figure believed to be between 20 and 25 percent of the distributors' gross on the movie. And part of that figure came from the fact Stigwood was the manager of Andrew Lloyd Webber and Tim Rice, who had originally written the musical the film was based on. He had fought off stiff competition from Harold Fielding, then regarded as British theatre's musical mastermind, and Lord Bernard Delfont, who with his two brothers dominated the British TV, film, and music industries, to sign the two—buying out their former manager for around £150,000 and shares in RSO so that he owned 25 percent of the income of Webber/Rice until 1979 and all rights to stage and film production of their works in the English-speaking world. After the success of the musical, the *Jesus Christ Superstar* movie had been the next step in his exploitation and promotion of their work. The trade magazine *Variety* had called it the 'biggest multimedia parlay of all time'. *Tommy* was a natural progression: another project that had begun in one medium was transplanted to another, with each supporting and reinforcing the other. It was a design later to be echoed in *Saturday Night Fever* and *Grease*.

Stigwood had made a fortune from *Jesus Christ Superstar*. Although he had no direct business interest in the original 1970 album (which preceded the musical and sold two million copies), once he began managing Webber and Rice he browbeat MCA Records into increasing the royalties paid on the album to the pair from 2.5 percent to 5 percent. This was typical of the hard negotiating Stigwood was infamous for; he even referred to himself as a 'ruthless bastard'. What he did with the musical was a creative master class and illustrated why The Bee Gees thought so highly of him.

First he'd hired fifty lawyers and spent $450k shutting down ad hoc productions based on the album that were springing up everywhere, particularly in America. Then he quickly arranged his own production, took it on the road, and in a year grossed $1.1 million. He presented a more lavish Broadway version in 1971, but it was in London, stripped back to basics, that the musical became a phenomena, playing to packed houses over seven years and 3,358 performances, taking seven million pounds at the box office. In total, *Jesus Christ Superstar* has been translated into twenty-two languages and earned more than a hundred million pounds. In 1973, Webber and Rice were honoured by the British government for export earnings of thirteen million pounds for the show. Stigwood had a hands-on role in making it a global success and was now considered one of the world's dominant forces in musical theatre. Although the groundbreaking hippie musical *Hair*, which Stigwood produced in London, had just closed after a hugely successful five year run, he had interests in myriad other stage productions, including *Oh, Calcutta!*; *Sweeney Todd*; *Sing A Rude Song*; *Pippin*; *John, Paul, George, Ringo and Bert* (voted best musical of 1974 by the *Evening Standard*); and *The Dirtiest Show In Town*.

If all this were not enough, Stigwood was also having phenomenal success in television, which is where he had begun his career, managing actors. In 1968 he had bought the company that represented the UK's best scriptwriters, Associated London Scripts (ASL), and two of its properties had been turned into popular American TV series with top ratings. *Steptoe & Son*, written by Ray Galton and Alan Simpson, had been transformed into *Sanford & Son*, running on NBC from 1972 to 1977. Johnny Speight's *Till Death Do Us Part* had become *All In The*

Family, running on CBS from 1971 to 1979, and widely regarded as one of America's greatest ever TV series. By virtue of his ownership of ASL, Stigwood had also profited from two highly successful *Steptoe & Son* films, released in 1972 and 1973 (the first, produced by EMI Films, grossed £500,000), and two film spin-offs from *Till Death Do Us Part*, in 1969 and 1972, the latter notable for featuring lead character Alf Garnett on an LSD trip. The ASL deal also brought Frankie Howerd to the RSO stable, and the camp comic had scored major success with his *Up Pompeii* BBC TV series and subsequent spin-off films, three of them released in 1971 and 1972.

He was a rich man. 'I'm not doing so badly,' Stigwood had told the *Daily Express* in 1972. The newspaper had then valued Stigwood's show business empire at nine million pounds. RSO had been a public company since 1970, and the success of *Jesus Christ Superstar* had trebled its profits, with the company raking in an estimated five million net in 1974. Share prices in RSO stood at £1.21; they had been initially offered at 37.5p. The Bee Gees were among RSO's major shareholders. Stigwood lived in a vast, thirty-six-acre, sixteenth-century mansion in Stanmore, Middlesex, complete with swimming pool, tennis courts, and go-karts. Here he hosted riotous and decadent parties, with fights and skinny-dipping the norm. There was also a holiday house in the South of France and, when in New York, a penthouse suite at the Waldorf-Astoria.

With the film industry in his sights, Stigwood was now looking at transferring all his activities to America. The Bee Gees might have been in danger of being left behind, but Stigwood tended to be loyal, and he had a soft spot for the Gibbs. He had not listened to Atlantic Records (which distributed RSO Records in America) when the label advised him to drop the group. Instead, he'd confronted the band. 'I got the feeling they weren't really listening to what was happening in the industry anymore,' he said. He then persuaded Atlantic boss Ahmet

Ertegun, his close friend, to give the group another chance, and together they had come up with the idea of putting the band in the studio with Atlantic producer Arif Mardin to record their new album, *Mr Natural*.

•

The Gibb brothers had always done what Stigwood said, ever since they'd first met him and he became their manager in early 1967. Back then he had just struck a deal to acquire controlling shares in The Beatles' management company, an audacious coup in a career already littered with bold moves. He was rated as one of the music industry's most flamboyant, visionary, and controversial figures, with a reputation for high living. He'd promoted The Rolling Stones and ran his own record label, Reaction, which put out records by The Who, including the major hit single 'Substitute', and the heavy blues-rock supergroup he managed, Cream. It was his association with their idols The Beatles, however, that most impressed the Gibbs.

'He changed our lives,' said Barry. 'For us he opened all the doors in the world. It was equal to having a hit record.' He was 'a blessing' and 'the man', said Robin. They even claimed that meeting Stigwood had been their destiny. Barry said that Barbara, who read the Tarot cards, 'told us about Robert before we met him'. 'A sort of middle-aged blond man will come into your life,' she predicted.

The Gibbs often spoke of their exit from Australia in mystical terms. They insisted that during a séance a spirit voice had contacted them to tell them they would be a great success in England. The truth was rather less palatable, and certainly not good for the image. Barry had turned twenty in September 1966, and at the time there was compulsory national service for males of that age in Australia, with conscripts obligated to give two-years full-time service. Since 1965, conscripts had been obliged to serve overseas, and for Barry that meant

Vietnam. The Bee Gees left Australia in a hurry—and inadvertently just as their success in the country reached its most fevered, with a single called 'Spicks And Specks' gaining massive national attention. The band were profiled in *Everybody's*, the country's best-selling national magazine; the *Sunday Telegraph*, Australia's biggest-selling newspaper; and featured on the cover of leading music paper, *Go-Set*, 'Australia's pop culture bible', which voted the Beatles-esque single 'Best Record of the Year' and made it #1 on its own music charts. The record broke around the country, making #3 on the Sydney charts and #1 in other cities, including Melbourne.

As well as a hit single, Barry left behind his new eighteen-year-old English bride. The brothers were maturing beyond the influence of Hugh, growing their hair and experimenting with drugs (chiefly the amphetamine Dexedrine) and new, more current musical styles. Barry said he wanted a shot at making it in UK, 'the doorway to international success'.

Despite the fact that a young Australian beat group, The Easybeats, had left Australia for London in the summer and quickly scored a major international hit with 'Friday On My Mind', Hugh was circumspect about The Bee Gees' chances of making it in the UK. He was advised by the Australian concert promoter Harry Miller, who brought acts such as The Rolling Stones to Australia for tours, to write to Beatles manager Brian Epstein and ask him to consider helping his sons.

When Stigwood took over the group he would tell of how Epstein had passed on Hugh's letter and the band's recordings with the highest of recommendations, and that this was how he had discovered the band. It was of significant benefit to be linked Epstein and The Beatles, the biggest group in the world. In fact, it was a contact at Polydor Records, which distributed Stigwood's Reaction label in the UK, who had tipped him off about The Bee Gees. The German company, determined to break into the UK market, was spending big and had recently struck a deal with The Bee Gees' Australian label to release 'Spicks And Specks' in the UK.

(Stigwood never let the truth get in the way of a good story. His own image as a pop Svengali even included the untrue rumour that he had trained as a hypnotist. The original Svengali created by George Du Maurier in his novel *Trilby* and immortalised in the 1931 movie *Svengali* was a ruthlessly maleficent hypnotist whose subject obeyed his every command.)

Stigwood worked the association with The Beatles endlessly and tirelessly in the early days of The Bee Gees. For instance, from the promise of the demos he heard, the Gibb brothers were, he said, 'probably the best new writers to emerge since Lennon and McCartney'. Soon it was Paul McCartney himself who Stigwood was claiming had told him to sign the band. The truth was, McCartney disliked Stigwood intensely.

Epstein had made Stigwood manager and joint director of his management company, NEMS, with an option to buy controlling shares, without first telling The Beatles. 'We told Brian that if he sold us to Stigwood, we would only ever record out-of-tune versions of "God Save The Queen" for every single record we make from now on,' McCartney said. Many others within The Beatles' inner circle disliked Stigwood, too, and had advised Epstein against taking him on. The Beatles' press officer and close aide, Derek Taylor, said Stigwood had 'a cavalier style that upset more people than it pleased'. Nat Weiss, the American lawyer who represented Epstein and the group, said Stigwood was 'a real carnival promoter … a man who had two cents to his name but could run up a bill'.

Stigwood was not middle-aged—he was only thirty-two when the band met him—but he adopted an older persona. His sandy hair, already receding, was styled into an elaborate comb-over, and he was paunchy, with a droll speaking voice that would soon become a deep croak. His lively blue eyes boggled outward, so he resembled a toad. Although he was born in Australia, and intuitively understood much about the Gibb brothers' background, he was cagey about revealing too much about his own background. Instead, he had adopting an upper crust, casual, old-fashioned English look as uniform: blue blazer, grey flannels, pale blue shirt. He was dripping in gold jewellery, and it was well known in the industry that, like Epstein, he was gay, but at the time he preferred to keep that private. He had handsome young males living in at his home and two male minders. Eric Clapton said Stigwood had fancied him when they first met (Pete Townshend told a similar story). 'He was an extraordinary character,' said Clapton. The Bee Gees said that when they first met he reminded them, with his 'sideburns and velvet lapel jacket', of Noel Coward, with his sonorous tones and talk of 'foul deeds' and 'chin wags'.

Although he described himself as an 'old bushwhacker', suggesting he was an unrefined country boy at heart, Stigwood was from a solid middle-class background—his father was an electrical engineer and his mother, whom he was closest to, ran a nursing home. They split when he was thirteen. His mother would go on to marry five times; Stigwood described her as 'totally wonderful and wonderfully insane'. Of his father, he said, 'I didn't like him and he didn't like me. I was too artistic.' In his teens he and his brother were sent to a private Catholic boarding school; Stigwood had hoped to become a priest after being an alter boy but found his homosexual tendencies difficult to overcome and lost faith when he was nineteen. Next he wanted to be actor, before settling for a job as a copywriter in a cutting edge advertising agency in Adelaide. Observers would later comment on the fact that he appeared to have had an unhappy childhood because of his homosexuality. 'You felt he was living some kind of lie,' one director who worked for

Stigwood said. 'I think he was living in a certain amount of shame with himself.' The story went that he had arrived in London in 1955 with just £5 in his pocket and in hot pursuit of an Australian girl he wanted to marry. He had told pals that when he returned to Australia it would be as a millionaire.

Stigwood tended not to dwell on his early years in London, which he spent selling vacuum cleaners door-to-door, or his two years with the charity SOS Children's Villages UK, working in a hostel for orphaned and abandoned boys in Cambridge, on nightshifts, overseeing the dormitories and preventing, he said, 'any flow of traffic after lights out'. By the late 50s he had begun to work in and around theatrical productions. He started with a small-time provincial company on the south coast before moving back to East Anglia and a job at the Norfolk Playhouse, a repertory theatre. There, Stigwood, twenty-five, with a broad role as general manager, painting the sets and also treading the boards, met an eighteen-year-old lad with model good looks called Stephen Komlosy. When, less than a year later, in June 1959, the venue went up for sale, Stigwood persuaded Komlosy to ditch dreams of university and pursue a career as a pop star, with him as manager.

Komlosy became Stigwood's first financier. His mother handled PR for the film side of the Rank Organisation and loaned the pair £5,000 (worth over £100,000 today) to open an office in London. Stigwood dreamed big. He wanted to be like Lord Delfont and his brothers, who owned a TV station, ATV, later to become ITV, and the only British channel to rival the BBC at the time; TV and film companies; a film studio; a controlling interest in Pye Records; multiple British theatres, including the illustrious Palladium; and a management agency that controlled many of the top UK music and acting stars of the day and represented the best American acts. Robert Stigwood Associates started as a model agency with one client: Komlosy. Stigwood sniffed out opportunities. He found that companies paying for adverts on ATV had big budgets but were finding it difficult to attract actors signed with the established theatrical agencies, who did not consider the work befitting their status. Stigwood signed up actors from the repertory theatre world and began supplying them to advertising agencies. Soon he was the go-to man for actors in TV ads.

Stigwood had not, however, given up on the idea of managing a pop star. He felt that one of his clients, twenty-three-year-old jobbing actor John Leyton, had the potential. Leyton had just landed a lead role in the hit 1960 TV serial *Biggles* and was gaining a following of female fans. The problem was that Stigwood was an outsider in the then staid music business, and Leyton was only an average singer. As a means to an end, Stigwood paid an independent producer—the only one in the UK at the time—£100 to make a record with Leyton. This was the legendary Joe Meek, and it marked the start of a significant bond between the pair that would go some way to revolutionising the British music industry. Meek had his own Willy Wonka-esque makeshift studio above a leather shop in a two room flat on Holloway Road, north London, where he famously utilised the bathroom, hallway, and stairs as recording areas to make the most experimental records of the era. His most famous track was the electronic 'Telstar', the first UK record to make #1 in America. The homosexual Meek was a troubled soul and could be vicious, bullying, and paranoid. He believed, for instance, that the major record labels were spying on him to steal his sound, and that he could talk to cats (which he would tape mewling in graveyards). In 1967, he suffered a breakdown and murdered his landlady, blasting her with shotgun, before killing himself.

Stigwood also struck up a close relationship with the fifty-seven-year-old chairman of EMI, Sir Joseph Lockwood. EMI was the country's leading record label, and Lockwood was also quietly gay. Stigwood made a clever tape-lease deal with Lockwood—a trick pioneered by American producers such as Phil Spector and taught him by Meek. It meant Stigwood (not EMI) paid for and controlled the recordings and retained ownership of the finished music. It was risky because Stigwood was gambling his own money up front, but it resulted, ultimately, in a greater share of profits and ownership of master recordings.

In 1961, Stigwood had his 'breakthrough': his first UK #1, 'Johnny Remember Me' by John Leyton. The single was produced by Meek at the peak of his powers. When Leyton was cast as a rock star in the new TV serial *Harpers West One*, Stigwood fixed it so that he performed the song, surrounded by adoring female fans, on the show. Stigwood had not been content to own just the star and the master tapes, he also signed up the man who wrote the song, Geoff Goddard, to his own newly formed publishing company: Robert Stigwood Associates Music Publishing. Stigwood loved the pop music industry, at the time dominated by a handful of key London figures, most of them gay, such as manager Larry Parnes (who had stable of young stars such as Billy Fury, Marty Wilde, and Tommy Steele) and songwriter Lionel Bart (who would later write the musical *Oliver!*). Both men, like Stigwood, were heavily involved with EMI. 'He became fascinated by it,' said author and pop impresario Simon Napier-Bell. 'He loved its trickery and tease, and the apparent ease with which money could be made.'

Over the next two years, Stigwood built up his own stable of pop stars. He dispensed with Meek and started to produce records himself, recruiting Meek's nineteen-year-old arranger Charles Blackwell to assist him. He also stole sixteen-year-old Billie Davis from Meek and put her in the Top 10. He owned every aspect of the process that it was possible to own in the era before independent record labels rose to prominence, also adding concert promotion to his repertoire. 'The idea was not to let anyone in from the outside,' said Komlosy. 'He is Svengali. He dominates you. He dominates your mind. He imposes his will. He is like a father and the children are all jealous of the father's attention.'

In 1962, Stigwood scored another #1 with the novelty song 'Come Outside' by actor Mike Sarne, featuring his fifteen-year-old secretary, Wendy Richard, as co-vocalist. The records were often terrible, but the success was unquestionable: Stigwood oversaw a remarkable seventeen Top 40 hit singles. His stable of stars made him a millionaire at twenty-nine. He bought a Rolls-Royce, hired a chauffeur, moved to plush new offices, sat behind marble tables, hung silk wallpaper, and threw tiger skins on the floor as rugs. 'I was very grand,' he admitted.

When The Beatles changed the pop landscape in 1963, Stigwood's actors-turned-pop-stars went out of fashion. Stigwood looked to stay contemporary: he briefly represented Tamla Motown in the UK. He bought a TV studio, where he made his own commercials under the name Robert Stigwood Commercials; invested in a music magazine, *Pop Weekly*; and began promoting tours by new, post-Beatles acts such as The Hollies. He made a small fortune promoting a 1964 UK tour co-headlined by The Rolling Stones and The Ronettes and lost it all and more promoting a prestigious Chuck Berry UK tour. He gambled on paying the American star a colossal fee of $15,000 a night, but Berry played to half empty houses outside of London. Next he booked a P.J. Proby tour, but the notorious American star cancelled and refused to repay Stigwood his £10,000 advance. The killer blow came when taped commercials were outlawed after a strike by the film technicians union, and Robert Stigwood Commercials was put out of business.

Stigwood's mini-empire imploded with debts of £50,000 (just short of a million pounds in today's money) and was declared bankrupt. 'My image was bigger than my money,' he said. 'I remember walking down the street and seeing the *Evening Standard* headline "Top Impresario Bust". I thought "top?" That can't be me.' Komlosy lost his house, and when Stigwood gambled away £400, earmarked to pay staff wages, at an illegal casino, Komlosy quit the company. Stigwood remained a life-long gambler.

It would take ten years for the affairs of Robert Stigwood Associates to be fully unravelled. One creditor exacted immediate payback. Stigwood had gone bust owing the Stones approximately £16,000. Keith Richards corned him at the Scotch of St. James nightclub and beat him to a pulp.

Komlosy went on to manage Lionel Bart, who was also a heavy gambler. Stigwood quickly found a new business partner, David Shaw, an ambitious City bond dealer who was looking for stars to enable a moneymaking scheme of his come to fruition. Shaw was proposing to allow the public to buy shares in stars and let the prices of those shares be governed by the income of the star. The star would be paid in shares—which they could trade—rather than cash. The trick of the scheme was in the tax margins: any profits from share dealing were subject to less tax than direct earnings. Shaw initially funded Stigwood with £25,000, soon followed by a further £15,000. He opened new central London offices and began his comeback. He had strong connections with The Who, via a relationship with the band's gay co-manager, Kit Lambert. (John Entwistle, The Who's bassist, said he found them in bed together.) He was soon the band's promoter, and he set up his own Reaction Records in 1966 to release their new material. Next he took on Eric Clapton's band Cream, launching them in America as support to The Who on a major US tour.

Stigwood chalked up as many misses as hits for Shaw, spending freely. To promote the handsome young singer Simon Scott, he had plaster busts made up of the star. For pop hopeful Oscar, formerly a teenage piano player with Screaming Lord Sutch, he sent out fake Academy Awards. Neither act stuck; Oscar failed despite Pete Townshend and

David Bowie writing songs for him. His real name was Paul Beuselinck, the son of Oscar Beuselinck, a powerful music business lawyer whose clients included MGM Films, Sean Connery, Richard Harris, The Beatles, and The Who. Stigwood would continue to nurture Oscar, who under the name Paul Nicholas would come good as an actor and pop star in the 1970s.

Infamously, Stigwood failed in his attempts to lure the country's leading mod group, Small Faces, to his roster. When their manager, the notorious Don Arden, found out about his overtures, he hired a small firm of heavies to attack Stigwood. It became one of the music industry's most apocryphal stories: how Arden had dangled Stigwood out his office window by his feet, threatening to kill him. Arden told me Stigwood had lost control of his bowels and that his cowboy boots were 'full of shit'.

Shaw and Stigwood switched their sights to The Beatles, and a deal was struck with Brian Epstein following what Shaw described as 'a dirty weekend' in Paris. In a three-bedroomed suite at the Lancaster hotel, they watched as Epstein took an alarming amount of drugs, including acid, and confessed to the unbearable pressure of running his music business empire. As well as The Beatles, Epstein's company NEMS oversaw the careers of a slew of acts such as Cilla Black, Gerry & The Pacemakers, Donovan, and Petula Clark. He talked about plans to retire to Spain to manager bullfighters. He was burned-out. Stigwood said he could manage all this and attract fresh talent. Epstein liked him. Shaw sought to finance a deal to buy NEMS, and Stigwood was installed as a manager and joint director of the company that employed eighty people. In September 1966 it was announced that Shaw and Stigwood had agreed to buy 51 percent of NEMS for a reputed half a million pounds. Polydor was putting up the money.

•

One of Stigwood first moves at NEMS was to sign The Bee Gees. Although he thought 'Spicks And Specks' only average—'very Beatles-ish'—he was intrigued to learn that the band members were barely sixteen when the song was written. 'I figure if boys that age had been able to turn out material of that calibre, they must have immense potential,' he said. He auditioned them at the plush Saville theatre in London's West End, part of the NEMS empire. They did their nightclub act for him, including the camp comic segment that featured their 'Puff The Magic Dragon' skit. Stigwood was impressed, and just seventeen days after landing in London, in February 1967, The Bee Gees were his. He took full advantage of their desire to be famous—and their lack of business acumen.

'These boys are completely uneducated,' Stigwood said. 'They don't even know how to spell. They write the lyrics out phonetically.' The contract was onerous. It initially lasted for five years and included recording, management and publishing. The Gibb brothers were put on a weekly wage of £25 each. 'We couldn't have been any greener,' Barry recalled. 'There are so many intricacies as to whatever became an agreement between Robert and us. There were so many side deals to which we had no knowledge.'

Epstein was unimpressed with the group. When Stigwood told him that, for just £1,000, he had bought a 51 percent of their song publishing for NEMS, Epstein responded, 'Well, that's a thousand out of the window.' The deal was more attractive to Hugh Gibb, who would receive a 2 percent royalty from any songs The Bee Gees wrote collectively or individually.

Stigwood saw great potential in the Gibbs' prodigious songwriting abilities. He would have NEMS acts Cilla Black, Billy J. Kramer, The Tremeloes, and Gerry Marsden all record songs by them before the year was out. It presaged a great many acts recording Bee Gee songs, including Dave Berry, Billy Fury, Adam Faith, and Manfred Mann's singer Paul Jones. Stigwood was most drawn to Barry, who would stay sometimes at his mansion on Adam's Row, a posh mews just off Grosvenor Square in Mayfair, where he lived with his manservant, Victor, and a small entourage. He also took Barry alone to New York to meet Nat Weiss, the lawyer who ran The Beatles' affairs in America, as his plans to launch the group developed.

Stigwood wanted to launch The Bee Gees as a real group, so they took on Colin Peterson on drums. As a child, Peterson had starred in a number of late-50s British films before moving back to Australia, where he concentrated on music, playing drums on several early Bee Gees recordings, as well as dating their sister Lesley. Like Barry, he was twenty, and had recently left Australia, and the threat of conscription, to live in London. Another old Australian pal of the band, twenty-one-year-old Vince Melouney, now living in London, joined on guitar, having likewise played on Bee Gees records in Australia.

The five-piece Bee Gees were presented to the public at a press-conference-cum-party to announce the signing of the band. Stigwood said it was 'impossible to overstate their international potential as performers and composers' and suggested they could be the 'new Beatles'. 'We can write a song about almost anything, to order,' said Barry. It was estimated that the initial campaign Stigwood put behind the band cost NEMS almost £50,000 (the equivalent of £800,000 today).

'I did a very big launch on them,' said Stigwood. He paid for 'Spicks And Specks' to get airplay on the influential pirate radio station Caroline, splashed out on new clothes for the group, and plastered the country with posters. He co-produced a new single, 'New York Mining Disaster 1941', that was released with indecent haste and gave the band their first Top 20 UK hit. Stigwood took out full-page adverts in the music press, proclaiming the group 'the most significant new musical act of 1967'. Beatle George Harrison said he had bought the single 'because it sounded so much like us'—so much so that a rumour circulated that the single was actually written by Lennon/McCartney.

'We came off the powerful Beatles hype machine,' said Robin. Stigwood enjoyed being around the group, loved their humour. 'We became good friends,' he said. 'Had lot of fun. They were incredible funny characters. Amusing ... lots of gags.' But he wanted more than a laugh. He 'wanted to really crack America quickly'. He sent out promotional copies of the single to radio stations with no signifier except NEMS and whispers that the group's name began with *B* and ended in *S*. Stigwood's 'scheme' worked, and some America DJs announced it as the new Beatles record. Lennon denied it, adding fuel to the fire. The record took off, and the band was invited to appear Dick Clark's *American Bandstand*. 'To crack America was the ultimate dream,' said Maurice.

Stigwood continued to clash with Epstein over the group. The pair argued over which American record label should handle the group in America: Epstein favoured Capitol, The Beatles' American label, while Stigwood preferred Atlantic, home of Aretha Franklin, Sam & Dave, and Otis Redding, to whom he had recently signed Cream. Stigwood got his way and was soon telling the UK press about the 'biggest record deal ever involving a new group', claiming Atlantic had paid an incredible $250,000 for the rights to Bee Gees records for America for the next five years. He introduced the American press to the band by sailing journalists around Manhattan on a luxury yacht he chartered, while a select few were flown in via helicopter. He wanted to give the impression the band was already superstars. 'Everyone is clamouring for Bee Gees songs,' he bragged.

Epstein grew increasingly upset over what he saw as Stigwood's personal extravagance. In London it had been turkeys from the local butchers or clothes from Harrods, all charged to NEMS. Now Stigwood wanted to charge the yacht to his personal account. 'What personal account?' Epstein fumed. He had already loaned Stigwood £10,000 out of his own pocket.

'New York Mining Disaster 1941' hit the American Top 20, and with that The Bee Gees' American career was up and running. They followed this with 'To Love Somebody', again written by Barry and Robin and co-produced by Stigwood. Robin and Barry had utilised their talent for mimicry and imagined they were writing the song for Otis Redding. A story emerged that Redding had actually asked the band to write him the song, but Barry would later admit he had written the song for Stigwood, who had requested it for his thirty-third birthday. 'Something along the lines of Sam & Dave or The Rascals,' Stigwood had instructed. 'It was for Robert,' Barry said. 'I don't think it was homosexual affection but tremendous admiration for the man's gifts and abilities.'

'To Love Somebody' was another Top 20 hit in America. Stigwood rushed out the band's debut album, which made the Top 10 in the UK and America. Then came the mammoth 'Massachusetts', the band's fifth single in just under six months. This time the song was credited to all three brothers and produced solely by Stigwood, who had ousted co-producer Ossie Byrne. Byrne had been with the group since Australia, where he developed the group in his own studio at his own expense. Described by Barry as a 'spirit guide', he had become their co-manager and travelled to London with them, co-producing, alongside Stigwood, the early hits. Now he was out. 'Robert wanted more production rights on the songs,' said Robin. 'Ossie had to step down. We had no say in the matter.'

'Massachusetts' was written as a 'send-up' of Tom Jones or

Engelbert Humperdinck, said Maurice. It was supposed to be a joke but Stigwood had insisted they record the song. He was finally in accord with Epstein, who declared the song 'beautiful' and predicted, 'It's going to be a world #1.' Epstein would not live to see 'Massachusetts' become the band's first #1 in the UK and across Europe, as well as Japan and Australia, peaking at #11 in America and selling five million copies in total worldwide. He died suddenly on August 27 1967, just a few weeks from his thirty-third birthday, from an accidental overdose of sleeping pills. The night before his death, Robin said he had heard Epstein, in tears, arguing loudly with Stigwood. At NEMS it became apparent immediately that The Beatles did not want to hand over control to Stigwood, who was also unpopular with many of the senior staff, including Epstein's brother Clive. There was a legal opinion that Stigwood and Shaw's deal was with Epstein alone and that it had therefore lapsed with his death. A statement was quickly issued by NEMS: 'Policies agreed between Brian Epstein and Robert Stigwood are now not practically possible.'

Stigwood and Shaw resigned from the board of NEMS and took all their assets to form the Robert Stigwood Organisation. 'I made the decision to go on my own, take The Bee Gees and Cream with me and focus my efforts on building their careers,' Stigwood said. It was rumoured that the 'amicable' parting involved a significant settlement for Stigwood and Shaw—a buyout in the region of £25,000. The pair persuaded Polydor to back the newly formed RSO with finances reputedly worth close to two million pounds. There was also a second 'very wordy' contract drawn up for The Bee Gees to sign.

RSO was immediately and hugely successful. Cream's second album, *Disraeli Gears*, was a major hit, hitting the Top 5 in the UK and America, while a single from the album, 'Sunshine Of Your Love', also broke into the American Top 5. The Bee Gees sixth and final UK single of 1967, 'World', sold over two million copies. They were now being featured on the front covers of the music press, with Barry pushed to the fore as the group's heartthrob, and voted 'Best New Group' by the *NME*. Barry and Robin spent Christmas at Stigwood's family home in Australia. 'He was almost like a parent,' said Barry. Stigwood made sure the momentum behind the group continued with a series of well-orchestrated publicity stunts.

When the Home Office quietly began proceedings to deport Colin Peterson and Vince Melouney back to Australia, both of whom were in the UK on temporary visas, Stigwood launched a massive 'Save The Bee Gees' campaign that made national headlines and cemented the band as a household name in the UK. Fans chained themselves to the railings outside Buckingham Palace, an elephant marched on Downing Street, a helicopter landed in the Chancellor of the Exchequer's garden, and there was a picket outside prime minister Harold Wilson's holiday residence in the Scilly Isles.

'The government is continually asking for help in the export drive and this group is potentially one of the biggest foreign currency earners for years,' Stigwood told the press, estimating that the band had earned $250,000 on foreign record sales in the past three months alone. The Bee Gees could, he suggested, earn as much money in record sales as The Beatles—maybe more. 'Even the Beatles hadn't sold so many million records around the world and conquered America in their first year,' he said, while Robin added, 'Others are awarded an MBE or a nosh at Buckingham Palace, but we are treated like criminals.' Stigwood created such an uproar that he was able to brag that 'finally the prime minister had to intervene'. In fact it was Roy Jenkins, the home secretary, who declared the band a 'social and national asset' and issued the two Bee Gees with the correct permits to stay. Ironically, Melouney would soon quit the group, blaming the 'overbearing and dictatorial' Hugh for treating him like 'an outsider'. Robin, he said, was also offhand with him, and with Peterson, never bothering to get to know either musician and sometimes criticising them onstage.

Stigwood also made the band's live shows events, hiring a thirty-piece orchestra to back them for a showcase headline at the Saville theatre, and then, in March 1968, at the Royal Albert Hall, organising what he called the most spectacular concert in rock history, with The Bee Gees backed by a sixty-seven-piece orchestra, a forty-five-piece air force band, and a large choir of forty. 'Quite a night,' said Stigwood, who said he had wanted to go one better than everybody else. 'Big things are happening for them, and there's no reason why their affairs shouldn't be treated with a certain amount of flamboyance.'

In America, two gigs in California, again with a thirty-piece orchestra, attracted 16,000 fans and earned the group $25,000, a notably high fee at the time. The group's US tour, which included a headline show at the Hollywood Bowl, would gross a minimum of one million dollars, Stigwood predicted. 'It's the biggest deal of its kind in showbusiness,' he said. In Europe, particularly in Germany, the group's concerts attracted crowds of over 10,000 and sparked hysteria. In Zurich, 20,000 fans swarmed the band, and in the crush and panic their driver ran over a girl, luckily just breaking her leg, while another girl was thrown through a plate glass door.

At the same time, Cream were sparking an even greater hysterical response. Their third album was a hit around the world, topping the American charts and peaking at #3 in the UK. The group announced they were splitting up after a huge American farewell tour—with a guaranteed £500,000 advance—and two farewell dates at the Royal Albert Hall, which Stigwood planned to film for a movie about the band he himself was producing. Stigwood was a millionaire again and, from his desk—an inch-thick slab of glass set atop four stone lions in his Mayfair offices, which featured a mahogany-panelled boardroom, executive suite, and a 'chairman's suite' with crystal chandelier and fake fireplace—he oversaw the metamorphosis of RSO from rock management concern to multimedia entertainment empire.

●

Stigwood had first tried to buy Associated London Scripts, which represented around thirty leading TV writers, while at NEMS. Now he struck a deal with the director of the company, Beryl Vertue, and bought a controlling interest in ASL from the company's founders, Eric Sykes and Spike Milligan. Vertue, who also managed Frankie Howerd, became a managing director at RSO, and her writers became part of the RSO family. Ray Galton and Alan Simpson, who wrote *Hancock's Half Hour* as well as *Steptoe & Son,* were particularly keen to write movie scripts.

The impact of the deal on The Bee Gees was immediate as they made a one-off show for Thames TV with Howerd, *Frankie Howerd Meets The Bee Gees*, written by Galton and Simpson. Aired in August 1968, the TV special showed off the band's comedy skills as well as their music as they acted alongside Howerd in ludicrous sketches, dressed up as vampires and Frankenstein. Next, Stigwood announced that The Bee Gees were set to star in their own lavish, £500,000 film, written by *Till Death Us Do Part* writer and new RSO employee Johnny Speight, and to be shot in Kenya. The story was said to be about five young men enlisted in the army as musicians but then pressed into service in the Boer War. Stigwood planned to produce the film, which was set to co-star Spike Milligan. The movie didn't get off the ground, but it was suggestive of how Stigwood foresaw all sectors of RSO interacting.

He was already thinking of further American expansion, too: in May 1968, Stigwood announced the opening of his American arm,

Stigwood-Fitzpatrick Inc. The president was The Beatles' former US attorney, Robert Fitzpatrick. From offices in New York and Los Angeles, Stigwood hoped to develop scripts, sign American acts, produce records, and set up an American music publishing company. His first choice of manager for his American operation was controversial. Soho club owner and music manager Rik Gunnell had an edge that suggested gangsterism. There was a story about Georgie Fame, who Gunnell managed, trying to switch management; Gunnell was said to have taken the keys to Fame's brand new Jaguar and rammed it repeatedly into the pillars of an underground car park. Handing the keys back, he said, 'If you leave me I'll do the same to your fingers and you'll never play the piano again!'

Stigwood bought the Bag O' Nails club, a London hotspot and favourite of The Beatles, from the notorious Gunnell, and also took a controlling interest in his music management agency, which handled acts such as Fame, John Mayall, Geno Washington, Alan Price, and The Jeff Beck Group. The association with Gunnell was problematic from the off. In 1969, Gunnell's fiancée, Jean Lincoln, a famous show-business agent, was found dead in his New York apartment. In 1972, Gunnell collected some $250,000 of John Mayall's tour money and vanished. He was removed as a director of RSO. Peter Brown, Brian Epstein's former personal assistant, who had assumed many of his duties after Epstein's death—and who had helped found and run The Beatles' Apple company—took over RSO in America, as president and chief executive officer, staying in the position until 1977.

Stigwood was restless. For him, work was life, and his employees and bands were his friends. He formed a production company with Chas Chandler, a former member of The Animals and now manager of Jimi Hendrix, who was tasked with finding and developing new talent. In 1968, he saw the hippie countercultural rock musical *Hair* on

Broadway and decided to produce it in London. The show had caused uproar for its sexual content, irreverence, profanity, and, above all else, nudity. The cast recording was already a huge seller, racking up three million sales, with some songs from it becoming Top 10 hits. Stigwood bought the British rights to *Hair* and opened the show in London on September 27 1968 at the Shaftesbury Theatre. It was a huge hit, running for just short of two thousand performances.

The Bee Gees continued writing mammoth hits. In 1968 they had 'Words', credited to all three Gibbs but a solo spotlight vocally for Barry, a #1 in Germany, Holland, Switzerland, Japan, Malaysia, South Africa, New Zealand, Singapore, and Australia, and a fifth Top 20 hit in America. Next came 'I've Gotta Get A Message To You', again written by all three brothers. It became their first Top 10 single in America, peaking at #2, and their second British #1. They said they had written the song with Percy Sledge in mind. Robin sang lead and had written most of lyrics. He also sang lead on the follow-up, 'I Started A Joke', another big emotional ballad that showcased his unique voice.

'Writing about emotions is seen as soft,' said Robin, 'but people love songs that melt your heart.' It was the sort of material they thought the public wanted from them, even though Maurice hated much of the music the band was making, particularly 'Massachusetts' and 'I've Gotta Get A Message To You'. But it was working. The Bee Gees' second album, *Horizontal*, released in September 1968, had advance orders of 250,000 in America alone, where it reached the Top 20, peaking at #4 in the UK.

Stigwood remained firmly in control of their career. 'I pick their singles,' he told the press. 'It's always left to me to make final decision.' Even so, he indulged the band and their growing egos. He oversaw the release of an album by The Robert Stigwood Orchestra full of grandiose orchestrated instrumentals of their hits. He hired the train used by the

Queen and The Beatles as transport for a German tour, and told the press, 'Many people have said a success story of the magnitude of The Beatles couldn't happen again; it's happening.' Stigwood said that they had sold ten million singles and three million albums to date, calling it 'an unparalleled achievement'. He predicted they would be millionaires in two years but admitted they lived as if they were already. Stigwood thought of the Gibbs as resolute troopers—'old professionals', he called them—hardened by being 'in entertainment as children'.

In fact, the intense burst of fame, a year of non-stop recording and performing, had crippled them. Both Barry and Robin had collapsed from nervous exhaustion. The group had also been handed massive advances against future royalties, and huge loans from RSO, and spent lavishly without forethought or prudence. Their spending was so over the top that Eric Clapton suspected Stigwood had 'creamed off' most of the profits from Cream to finance The Bee Gees.

'It was impossible to keep our feet on the ground,' said Maurice. 'It was so hard to handle sudden success. Everything was going so fast. The swiftness of our success was scary.' Still only eighteen, Maurice lived in affluent Belgravia and bought John Lennon's black-windowed Mini Cooper, a Rolls-Royce Silver Cloud, and an Aston Martin DB6. He got himself involved with a party scene that revolved around hard-drinking Brit actors Richard Harris, Michael Caine, Peter O'Toole, Oliver Reed, Alan Bates, and Albert Finney. 'The whole gang of us, the London Mafia, used to go around together drinking a lot,' Maurice said. He grew more flamboyant and extroverted and started crashing his cars. The Rolls-Royce went into a tree; the Aston Martin was driven off a pier and abandoned. It was rumoured that the cost of his car collection alone would soon top one million. 'By the time I was twenty-one I had five Rolls and six Aston Martins,' he said.

Maurice's relationship with Lulu—at the height of her fame having just scored a huge American #1 with 'To Sir With Love' and been chosen to representing Britain in 1969's Eurovision Song Contest—raised his profile to such an extent that he eclipsed both of his brothers. 'No one knew me until I met my wife,' he said. 'Barry had the sex [idol] image, Robin's got the voice, and all I do is stand there and play my guitar.' From the start there was a sense that Stigwood had played matchmaker to the pair, teasing her away from Monkees singer Davy Jones and telling the press she was madly in love with Maurice. Their engagement was announced on TV, on the *Happening For Lulu* Christmas 1968 Saturday-night BBC1 TV special. On the show, Maurice played piano accompanied by an orchestra, and the couple duetted on the Donovan song 'What A Beautiful Creature You Are'. When they married a few months later, three thousand fans showed up. It was the showbiz marriage of the year.

Maurice was suddenly front-page news. '[We were] the king and queen of the world,' said Lulu. 'We thought we were fabulous.' They bought a new home in Highgate, where Ringo Starr was a neighbour. He and Maurice became drinking pals. 'We were going to [the newly opened] Tramp [club] every night, parking our Minis at the Speakeasy and driving home blitzed,' said Maurice. He wrecked a Bentley convertible, bashing his face up, but passed it off as nothing. He emerged from a crash in his Rolls-Royce Silver Cloud with a broken nose and two black eyes. Barry drove him to hospital. He was a mess, a drunk. He fell down the stairs at Stigwood's office and broke his arm. Money didn't matter to him. 'Cheques arrived for hundreds of thousands of pounds,' said Lulu. Maurice didn't even know what the money was for. The partying went on. 'The doorbell would go at 3am and it was [David] Bowie and Rod Stewart, and we'd get the bar open,' he said.

Even though he had acted as best man at the wedding, Robin was jealous of the attention Lulu and Maurice got. By 1968, his ego was out of control. He felt he had established himself as a lead vocalist equal to Barry and deserved an equal share of the limelight, challenging Barry's role as group leader. He began to dislike Stigwood, who seemed to always prefer Barry. He grew his hair and refused to have it cut when Stigwood ordered him to do so.

There was also a growing resentment over songwriting credits. A straight three-way split between the brothers did not represent how hits such as 'I've Gotta Get A Message To You' or 'I Started A Joke' were put together. Often, Maurice was not involved at all. Barry admitted the songwriting credits were a 'difficulty': 'One would write it but it would go down as B. R. & M. Gibb … the problem comes when it's a hit song and the person who actually wrote it realises he is missing out on the prestige of having individually written the song and also two-thirds of royalties.'

Robin was highly strung and sensitive to criticism; 'more artistic than the others in every way', said his mum. He was also addicted to pills, specifically speed and downers. 'I used to wallow in all those pills,' he said. 'He was in his own world,' said Barry. 'Robin suffered a lot. The pressure and fame got to Robin the most … the whole period is just constant speed. Dexadrine. We were all into pep pills, purple hearts and any other kind of speed we could get our hands on. It was hard to know what time of day it was. We just went from one thing to another. It never stopped … we were too green to see the dangers, the paranoia and illness. Robin was seriously ill.' The nervous breakdowns kept on coming. 'Everything was so intense,' said Molly, Robin's new wife, two years his senior, whom he had met when she was a secretary at NEMS. Molly said Stigwood 'manipulated' the group 'like puppets' and fuelled the unease between the brothers.

Above all, Robin was haunted by an incident that happened early in his relationship with Molly when they had been involved in a horrific train crash that had killed fifty-three people and left eighty severely injured. It was the worst rail disaster in England for ten years. Eleven of the twelve coaches had derailed. The first class carriage Robin and Molly had been on was spared. Robin had pulled dying people out of the wrecked carriages, stepped over mutilated bodies and severed limbs, and heard the screams for help as medics carried out amputations by the railway line. After the accident, his natural introspection tipped over into reclusive behaviour. He stayed home in his luxury apartment in Knightsbridge, taking copious amounts of speed and writing songs. He thought a lot about God, how his carriage must have been spared 'for a reason'. He suffered delayed shock and didn't sleep for 'a long, long time'. Barry told the press that Robin was 'twice as serious' about everything since the crash. 'He can't take life as a joke anymore,' he said. 'He's very quick to criticise everybody at every moment … he gets into terrible tempers and terrible moods … he's a very nervous person now, but he writes better music!'

The rivalry between the three brothers was obsessive, said Lulu, the tension vicious as they began to fight aggressively. It seemed to be Stigwood's attention they all wanted, Lulu writes in her autobiography, 'especially Mo and Robin'. Barry admitted Stigwood could be 'disruptive' and 'played favourites', that sometimes 'it was like a popularity contest'. The resentments were piling up. Maurice also began to challenge Barry's dominance over the group. He reacted angrily when Barry spoke out against his marrying Lulu, saying his brother was too young. Barry, now twenty-two, was thinking of his own teenage marriage, the recent ending of which had been acrimonious and led to him having a mental breakdown. He told the press he had kept the marriage secret because he didn't want to 'spoil my image'. Now he was hooked up with model Linda Gray, who at seventeen had been Miss Edinburgh 1967 and a hostess on *Top Of The Pops*. In London, Jimmy Savile had been looking after her for her parents—which, in retrospect, must have been a highly problematic relationship.

Gray was glad to meet Barry and escape from Savile. They lived in a duplex penthouse flat in Eaton Square with a roof garden and a fountain in the lounge. Barry had stopped Linda from modelling. He employed Keith, his sister Lesley's husband, to work as his PA, and kept two servants. He was looking beyond the group now and producing other acts, such as Australian outfit The Marbles—their name chosen by Barry—who scored a Top 5 hit in the UK with a song written by all three brothers. He was also involved with a new Australian girl group, a teenage male singer, and an eleven-year-old girl singer who was a friend of the Gibb family. Barry also told the press he wanted to be a film star.

He lived an opulent lifestyle, spending small fortunes on Carnaby Street clobber, boasting of his £16,000-a-year clothing budget, and over-the-top jewellery, thinking nothing of dropping £20,000 on the many rings and bracelets he wore. He made the news when he had jewellery worth £8,000 stolen on holiday in Australia. There was little sympathy from the British public—the average annual wage in the country was less than £1,500. There was even less sympathy when he got caught smuggling jewellery into the UK, trying to evade customs duty on a £3,000 watch. He was fined £2,000, plus £500 for making a false statement.

Barry could not stop showing off, though. He said he owned six cars, including a Rolls-Royce and a Lamborghini that he claimed he cleaned with cashmere sweaters (leading Robin to claim that he cleaned his shoes with his suits). It was reported that the band was earning three million pounds a year, and Barry felt he was sitting on a 'ludicrous amount of money', estimating he was bringing in half a million a year. Stigwood, he later complained, never gave the group any guidance about their finances, the structure of which the band never fully understood.

In many ways, Barry was as unhinged as his younger brothers, stoned, firing a BB gun at the chandeliers hanging from his ceiling. He collected firearms. In fact, he had recently been arrested for firing a .38 revolver at what the courts described as 'a thirty-four-year-old man from Edinburgh ringing his front door bell demanding money'. Barry said the same man had also been making harassing calls to his home. Barry was fined £25 for possessing the German Luger without a firearms certificate. He later admitted the band had 'got too big for our boots' and 'lost contact with real world'.

●

The carefully constructed image Stigwood had created around the group shattered during their debut American tour—the one Stigwood had predicted would generate a million dollars. Ticket sales were shockingly poor. Concerts cancelled. Shows in Los Angeles and New York, at Forest Hills, were good, but the 'shows were papered to an extent', said Barry. 'The tour was a wash out.' Robin, who was still not sleeping, collapsed and was hospitalised due to severe nervous exhaustion. The band would not play America again until 1971, and it was not until the success of *Saturday Night Fever* that they finally became a profitable touring act.

The Gibbs' private lives continued to unravel. All the group's wives were getting poison from fans. 'We were in total chaos,' said Barry. The pressure, he said, was unbearable. 'There was too much money and we stayed to ourselves, surrounded by hangers on. We were nervous wrecks.' He announced he was going solo, telling the press he had received several film offers in Los Angeles. 'It's now or never for me,' he said. 'I want to be a big star in the mould of Bob Hope or Bing Crosby.' The Bee Gees, he said, 'were formed with the intention of a short-term future—get in, get some money, and get out'.

Such was the dysfunction between the three brothers that Robin said he only heard about Barry's plans via the press. Leaving The Bee Gees, however, was not as easy as Barry imagined. Stigwood had him contractually tied to the group for a further two years. 'I have said I shall be leaving The Bee Gees and I stand by that,' Barry said, 'but I shall fulfil existing commitments.' The atmosphere within the group hit a new low. All three brothers now wanted to go solo. 'We'd become enemies,' Maurice said. 'The magic was lost.' As the rivalry intensified, the hits started to dry up, especially in America, where they struggled to make the Top 40 in 1969. 'We could no longer deal with each other,' said Barry, 'The three of us drifted apart—in fact, I'd say the four of us drifted apart, including Robert.'

Stigwood was occupied with, among other things, the launch of Eric Clapton's new group, Blind Faith. He executed his most ambitious concert to date for them: a free gig in June 1969 in London's Hyde Park for over 100,000 people. Clapton was a superstar, voted the world's top musician, and the Hyde Park curtain-raiser was followed by hugely profitable Blind Faith tours of Europe and America, where a sell-out Madison Square Garden gig in New York to 20,000 was the highlight of a seven week concert schedule. 'Stigwood didn't give us time to think,' complained Clapton. The band's hastily recorded debut album went to #1 in America and the UK, selling half a million copies. The band's huge commercial success also stimulated Cream back-catalogue sales and led to Stigwood picking up the Trendsetter Award from *Billboard* magazine in America 'for popularising the concept of free admission open-air concerts in Britain, and for backing the London presentation of *Hair*—thus setting a new style in musicals'.

Stigwood did try and reinvigorate The Bee Gees, urging them to make a concept double album, a rock opera: 'something that could be put onstage', said Barry. But the band was not on speaking terms, and

Robin's health was poor. 'There was no communication between him and me and Maurice,' said Barry. 'It just got way out of hand.' There were blistering arguments in the studio, and to complete the project the brothers had to go into the studio one at a time. When it came to choosing the first single from the album, called *Odessa*, Robin demanded a song he sang lead vocals on, 'Lamplight', calling it 'the strongest thing we've ever written', predicting it would be #1 for weeks. Stigwood favoured a song Barry had sung, 'First Of May'. Robin threatened to remove all his songs from the album, changed his phone number, and refused to answer the door.

Stigwood brushed away Robin's tantrum and said he'd not yet chosen a single that all three brothers had liked. 'Somebody is always going to be unhappy,' he said. Stigwood added that he usually made the right decision, citing the twenty-five million singles the band had sold to date. He told the press Robin 'had one of the finest pop voices of all time' but called Barry a fantastic solo singer in his own right.

Robin quit. It was March 1969, just two years after they'd signed with Stigwood. Robin was nineteen. He said his dislike of Barry had turned slowly to hatred, and that he had felt like a prisoner in the band. He spoke out against Stigwood. 'Maurice and I were neglected, publicity-wise,' he said. 'It had been all Barry.' Barry responded by calling Robin selfish, arrogant, and condescending. 'Robin wants to sunbathe in the spotlight while the rest of the group stand in the shadows,' he said. 'He is rude, unwell, with a big persecution complex. He thinks everybody hates him.'

Stigwood said the same thing: 'Robin tends to think the whole world is against him. He has no confidence at all and can be hurt by the pettiest of remarks which is silly since every artist must expect to receive a few knocks.' He told the press that Robin had been hospitalised and was 'under great strain', recovering from a 'minor breakdown'. As soon as he recovered, they would be able to discuss his future with the group, Stigwood added.

'They make me sick,' Robin responded. He said he was going solo. Stigwood said he had Robin under contract for two more years and would take legal action 'against anybody who purports to issue a recording by Robin in breach of the Stigwood Group of Companies'. He infuriated Stigwood further by failing to appear for scheduled TV appearances on *Happening For Lulu*, Lulu's new BBC1 TV series (which would run until 1975) and a BBC2 live concert special. Stigwood persuaded Lesley, now a mother of four, to stand in for her brother at the gig and talked about launching her as a solo star. He said there was a tour of America lined up for the group, including a gig at Madison Square Garden, and that the 'show would go on' with or without Robin.

Now Hugh got involved. 'Barry and Maurice have got to show Robin they can do it without him,' he said, suggesting younger brother Andy as a possible future replacement for Robin in The Bee Gees. Andy had just turned ten. Barry told the press he would never work with Robin again. He said they were now 'dire enemies', laughing at Robin's solo ambitions. 'I've been writing for nine years, he's only been writing for a few years,' he said. Maurice said that Barry was 'so full of pride he couldn't understand why Robin had done it'. There was talk of replacing Robin with former Cream and Blind Faith bassist and singer Jack Bruce, now that Blind Faith were splitting after just over a year together. There were unknowns auditioned, too, but Stigwood blocked all moves to replace Robin, suggesting Maurice sing more lead. RSO hurriedly put together a hits album, *Best Of Bee Gees*, which temporarily patched over the discord, going Top 10 in the UK, America, Canada, and Australia.

Three months after announcing he was quitting the group, Robin issued his debut solo single, 'Saved By The Bell'. It rose to #2 in the

UK and was huge hit around Europe, although not in America, where in barely scraped into the Top 100. In interviews, a manic Robin did himself few favours, claiming to having written one hundred songs in ten weeks, six destined for Tom Jones, plus a book of stories and poems ('I'm a great admirer of Dickens'), two films, and several musicals, one based on *A Christmas Carol* called *Scrooge* and another based on the life of Henry VIII.

'I can move into films at the flick of a finger,' he said. 'I'm ten times better off than before. I have no intention of returning to the group. I would rather sweep roads or lay carpets.' He outlined plans for high-profile live shows billed as 'An Evening with Robin Gibb', with 'ninety-seven-piece orchestras' and 'sixty-piece choirs'. He suggested he was the real artist in the band; that Barry was more concerned with 'publicity' than recording; and compared himself to Bob Dylan. His interviews were also dotted with conspiratorial references to MI5 and secret nuclear warheads. Soon he was talking about becoming a film star and having a hundred-piece orchestra backing him on a tribute he'd written to Winston Churchill.

Robin's single, which Maurice claimed was a product of Bee Gees sessions, had been issued by Polydor, the same company Stigwood had put out all The Bee Gees records with in Europe, and he was being loosely managed by a Stigwood employee, Chris Hutchins, on behalf of RSO. Robin was determined to extricate himself from the control of Stigwood completely. RSO, however, would not allow him free from his contact. There was a stalemate. Robin's finances were uncertain. He and Molly had just moved out of London into a new mansion in Surrey, and he continued to spend extravagantly, treating himself to a £6,000 Mercedes that he gave away the next day to his PA. But with lawyers wrangling over his future and his cash flow drying up entirely, the foolishness had to stop.

'Absolutely crazy nightmare,' said Molly. 'Terribly unpleasant.' She said the couple was forced to pawn items from their new home to get by. 'I was told he had gone through an extraordinary amount of money,' said Stigwood. Soon, Robin was emboldened to announce he had signed a new management contract with Vic Lewis, the managing director of NEMS. The deal, it was claimed, was worth at least £400,000 a year. Lewis had been an adversary when Stigwood was seeking control of NEMS in the aftermath of Epstein's death. Now RSO issued writs against Lewis and NEMS, restating that Robin was under exclusive contract to RSO for agency, management, recording and publishing for another two years.

Hugh became embroiled in the dispute. 'My wife can't take anymore,' he said, and in September 1969 he went to the High Court to try to have Robin declared a ward of the court, 'for his own protection'. Usually this would apply to either a child under eighteen or an incapacitated person whom a court can take legal responsibility for. Robin was two months from being twenty. Hugh clearly felt he was incapacitated. 'Certain people around him are trying to rip him off,' Hugh said. 'I can see what is happening. We believe he is almost a prisoner in his own home. He is very heavily guarded.' Robin called it 'ridiculous' and suggested Hugh was 'just making a fool of himself'. In another interview he warned his father that he might end up with 'concrete boots' if he persisted in the court action.

Finally, in November, Stigwood let Robin go. 'They [Barry and Maurice] were so upset by Robin's departure that we had to release Robin from the company,' he said. 'That was really the most difficult part of it.' He made one of his famously tough deals: a NEMS spokesman said Robin had been forced to relinquish his shares in all the Bee Gees songs in return for his release from the RSO in all areas. It was said that he had sold his shares in the songs to Stigwood for £40,000. RSO's publishing arm, Abigail Music, would also control Robin's new songs for the next five years.

While the dispute with Robin unfolded, Maurice and Barry had filmed lead roles in an hour-long BBC TV special called *Cucumber Castle*, which was advertised as having been 'devised and written' by The Bee Gees and described by Maurice as 'a Tudor period comedy with breaks for our songs and top line guests'. It cost £50,000 to make and was shot at Stigwood's impressive Stanmore spread, where a Scottish castle was removed brick by brick and rebuilt in the grounds. It was a camp, kitsch, and packed with silly skits. The brothers had starring roles as the idiot sons of a bedridden king, played by Frankie Howerd, with guest appearances by Vincent Price, Lulu, and Spike Milligan. In one memorable scene, Maurice and Barry were dressed as oversized ducks. 'We've waited two years to do this film,' said Maurice. There was talk of a thirteen-week spin-off TV series and a soundtrack album.

After filming was complete, Stigwood unceremoniously fired Bee Gees drummer Colin Peterson via a short letter, signed by Maurice, Barry, and Hugh, and delivered by Stigwood's chauffeur. Peterson had not contributed to the music significantly since he joined but he was a family friend and had actually found the Gibbs a house to stay in when they first landed in London. 'We were pressured to do it,' said Barry. Peterson had been asking questions about business, wondering how Stigwood could best manage the group with so many conflicting interests. How could he, for instance, manage the band, be their promoter/agent, own their master recordings, *and* be their publisher? Would he put the publishing and recording interests of RSO over the interests of the group? 'He had complete control over all aspects of his acts,' said Peterson, who took his case to High Court, where he lost his right to a share of the band's royalties. He ended up working as a painter and decorator.

Ultimately, the BBC did not commission a series of *Cucumber Castle* and postponed the screening of the special until Christmas 1970. A single from the soundtrack, 'Don't Forget To Remember', made #2 in the UK in August 1969. The song was a country & western pastiche written by Maurice and Barry and evoking Jim Reeves. It was a smash in Europe and Australia, but like Robin's single it failed to make any impact in America. Barry tried to put a positive spin on the future for the band, talking of a concert tour with a 'big orchestra' before Christmas and star parts for himself and Maurice in a movie version of *Hair* 'to be made in three months' (in response to which an RSO spokesman was forced to concede that RSO had not yet got the films rights to the musical).

'We're having a ball,' said Maurice. 'We know we don't want to split up.' Barry said he and Maurice were much closer now, 'working much more together'. It was rumoured that they were working with George Harrison and Eric Clapton on a new album. 'We've always been the closest brothers,' said Barry, explaining how 'they both loved ballads'. He talked of a complete partnership in business, and of how the pair planned to set up a record label and production company. In the studio, however, they tended to work separately while writing and producing for soul singer P.P. Arnold, Samantha Sang (an Australian seventeen-year-old, real name Cheryl Gray, whom Stigwood suggested would be as big as Barbra Streisand), and The Marbles (whose singer Stigwood suggested could be a new Tom Jones). Maurice, on his own, produced a surprise Top 20 hit in America for the Australian group Tin Tin, 'Toast And Marmalade'.

Despite their claims to the press, Barry and Maurice were no longer close. 'I find it easier to talk to Robin,' Maurice admitted. Barry had become a recluse, preferring to watch TV or read books on UFOs and mysticism than to go out clubbing. Maurice was still doing plenty of the latter, often with Lulu's brother, Billy Lawrie. After the second single from the proposed *Cucumber Castle* soundtrack album, 'I.O.I.O.', failed to make the charts in America or the UK, The Bee Gees called it quits. Barry said the final straw was when he had showed up at the studio to begin recording a new album and Maurice hadn't. He had gone to Australia with Lulu to promote *Cucumber Castle* instead, but no one had told Barry, who said he 'felt isolated and rejected'.

In December 1969, Barry officially announced the end of The Bee Gees, citing legal problems. 'As from today, I'm solo,' he said, describing the previous months as a 'traumatic experience' and 'the biggest nightmare'. The press intrusion into the fallout with Robin had made the lives of the Gibb family 'hell'. He described himself as 'miserable, disappointed, completely disillusioned, [and] heading for a breakdown'. He said he had started the group when he was nine, and now he'd had enough.

CHAPTER THREE

HEALTHY SHADE OF BROWN

ARIF MARDIN
BARRY, I HAVE AN IDEA. TRY SINGING THE CHORUS IN FALSETTO.

Eric Clapton had stepped out of the limelight after Blind Faith split up in late 1969. For a while he had played the hired hand to the Plastic Ono Band, Delaney & Bonnie, and George Harrison. In late 1970 he released a debut solo album that failed to chart in America, and then returned with a new group called Derek & The Dominoes. He was fed up of being a 'superstar' and hoped to hide behind the 'Derek' persona. Stigwood reacted by launching a 'Derek is Eric' publicity campaign, but the band's debut album, while still an American Top 20 hit, failed to reach the heights of Cream or Blind Faith.

Clapton was, at the time, hooked on heroin, cocaine, and booze. He was also infatuated with George Harrison's wife Patti Boyd, about whom he had written the Dominoes track 'Layla', but she had rebuffed his pleas that she leave Harrison for him. Clapton had told Harrison he loved Boyd at one of Stigwood's Stanmore parties. His heroin addiction soon consumed him, and he famously passed out onstage in 1971 at a charity gig. It would be a couple of years before he was deemed fit enough to be back onstage and Pete Townshend organised a comeback concert for him.

During the hiatus, Stigwood had continued to exploit Clapton's back catalogue with albums such as the 1972 compilation *The History Of Eric Clapton*, a Top 20 hit in the UK and Top 10 in America, which had finally made a rereleased 'Layla' a hit. There had also been several Cream compilation albums, and Clapton's 1973 comeback concert was released as a live album, hitting the Top 20 in the UK and America. By 1974, the twenty-nine-year-old Clapton was no longer using heroin, although he was still drinking heavily. He said the only pressure Stigwood had applied to him while he had spent close to three years strung-out and non-productive was when his habit had hit its peak and he was spending the equivalent of thousands of pounds a week in today's money on heroin. Funds were running low, Stigwood warned him.

'Through the course of my addiction, Stigwood always had faith that I would come through,' Clapton said. 'Even though it was an enormous gamble, he stuck by me.' When the pair sat down to plan a future, Stigwood asked, 'What do you want to do? Because I know what I want you to do.' Clapton said, 'Well, I've got all these ideas, and I think I want to make a record.' Stigwood answered that was good because he had already booked Criteria Studios in Miami, where Derek & The Dominoes had recorded, and Atlantic Records producer Tom Dowd, who had produced Cream and the Dominoes album. 'It had all been prearranged,' said Clapton. 'I remember thinking how great it was that he had shown such foresight in putting together something that I could just step into.'

Stigwood had rented a luxury house, 461 Ocean Boulevard, right on the seafront in Miami Beach, for Clapton to stay in while recording. He had also lined up Yvonne Elliman, twenty-three, to provide backing vocals on the album. Elliman had played Mary Magdalene in *Jesus Christ Superstar* on Broadway in 1971 (and scored a hit single with a song from the musical), and in the hit 1973 movie version, her performance in which had been nominated for a Golden Globe. She embarked on a short-lived romance with Clapton in Miami, while the resulting album, named *461 Ocean Boulevard*, was cut quickly, in a month, and released in July 1974. Clapton had not wanted to include the lead single, 'I Shot The Sherriff', on the album but Stigwood had sniffed a hit and forced the issue. He was rewarded with Clapton's first American #1 single. The album also reached #1 in America and was a hit all across Europe, peaking at #3 in the UK. Stigwood sent Clapton out on a massive six-week, twenty-eight-city tour of North American stadiums, where he played to up to seventy thousand people a night.

Clapton's success could be in no starker contrast to that of the ailing Bee Gees. After their humiliations in Batley and the cabaret clubs, Barry had sought to rally the group. 'This is never ever going to happen to this group again,' he said. However, their new album, *Mr Natural*, their first since January 1973, was a flop when it was finally released in July 1974. 'A disaster,' Maurice said. It peaked at #178 in the America charts, while the three singles from the album all sold poorly. Only one of them, the title track, made the charts anywhere in the world, peaking at #11 in Australia. RSO booked them on a three-month world tour to support the album. There were no shows scheduled for the UK, but the band retained a following in Australia and the Far East, in Japan, Hong Kong, Malaysia, Thailand, Indonesia, and the Philippines—countries they had played often over the past few years as the scrambled for money. The dates in America proved disastrous, however, and were marked by poor attendances.

In Japan, The Bee Gees crossed paths with Eric Clapton, who was also touring the country. Here the two acts were more equal and socialised easily. They discussed music and The Bee Gees' desire to rise up again as a contemporary force. Clapton's guitarist, George Terry, who was from Miami, suggested that if the band really wanted to go down a new path they should record in Criteria, the studio where Clapton had revitalised himself. Clapton told Barry it was a good idea and to speak to Stigwood. 'Maybe the change of environment will do something for you,' Clapton advised. Maurice said Clapton showed them a picture of the *461 Ocean Boulevard* cover, which featured Clapton posing in front of the Miami property, all white stucco and Cuban barrel tile roof with a single palm tree in front, and said, 'Rent that place and live there, record and get a sun tan.'

At this point The Bee Gees' drummer at the time, former Amen Corner member Dennis Bryon, spoke up. Bryon's musical career had nosedived since Amen Corner hit #1 with '(If Paradise Is) Half As Nice' in 1969, and he needed the steady wage the drum stool in The Bee Gees offered—a £30 a week retainer plus additional fees for each show. Stigwood had been threatening 'big changes' if the band's next album did not have a hit on it, and Bryon feared for his livelihood. Although he had been in the band for over a year, up until now he had not dared share his opinion about their live shows: that the songs were 'out of date' and there were 'too many ballads and not enough R&B or funk'. Now the twenty-five-year-old spoke quietly and carefully to 'the leader', Barry, who he knew liked 'coming up with the ideas himself'. He suggested ditching the local orchestras the band had been hiring for each gig on the tour and putting together 'a real band': two guitars, bass, drums, Hammond organ, synth, horn section, and 'even percussion'. Barry, he said, was nonchalant. 'If you think it's a good idea, you put it together,' he said.

●

It had been almost four years now since the Gibbs had regrouped and they found it hard to be enthusiastic about a future for The Bee Gees. They had all known *Mr Natural* was a disjointed, half-hearted effort, but its failure had hit them hard. Although they had made some money from the three-month world tour, the dates had not been 'fulfilling', said Robin, who wondered again about trying to resurrect a solo career cut short when the Robert Stigwood Organisation was floated on the English stock exchange in July 1970, turning it into a public corporation. It had been a brave and highly unusual move by Stigwood—an innovation driven by his business partner David Shaw. Shares in the company had initially floundered, however. Brokers Sebag had offered two million 10p shares at 37.5p, but by the end of the first day of trading only 540,000 had been taken up by investors. A few days later, the shares were selling at roughly one third of face value. It had been speculated that the value of the Stigwood Group of Companies was three million pounds (over forty million today), but the financial markets now dictated the genuine value, and it was badly down on expectations.

For the Gibbs, Clapton, and all the other significant RSO acts, this was a worrying time. Up until now, to avoid high rates of personal tax, RSO artistes had never been paid directly. All monies were instead collected by RSO, which paid a lesser company taxation, and then loaned to the acts. If a Bee Gee earned a hundred pounds, he might lose 96 percent to the taxman. If RSO received the cash instead it would be liable to 50 percent company taxation. That would leave fifty pounds, tax paid, within the company. RSO would then 'lend' the Bee Gee the fifty pounds. The system had been elegant, legal, and for a period successful. But the balance between loans, profits, and spending had spiralled out of control, and soon there was an almost £600,000 black hole in RSO finances, the loans they had paid to artists as yet unearned. Although the company had few fixed assets—just an office and a handful of cars—it had an inner strength in the song publishing copyrights it owned, fees for which would keep coming in, but it also had a massive cash-flow problem.

Asked to pay back the loans, the individual Bee Gees had been put in a difficult position. They did not have the money. They had spent it. Barry was planning his wedding to Linda—his best man was the gay fashion kingpin John Stephens, who owned numerous shops on Carnaby Street—and had just moved to a grand house in Gerrards Cross, Buckinghamshire, with an enormous driveway and full-size snooker table, the walls papered with gold records. Linda said the couple had spent lot of money 'when they didn't have it in liquid cash'. She said Barry was spending 'advances and loans', and then all of sudden 'the office' asked them to pay back the debt. To complicate things further, the loans and advances had not come direct from RSO but via Polydor. The Bee Gees could work off their debt by making money for Polydor, producing records for which they had already been paid. But The Bee Gees had just split up.

It was then that Shaw cooked up the floatation idea. The Bee Gees were told it would resolve their debts in one go. In return, for the sale of their songs and master recordings, they would get shares in the public company. All the RSO acts were offered the same deal. It was a stressful period. Gangsters tried to grab control of RSO; Barry claimed he and his brothers received death threats and 'threats to our families' to sell their shares pre-floatation at knockdown prices. 'Major people,' he said 'were harassing us and persecuting us.' Heavies would appear late at night, banging on doors. 'I can't say who sent them, various major concerns,' he said. 'One night I was lying in the hallway with a gun, pointing at the front door.' Stigwood said Robin had been pressured harder than anyone to give up his shares. Ultimately, he did, but not to gangsters. Instead, they went in a nasty, hard-fought boardroom battle between the lawyers at NEMS and RSO as he sought to pursue his solo career.

In the final reckoning, Polydor, the major financier of RSO, held most of the shares. Next came Stigwood, with shares worth over half a million pounds; then David Shaw, with shares worth £400,000. Barry was next, with shares worth £166,000; then came Maurice, whose slice was worth £112,000. Clapton had shares worth £27,000, while Frankie Howerd's shares were worth £38,000. Following the flotation, called one of the 'biggest flops in recent years' by financial experts, the value of these shares plummeted. Barry said the value of his shares had £36,000 wiped off them, while Maurice was down £24,000.

'For some reason best known to itself the City looks upon the showbusiness world as a poor relation,' Stigwood said at the time. 'We are going to show how wrong the pundits can be and make them eat their words.' Although the floatation had wiped off approximately a third of RSO's debt, there was still a major cash-flow issue within the company, and there was talk within the City of the company folding. 'Diabolical nonsense,' said Stigwood. 'My people will bring in an annual profit of £250,000. The public has been buying. But the institutions are fence sitting, hoping for a low opening price. If I misjudged things as much as the City does, I would not be in business a fortnight.'

Barry had nothing left in the bank—'only shares in RSO'. His solo career had failed to take off, with a debut solo album left unreleased following a flop debut single. He was bitter, claiming that Polydor had sabotaged his career to force him to reform the band, but the floatation, he said, had made him 'hard, more steely', made him realise the music business 'wasn't all stars and flowers'. Stigwood had suggested The Bee Gees reform prior to the floatation of RSO. With Blind Faith finished and Clapton faltering, he wanted a hit to buoy the market. Now, with the company in dire straits, the band's finances precarious, the situation demanded it.

'We grew up fast at that point,' said Barry. There was a lot at stake. Robin, who needed to be bought out of his NEMS contract for a figure rumoured to be £50,000, described a night spent with lawyers arguing over how to redistribute RSO shares between the three of them and the next morning meeting at Stigwood's offices and reforming over champagne on the roof garden before heading to the studio to record. 'Spiritually, our heads weren't in it,' Barry said. 'We were still upset with each other ... everything we did was for the corporation. Shareholders and speculators needed some confidence. It was all done legally, everybody had their lawyer in the room ... there was a battle going on over who could get the most amount of shares.'

The band announced their reformation in August 1970, one month after the floatation of RSO. Maurice told the press that 'we all want to get the good vibrations back into the company'. He too had released a flop solo single and had been reduced to writing commercial jingles for TV adverts, his music selling shoes, toothpaste, and package holidays. He was drinking more heavily than ever, and his marriage to Lulu, who had recently thrown an ashtray at his head, was disintegrating. Stigwood had tried to keep him on an even keel with a role in musical he was producing, *Sing A Rude Song*, based on the life of music-hall performer Marie Lloyd and starring Barbara Windsor, but Maurice had not enjoyed 'dancing around like a half-assed clown' and the production had failed, with the original cast album that Maurice produced for the show buried.

'I always instinctively knew that they'd get back together,' said Stigwood. 'Individually they are creative people. Collectively they are the best pop group in the world.' They quickly knocked together an album, *2 Years On*, for release in November 1970. The lead single from it, 'Lonely Days', became their biggest US hit to date, peaking at #3, selling over one million copies worldwide and, crowed Stigwood, reaching '#1 in 14 different countries'. Robin bragged that the song, credited to him and Barry, was written in ten minutes. 'I could never envisage composing with anyone but Barry,' he declared. 'He brings out the best in me … it's like a spiritual thing when we write.' The single helped carry *2 Years On* into the Top 40 in America. In the UK, however, the band could not catch a cold. 'Lonely Days' failed to make the Top 20, and the album did not even chart. Stigwood blamed the bad press surrounding the acrimonious split, claiming it had turned the 'English public' against the band.

The Bee Gees focused their efforts on America, and at the start of 1971 went to #1 there with 'How Can You Mend A Broken Heart?', a song Barry said was about 'how we felt coming back together'. Again, the song was credited to just Robin and Barry, the pair having channelled crooner Andy Williams to come up with the gentle, maudlin, ballad. It would quickly become a standard, covered by artists such as Johnny Mathis, Al Green, Cher, and Barry Manilow. The single propelled a second comeback album, *Trafalgar*, into the American Top 40, and saw the band nominated for their first Grammy in the category of best vocal performance. 'How Can You Mend A Broken Heart?' went to #1 in Canada, Singapore, Malaysia, and Hong Kong but was another disappointing flop in the UK, as was *Trafalgar*.

Although it was a sore point, the band were able to overlook the dire situation in the UK and revel in their success in America as they made a succession of high-profile appearances on popular US TV shows. There was talk of the band making an American TV series and a film—a Western spoof or a horror movie. In terms of bolstering the value of RSO, The Bee Gees had more than delivered. Barry said the 'public company' was now worth about twenty million dollars, and 'as major shareholders we have enough security for us to live in comfort for twenty years or so.' What he did not expect, then, was such a rapid fall from grace.

'It happened too fast, the power took hold again,' Barry later reflected. 'We thought, God, we're at the top again, we've made it.' But then tickets for an American tour failed to sell, and several shows, including one planned for the prestigious at Carnegie Hall, were cut. The remaining shows were fraught with familiar problems. One member of the backing band said there was an 'extreme amount of substance abuse' on the tour. 'We were young, successful, famous, wealthy, and fully involved in the early 70s music business of sex, drugs, and rock roll,' he said. Robin, who was taking prodigious amounts of pills washed down now with Southern Comfort, collapsed and was hospitalised. Maurice, a victim of excessive boozing, was next, suffering what he called a 'nervous collapse'.

After two further Top 20 American singles in 1972—one of which, 'Run To Me', also made the UK Top 10—a third comeback album, *To Whom It May Concern*, bombed, failing to chart in the UK and just scraping into the US Top 40. It was over. The Bee Gees travelled on Greyhound buses during a disastrous thirty-city American tour. The orchestras they assembled were often made up of college kids; the gigs were never full, and often empty. The brothers lived in a bubble, still booked into luxury hotels while their band members and crew were treated poorly. Hugh went on the road with them, acting as a lighting advisor, as did their youngest brother, Andy, just turned fifteen. Hugh was planning to drop him into the group soon. 'He's basically on this tour watching us and studying us so he knows what to do when he joins us, which will probably be in about a year,' said Barry. The material they were cutting was getting worse, however, and their singles routinely failed to chart.

Stigwood, meanwhile, was high on the success of *Jesus Christ Superstar*, growing more powerful, and hungry for expansion. In 1973 he launched his own record label, RSO Records, appointing Al Coury—a forty-year-old Arab-American who had been a vice president of marketing, sales, and promotion at Capitol Records in America, working closely with The Beatles and overseeing the solo careers of Paul McCartney and John Lennon—to run it. The Bee Gees had fulfilled the eight-album deal Stigwood had struck for them with Polydor, and Eric Clapton was also free of obligations. So Stigwood had both acts commit to RSO Records, as well as new signing Jimmy Stevens, who was being produced by Maurice.

Stigwood had ultimate faith in himself. He swiftly negotiated manufacturing and distribution deals for RSO Records with Atlantic in North America and Polydor for the rest of the world. Stigwood had a long and cosy relationship with both labels, so little changed except for the percentage he took from record sales and the logo on the discs: Stigwood chose the soon-to-be-familiar RSO Records red cow after being gifted an Akebeko, a traditional Japanese red cow toy that was said to be a symbol of good health and good fortune. ('I thought, Good health and good fortune, that's appropriate. Just write RSO on it,' he said.)

The Bee Gees signed to RSO Records for five years and eight albums. Stigwood was now their manager, publisher, record label, and agent. Until Clapton released 'I Shot The Sherriff' and *461 Ocean Boulevard*, however, RSO Records struggled to ignite. The label's first album, *Life In A Tin Can* by The Bee Gees, was a disaster, failing to make the Top 40 in the UK or America, with sales barely reaching the tens of thousands. The album spawned one desultory single that went nowhere. In an attempt to reverse the slide, Stigwood filled the 2,500-capacity Royal Festival Hall in London for the band and hired the ninety-two-piece London

Symphony Orchestra to back them for a comeback show in February 1973. It did not convince anyone, though, and a planned UK tour had to be cancelled due to poor demand for tickets.

The three brothers rarely socialised together, and cash was drying up. Maurice was drinking a bottle of Scotch in the afternoon before hitting the clubs, and his relationship with Lulu was a mess. She called it 'an experience beyond my worst nightmare' and 'a showbiz dream gone wrong'. By August, *Billboard* was reporting that the band planned to junk an entire album. Batley beckoned. 'The Bee Gees' sound was basically tired,' Barry said. 'We needed something new. We hadn't had a hit record in about three years. We felt that was our lifespan. We didn't know what was going to happen.' But for the close relationship between Stigwood and the co-founder of Atlantic Records, Ahmet Ertegun, it would have been the end of the group. At the time, the pair were investing half a million dollars of their own money into co-producing a camp and absurd disco-tinged musical, *Rachel Lily Rosenbloom*, on Broadway. Ertegun had hoped to persuade Bette Midler to star in the show. She passed, and Stigwood would eventually axe the show after terrible preview performances.

Stigwood and Ertegun informally discussed the future of The Bee Gees. Ertegun did not particularly think they had one. Although the label was famous for its illustrious R&B catalogue and acts such as Aretha Franklin, Ray Charles, and Sam & Dave, more recently he had steered the label toward rock, scoring huge success with English acts such as Led Zeppelin, Yes, and Bad Company, as well as Crosby, Stills, Nash & Young. To Ertegun, The Bee Gees were hopelessly out of step. Stigwood, who had given the label The Who, Cream, and Blind Faith, as well as the 60s Bee Gees, was able to persuade him to give the 70s version another roll of the dice.

Planning a radical overhaul, Stigwood was keen to put the group together with producer Thom Bell, a key figure behind the Philadelphia soul sound, the dominant force in black American music at the time. Bell was a pioneer of the lush instrumentation of disco, which was popular in gay clubs, and had made his name working with The Stylistics and The Delfonics. He was also having huge success at Atlantic with The Spinners, winning him a Grammy for 'Producer of the Year' in 1975. Stigwood was alive to the nascent sound of disco, which began to coalesce in 1974 in New York, with the world's first disco conference organised by *Billboard* magazine at the Roosevelt Hotel. The Stylistics, who scored a huge hit in 1974 with 'You Make Me Feel Brand New', would become firm favourites of The Bee Gees, alongside Al Green and Otis Redding.

It was Ertegun who suggested the band work with Atlantic's in-house producer and arranger Arif Mardin, who alongside the label's co-founder Jerry Wexler and producer Tom Dowd had been responsible for establishing the famed 'Atlantic sound', producing hits for acts such as Aretha Franklin, Carly Simon, Diana Ross, The Rascals, Dusty Springfield, Cher, Hall & Oates, Willie Nelson, Average White Band, The Manhattan Transfer, and Bette Midler. Despite having won twelve Grammys and produced close to sixty gold and platinum records over the course of his career (and later being inducted into the Rock and Roll Hall of Fame in 1990), the forty-one-year-old R&B specialist, known as 'doctor of music', was an undemonstrative figure in the studio, more of a thinker than a talker. But when Stigwood told The Bee Gees they were going in the studio with Mardin, they reacted furiously. In the face of a career unravelling, they continued to delude themselves. They argued that, having produced their previous four albums themselves, they did not need any help in making records. Stigwood forced the issue. 'They needed an injection,' he said. 'Arif was terrific for them.'

The initial sessions were stilted. The diplomatic Mardin tried to guide the group, tactfully, toward a more contemporary American sound. He suggested they listen to Stevie Wonder and The Delfonics and played them his recent work with the popular Scottish R&B act The Average White Band, suggesting their 'blue-eyed soul' be a prototype for The Bee Gees. Their disco-funk single 'Pick Up The Pieces' was destined to be a huge hit. The band also listened to the 1973 Hall & Oates album *Abandoned Luncheonette*, which Mardin had produced, and explored the work of soul singer Donny Hathaway, whom Arif had also produced. Robin and Maurice remained circumspect of the stranger in the studio, but Barry warmed to Mardin. 'He makes you know that he knows what he's doing without being heavy with it,' he said. The new album, he told the press, 'will be a distinct new sound for The Bee Gees'. Mardin's advice was simple: 'Leave The Beatles alone and get into American music.' It would take years for Maurice to appreciate Mardin's input. 'He showed us the right track,' he said in 1979. '*This* was the track leading to R&B and hits, and *that* was the track leading to lush ballads and forget it, and he just shoved us off that track and right up this one.'

Although the resulting album, *Mr Natural*, was a flop, and the band were still bruised from the ignominious cabaret dates, the experience of working with Mardin awoke something in all three Gibbs. 'We knew we could do better work,' said Barry. 'We were writing in the past,' said Robin. Unfortunately, it was the final straw for Atlantic Records. Ertegun had put them with Mardin as a favour to Stigwood. It had been, as far as the label was concerned, a waste of time. A frustrated Jerry Wexler said 'enough'. He told Stigwood to forget about The Bee Gees.

●

It was lucky for the Gibbs that by late 1974 RSO was in such good shape. The public company was almost debt free, thanks largely to the success of Clapton, and cash rich due to the ongoing success of *Jesus*

Christ Superstar. Stigwood had financed *Tommy* and was gambling on making his mark in Hollywood and moving his entire business empire to America. He did not want to leave the Gibbs behind. 'He took us with him,' Barry said. 'It was the opening of the Americanisation of this group—we had to find a new direction.'

Barry relayed to Stigwood Clapton's advice about recording in Miami to get some 'fresh ideas'. Stigwood booked Criteria Studios and producer Mardin for the entire month of January 1975. Mardin had enjoyed working with the group and, unlike Wexler, thought the band had potential, particularly with their close harmony singing. 'They sing like angels,' he said. 'Only Arif, of all the Atlantic people, kept faith in us,' said Robin.

Before the sessions began, drummer Dennis Bryon suggested hiring a new permanent keyboard player, Blue Weaver, who had played keyboards alongside him in Amen Corner. The two had been in bands together since they were boys. Weaver had fallen on hard times and had been driving a cab to support a young child and wife. He was, however, just getting back on his feet, gigging with Mott The Hoople, Lou Reed, and The Strawbs and was unsure about joining The Bee Gees, whose career appeared to be in terminal decline. 'It was the lowest ebb that the three brothers had been,' said Weaver. Bryon himself had joined the band on the suggestion of their long-time guitarist Alan Kendall after moving into a London flat in the same house as him. Kendall, an amiable northerner with a wife and two young children to support, had been a fixture in The Bee Gees since 1970, joining the group from RSO act Toe Fat. Bryon was more ambitious. Prior to joining the band he had been acting as tour manager to groups such as Supertramp and Peter Sarstedt.

As a favour to Bryon, Weaver accompanied the drummer and Kendall to the Isle of Man for rehearsals at Barry's new home. He had listened to *Mr Natural* and felt that there were elements there that they could take forward. The atmosphere was relaxed. Linda baked space cakes and Barry showed the others around the Bay of Douglas, where they did a bit of fishing. They dined on fish and chips—'the best in Douglas', Barry assured them. Weaver had shipped over an ARP 2600 synth and a Moog—cutting-edge equipment that, Bryon explained, meant they could discard the orchestra for live shows and become a proper band. They jammed. Barry was impressed with the synthetic string sound Weaver could manipulate from the machines and asked him to accompany the band to Miami.

When they arrived, the weather was hot for the time of year, and Golden Beach was beautiful, just out the back of 461 Ocean Boulevard. The house had a huge entrance hall, a grand staircase, high ceilings, and marble floors. The only downside was that the three Gibbs, along with Weaver, Bryon, and Kendall would all be sharing the one property. Bryon recalled 'many arguments and squabbles' between the brothers. Robin, a strange mix of crude humour and terrible seriousness about his craft, didn't socialise much, and the band found it hard to get to know him. Maurice was drinking and clowning about and Barry was stoned, chilled. 'The drink and drugs didn't stop when we went to Miami but we were determined to change,' said Maurice. 'We decided that it was out big chance to get serious about out music again.'

The recording at Criteria began on Monday January 6 1975 and would finish over six weeks later, during which time the band was transformed beyond recognition. The brothers did not have an album of finished songs written, so they wrote new material in Miami. 'Unorthodox,' was how drummer Bryon described their methods. 'They loved echo on their voices, so they wrote in places that had natural echo, toilets, entrance halls,' he said. He watched the three of them, Maurice and Barry on guitars, write songs from scratch. It seemed to be the one time they could enjoy being together. 'They were always laughing when writing,' said Bryon. 'From out of laughter would come an incredible melody and bits of lyrics. Barry would say, That's good, sing it again, then Barry might embellish it.'

This time around, Mardin was accepted by the brothers as an integral part of the process. They listened when he suggested making crucial changes to tracks. 'Why don't we start with the chorus, it's a stronger melody line,' he would say. 'Put that verse there and that chorus there.' Barry thought of it as 'uncle advice'. 'He doesn't take the song away from you, he just places it where he thinks it should be,' he said. 'He brings out best in people.'

Criteria was just a short drive from the rented house, in a long two-storey building. Clapton was not the only superstar to have recorded there. James Brown had cut 'I Got You (I Feel Good)' at the studio in 1965, and The Average White Band and The Allman Brothers had recorded there. Atlantic had a strong connection with the studio. Tom Dowd had helped refine the recording and mixing consoles, and many Atlantic acts, including Aretha Franklin, had made records there. Mardin was comfortable at Criteria, and the new band began to relax into the recording. With Maurice often drunk, Weaver diplomatically took over from him on piano, and often played his bass parts on his synthesiser. Mardin was particularly enthusiastic about the band's use of synth sounds. Barry found inspiration from sitting in with Weaver, Bryon, and Kendall as they jammed, writing album track 'Come On Over' over a country-ish drum pattern. Olivia Newton-John would take a cover version of the song into the American Top 20 in 1976, but it did not impress Stigwood when he visited the studio, thick with cold, swigging Scotch and Coke. He had hoped The Bee Gees would find a new direction in Miami, but 'Come On Over' and other new tracks such as 'Wind Of Change' were the same old Bee Gees ballad style.

Stigwood had been on holiday to Brazil, to witness the Rio Carnival, and had heard the growing influence of disco even in South America. 'I told them I wanted to scrap a lot of the things they'd done, and I'd like them to start again,' he said. 'I would swallow the costs, not to worry, but to really open their ears and find out in contemporary terms what is going on.' The band, said Maurice, was 'devastated'. Stigwood sat on Golden Beach with them and apologised for having been so distant of late. 'I'm determined to get involved again,' he said, before reiterating his instructions: 'Listen to what is going on in the business.'

Stigwood pointed out the success of acts such as Barry White, KC & The Sunshine Band, and Donna Summer, all of whom were riding the new disco boom in America, with TV shows such as *Soul Train* and *Dance Fever* now featuring the music and radio stations programming exclusive disco shows. *Billboard* magazine had begun running a disco/dance chart. The scene was exploding. In 1974 there had been 1,500 discos in America. That number was now 10,000, with 500 discos in New York alone. Disco was set to be the sound of America in 1975, dominating the Top 40 as the movement went from hip underground sound to mainstream, with Van McCoy's classic 'The Hustle' a trailblazing #1 hit, selling eight million copies. In fact, five of the ten biggest-selling American singles of the year were disco songs by Earth Wind & Fire, Labelle, Shirley & Company, Ohio Players, and Kool & The Gang, who had an incredible run of #1 hits with disco-influenced songs such as 'Spirit Of The Boogie'.

Miami rivalled New York as America's main disco city. The sound here was heavy with Caribbean and Latin influences. There was a mega club called 1235, where cocaine was commonplace. Miami was also home to the country's main disco label, Henry Stone's TK Records, which had released such classic disco cuts as George McCrae's 1974 'Rock Your Baby' (sung in falsetto), while its biggest act, KC & The

Sunshine Band (who had written 'Rock Your Baby') were dubbed 'the kings of disco', scoring a run of huge monster #1 hits in 1975 such as 'Get Down Tonight' and 'That's The Way (I Like It)'.

Barry Gibb was neither a clubber nor a disco fan. He loved his cups of tea and nights in front of the television. Criteria staff engineer Karl Richardson was, however. Richardson, in his late twenties, had been a disc jockey before he joined Criteria in 1967. He had worked the Eric Clapton sessions and even helped design some of Criteria equipment. He clicked with Barry and guided him through the current sounds that moved Miami's dance floors—soul, funk, R&B, and, above all, disco. 'Here was a new culture to absorb, to base our music on,' said Barry. 'Peopled wanted to dance.' At 461 Ocean Boulevard, the brothers tuned in to Miami radio stations (both Top 40 and the increasingly powerful FM stations), the whole band getting into what Mardin called 'a closer relationship to what's happening on the Top 40 music scene'.

'We were listening to a lot of radio and we tried to get an idea of what people wanted to hear,' Barry said. What he noticed, above all, was many hits were 'locked into the groove'. 'So we moved into that area,' he added. 'There was so much of this kind of music going on around us and we wanted to do it, but we want to do it better if we could … we knew we couldn't go in there and make another album that wasn't going to go. We knew this was it. If this album doesn't work, it's really the finish for our recording career.'

The Gibbs came up with a new, funky, Latin and disco-tinged up-tempo song called 'Lights On Broadway'. 'What's with the lights?' asked Mardin. 'Why not nights? "Nights On Broadway" is sexier.' When they came to record the vocals for the retitled track, the three brothers, gathered around just the one microphone, began an impromptu version of 'You Make Me Feel Brand New', attempting to ape The Stylistics' distinctive falsetto sound. They began goofing around, exaggerating the falsetto, before breaking up laughing. Mardin spoke to them from the control room. 'Barry I have an idea,' he said. 'Try singing the chorus of "Nights On Broadway" in falsetto.' It was clear to Mardin that Robin's elegiac vibrato was not suited to the dance floor. 'I asked Barry to take his vocal up one octave,' said Mardin. 'The poor man said, If I take it up one octave I'm going to shout and it's going to be terrible. He softened up a little bit, and that's how their falsetto was born. Robin and Maurice joined in [also in falsetto]. We had the chills. This was a hit.'

Mardin returned home to New York most weekends to take a break from recording. It had been a frustrating first couple of weeks in the studio. Much material had been scrapped, and even after Stigwood's pep-talk, the newer songs remained chained to the band's old songwriting patterns, musically and lyrically. Even 'Nights On Broadway' was only half way to where Mardin imagined the band could go; it was still anchored to a Beatles-style structure and melody, especially Robin's parts. Barry was also reluctant to change his style of singing. Mardin heard the future in the falsetto, however, and wanted the band to use it more, saying it was like The Stylistics or Brian Wilson. 'They're not afraid to do that,' he said. 'Go and think about it and expand. You know, write with that voice.' The band was unsure. As he prepared to leave Miami, late on a Friday afternoon, Mardin pulled Barry to one side. 'If you're ever going to do something different, now is the time,' he said. 'Set your mind to that. Look at what's happening now, rather than what's happening to you. Your mind seems to be stuck in one place.'

The Bee Gees were at the crossroads. 'We had already cut "Nights On Broadway", so I could see a new direction,' said Mardin. When he returned from New York on Sunday evening, Barry played him a new song they'd come up with, 'Drive Talkin''. Robin said they had written it in the car on way over, inspired by the sound the car made as it crossed the four-mile long Julia Tuttle Causeway bridge that connected

Biscayne Bay to Miami, echoing the rhythm of the wheels as they hit the lines of reinforced steel girders. Mardin sent the brothers upstairs to finish the song and said he would record it while it was fresh. They did, but the recording was a mess, although they had by now retitled the song 'Jive Talkin''. Mardin sensed there was something worth persevering with and pored over the recording, finding a few bars that he felt had some sort of magic about them and then playing them back to the Gibbs. 'He gave us groove,' said Maurice. 'He said, This is what the tempo should be.'

Mardin also liked the title: 'jive talking' was a black expression for bullshitting. The band had not realised. They had obviously heard the expression, but they believed the 'jive' was a rock'n'roll dance. They changed the chorus line, 'You dance with your eyes', to 'You're telling me lies'. Blue Weaver came up with the distinctive bass line on his Arp synth. 'Maurice was not in the studio,' he said. A similar sound had been created by Stevie Wonder and used on his hits 'Living In The City' and 'Superstition'. Mardin had the band playing along to a metronomic click track so he could take a chorus, duplicate it, and drop it in elsewhere. It meant the song was locked into a groove. Barry sang the song, hesitantly, in falsetto. Mardin encouraged him. 'Experiment with your voice,' he said. 'Take it places it's never been.'

'Those were some of the most memorable sessions—some of the touchiest, at least in the beginning, but also the most rewarding,' said Mardin. 'It was exciting to see Barry and his brothers come up with these new songs.' Barry would acknowledge the importance of Mardin in the process of rebooting the band. 'He brought the magic out of us again,' he said.

At the time, the band were unsure about 'Jive Talkin''. It sounded to them like a joke—especially the chorus and the musical breaks, which were a pastiche, really, of The Stylistics. Stigwood had no such doubts.

'As soon as I heard the tapes I flew to Miami,' he said. 'He knew it was going to be a smash,' said Maurice. 'We were only kidding,' Barry said. 'You were only kidding the night we did "Mining Disaster",' Stigwood said. 'Let me hear that again.' Stigwood told them, 'You've found it, stay on that course.' Ahmet Ertegun at Atlantic was also impressed with 'Jive Talkin''. 'Wow, this is dance music!' he said.

For the final two weeks at Criteria, the band and Mardin worked up to eighteen hours a day in the studio. 'It became like something out of a movie, with everybody being incredibly creative and dynamic,' said Mardin. Barry began to explore the falsetto voice. 'That sound can be looked upon as very feminine, so we had to be careful,' he said. 'But then we looked at other groups like The Stylistics, who had an enormous amount of success with that sound, so we just went for it.' The falsetto was a very popular voice in disco, being used on many of the big chart hits in America, such as 'I Wanna Dance Wit' Choo', and within R&B, too, although The Stylistics often counterbalanced the falsetto with deeper, more resonant voices. Frankie Valli of The Four Seasons was also a strong influence on the group's developing vocal style.

'Frankie Valli and Brian Wilson,' said Maurice. 'They were a tremendous inspiration—"Big Girls Don't Cry" and "God Only Knows"—because it made you unafraid to do that.' Maurice was also quick to praise Mardin, who enhanced the new material with his trademark orchestral strings, brass, and percussion. 'He was brilliant, full of ideas,' he said. 'He knew all the feels and the grooves and was so experienced. Arif taught me areas of bass I never thought I could play.' He had also taught the group the importance of strong beats—a blueprint for their future recordings.

Stigwood had no doubt 'Jive Talkin'' was going to be the lead single from the album, predicting it would be a #1 record. He also knew he needed to be creative with the marketing for the new single. The band was so out of fashion that it was feared just their name would prevent the single being played by radio DJs. RSO Records was expanding, with Bill Oakes brought in to handle much of the day-to-day business of the label from the company's New York office, and Al Coury assuming the title of president. Oakes, an Englishman in his mid-twenties, had worked for The Beatles and had once been Paul McCartney's assistant. He was the husband of Yvonne Elliman, who was now signed to RSO as a solo act while still working as a backing vocalist with Eric Clapton.

'It was hard just getting The Bee Gees back on the radio, because they were virtually blacklisted,' Oakes said. Stigwood came up with a plan to obfuscate the name of the band—a trick that had worked back in 1967 with 'Mining Disaster'. He had Oakes send out unmarked cassettes and vinyl of 'Jive Talkin'' to critics and DJs. Within hours, the label was getting feedback, said Oakes. 'Who is this? It's amazing.' *Rolling Stone* magazine would later write that only 20 percent of DJs could identify the song as being by The Bee Gees. Having said they liked it before the discovered whch band was behind it, it was 'hard for them not to play it', said Coury, who was to take a keen interest now in the Bee Gees career. 'That again was Stigwood's genius,' he said. In the UK, Polydor sent out a pleading press release, asking for the single to be given a chance: 'It is totally unlike anything they have recorded in their entire career and extremely funky.'

'Jive Talkin'' was released in May 1975 as The Bee Gees began an eight-week, forty-date tour of America. The set mixed the new album material with their old hits (Yvonne Elliman guested on 'To Love Somebody') and familiar cover versions such as 'Bye Bye Love', 'Lollipop', and 'Happy Birthday Sweet Sixteen'. It was the first time they band had played without an orchestra. Weaver and the classically trained Geoff Westley, twenty-five, who had conducted *Jesus Christ Superstar*, played keyboards. Maurice was on bass. 'For years people said that because we always worked with an orchestra they never knew if we were any good as a band,' said Barry. 'It was time to let everybody hear us as a band.'

The opening dates were spirit-sapping, a low point in their touring history—worse even than Batley. In Ohio, they played to 500 people in a venue that could hold almost 10,000. There were plenty more empty seats as the tour crawled to its halfway point and a much needed break. Radio stations in America had by now started to get behind 'Jive Talkin'', and the single was starting to climb both the American Top 40 and the separate, black R&B charts. The track was covered by black funk band Rufus, who included it on their late-1975 album *Rufus Featuring Chaka Khan*, a Top 10 album in America.

'We're an R&B group with a lot of soul in our hearts,' said Robin. The Bee Gees plugged the song on TV, appearing on the popular *Tonight Show With Johnny Carson* and *Midnight Special*, debuting a new, sexier look. With their Miami tans, manly beards, tight flares, open shirts, hairy chests, sunglasses, and gold medallions, the band had a new image to go with their new sound. 'Jive Talkin'' was in the Top 10 by the time the tour resumed in Los Angeles, and was soon at #1. The 8,000-seat venues the band was booked into became less noticeably empty. By the end of the tour, a second single, 'Nights On Broadway', was climbing the American charts.

'Jive Talkin'' crossed over from America and became a huge hit in the UK, peaking at #5, and in Germany and Australia. Barry told *Hit Parade* magazine, 'We're definitely back on the inspirational path. Everybody's dancing now and people should be able to dance to our music.' Atlantic was still unsure how to market the group in America, though. For the new album, titled, *Main Course*, they had opted not to use a photograph of the band on the cover. 'Atlantic didn't want black people to know the group wasn't black,' said Al Coury. Released in

June, the album would climb to #14 on the American charts, reaching #1 in Canada, selling almost one million copies worldwide (including 500,000 in America and 200,000 in Canada). It was the band's best-selling album to date.

'Our music has changed,' said Barry. 'It's more rhythm and blues now. This is best record we've ever made.' He would later reflect on how '*Main Course* was when we started to turn black … or blacker … a healthy shade of brown'. Stigwood organised a lavish party for 450 people on an outdoor skate rink at New York's Rockefeller Centre to celebrate the success. It was billed as the band's twentieth anniversary in showbusiness. They arrived in a stretch limo, to be greeted by paparazzi flashbulbs. Stigwood unveiled a huge piano-shaped cake and kept guests amused with his quick and dry wit. He told of how Jack Bruce had listened to *Main Course* and said it was by 'the best new black band' he'd ever heard. When he played Mick Jagger the album, he said, the response had been similar. 'That's fucking dynamite, some new group you've signed up?' Jagger said. The Bee Gees were back.

'Nights On Broadway' peaked at #7 on the America charts in September, but like *Main Course* it failed to chart in the UK, where the band was called a disco group as a 'sort of put-down', said Barry. 'People said we had "stepped down" to be a disco group,' he said. 'We don't think disco is bad music, we think it's happy and had has wide appeal. We decided we would try something light-hearted.'

There were also accusations that the new direction was a cynical move to appropriate black sounds and capitalise on the disco market. Robin was particularly prickly about this. 'If anything, we have contributed to today's disco music popularity,' he said. If not in the UK, 'Nights On Broadway' was a hit in many other European countries, with Stigwood, who proclaimed that the band had 'the beat of the dance floor in their blood', organising lavish press parties in Copenhagen, Hamburg,

Amsterdam, Brussels, Milan, and Paris. 'We had gone from oblivion in 1974 back to suddenly everybody wanting to know, due to this falsetto thing,' said Barry.

In interviews, The Bee Gees immediately began talk of making a film, either a western or 'a chase film'. A third single from *Main Course*, 'Fanny (Be Tender With My Love)', reached #12 in America and #2 in Canada, but again failed to chart in the UK. Maurice married Yvonne Spenceley, the girl he'd met at Batley, who was now heavily pregnant. Barry, his leg in plaster after a nasty fall, was best man.

●

The resurgence of The Bee Gees topped a remarkable year for Stigwood and RSO. Eric Clapton, despite still struggling with booze and drugs, had followed the success of *461 Ocean Boulevard* with another hit album. Andrew Lloyd Webber, having ignored Stigwood's suggestions to develop a musical version of Peter Pan, had delivered a follow-up to *Jesus Christ Superstar*. The new West End musical *Jeeves*, based on the P.G. Wodehouse stories, was only a minor success, but Stigwood was heartened to hear that Webber was reuniting with Tim Rice to write a new musical based on the life of Argentine political leader Eva Peron. The pair intended to write it as a musical album, as they had done with *Jesus Christ Superstar*, and Stigwood saw another mega-hit brewing.

Most satisfying of all, *Tommy*, which had premiered in March, backed by a splashy and exuberant PR campaign, had been a huge hit at the box office, grossing a remarkable $34.3 million. Stigwood had worked hard on the movie, organising a series of press stunts that included a party in a subway in New York, where he served lobsters, and a lavish event on a yacht moored at the Cannes film festival. He had made millions from the clever distribution deals he had secured for the film's release. Stigwood enjoyed telling how having been unable to find a distributor in France he had decided to hire cinemas and show the film himself. He had taken a million dollars out of the county when, he said, the best distributor's bid had been $50,000.

Stigwood had two more films ready for release in early 1976. He was executive producing a British gangster movie called *Bugsy Malone* in association with Paramount Pictures that featured only child actors, including a thirteen-year-old Jodie Foster. RSO Records was releasing the film's soundtrack. (While grossing only $2.8 million at the box office, the film would be a critical hit, picking up numerous awards, including an Oscar for 'Best Original Song Score', which would help turn the soundtrack into a sizeable hit.) He was also involved in a Mexican film based on a real-life plane crash in the Andes in 1972, when passengers had been reduced to eating the dead in order to survive. Allan Carr, who managed major stars such as Ann-Margret and Peter Sellers, had brought the film to Stigwood. They dubbed and trimmed the Mexican original, retitled it *Survive!*, and struck a distribution deal with Paramount. It would make the pair a great deal of money, despite poor reviews. Also via the flamboyant thirty-eight-year-old Carr, who had a background in theatre production and a hand in creating Hugh Hefner's *Playboy* empire, and was a party giver on par with Stigwood, RSO had recently bought the film rights to the long-running Broadway musical *Grease*.

Remarkably, RSO was also juggling two huge US TV hits. Beryl Vertue had sold CBS the series *Beacon Hill*, its concept loosely based on the hit British series *Upstairs, Downstairs*, which Vertue had been responsible for helping sell to the BBC, as she handled one of its original creators, Jean Marsh. *Beacon Hill* was heavily hyped, with the first episode costing a whopping $900,000. It was also an instant hit, with a 43 percent audience share, reaching between sixteen and twenty-three million viewers. It could not maintain those numbers, however, and was cancelled after eleven episodes. Vertue had also sold *The Entertainer* to

NBC as a TV movie. There had already been an acclaimed film based on the 1957 John Osborne play, starring Laurence Olivier, released in 1960. The play had recently been revived onstage and the RSO film production, filmed in Los Angeles and starring Jack Lemmon, would be a success, earning five prestigious Emmy Awards nominations.

Vertue spoke in glowing terms of Stigwood's ability to expertly promote these projects, and his success in America, across music, film, and TV, attracted a new level of media scrutiny. In a major *New York Daily News* article, the executives at RSO were famously described as the 'Velvet Mafia'. *Rolling Stone* magazine meanwhile described RSO as a 'family company', adding, 'Everywhere you look an unusual camaraderie is evident. The people who work here share an enthusiasm that is less than a cause but more than just a well-paying job. It seems to be a cult of personality attached to Robert Stigwood himself.'

RSO was still a public company in the UK, and despite the overwhelming success of 1975, with predictions of another five million pounds in profit, accounts dated September 1975 showed a net loss of £370,000 after tax. These were deadly figures for a public company. The profit from *Tommy*, *Jesus Christ Superstar*, RSO Records, and the TV division had been eaten up by hidden costs such as a forced £750,000 buy-back of a 15 percent stake in RSO Productions and the collapse of a minor bank called Roynton that RSO had bought, losing the company £220,000. The RSO assets remained difficult to quantify, since they were largely held in music publishing and artist contracts, with future earnings seemingly dependent on the gut instinct of Stigwood. The German owners of Polydor, which owned the majority of shares in RSO, were unhappy. They saw the public status of RSO as a liability. Share prices didn't necessarily reflect the true value of the company.

To Freddie Gershon, the answer seemed simple: take RSO private. Gershon, an American showbusiness lawyer, had been working with

Stigwood since 1971, when he had dealt swiftly with a 'personal matter arising from an automobile accident'. Since then, Gershon had grown increasingly influential at RSO. He had graduated from Columbia Law School in 1964 and represented film and stage directors, playwrights, and the rock band Chicago before becoming counsel to the Robert Stigwood Group Ltd for America, representing all aspects of *Jesus Christ Superstar*, Blind Faith, Derek & The Dominoes, Eric Clapton, The Bee Gees, and the financing of the *Tommy* film. Gershon said that when he first met Stigwood, he had asked him to reveal his number-one goal. 'To get out of the UK and to bring my public company private,' Gershon recalled him saying.

Although much of RSO's current activity was channelled now through its New York office, RSO was still based in the UK. Stigwood's long-term business partner, David Shaw, disliked America, preferring weekends in his Norfolk mansion with family. They had been squabbling about Stigwood's expenses—notably the $350,000 he had just splashed out on a luxury Central Park apartment in New York. As Stigwood leaned heavily on Gershon for advice, the arguments with Shaw grew increasingly bitter.

Stigwood had a tremendous desire now to go for the big stakes in America. He was especially keen to expand his role in movies, but he argued that a move to America also made sense in terms of the music industry: almost half of all record sales were American, with Japan and Germany second and third. The UK only represented 9 percent of total sales worldwide. Running RSO out of the UK made little commercial sense, and it was actually a hindrance. Gaining credit in America was impossible, because the company had chiefly British assets, forcing Stigwood to take money out of the UK to invest in America, where financial rules meant the company had to pay a mark-up on the cost of foreign money for investment purposes.

'Instead of wheeler dealing, Robert had to slow down and think about the balance of payments and whether the company had enough dollar bills,' said Gershon. 'None of that ought to come into your judgment on a deal.' American ambitions and a British base were not compatible. Taking the company private would solve that problem, too. Gershon structured a deal where RSO became part of a reorganised US-based company that would buy all the shares in the UK public company—a reverse takeover.

Stigwood had already sounded out potential financers of the deal. He planned on selling one third of RSO to Warner Communications, the company that owned Atlantic Records. Ahmet Ertegun had recommended the purchase to the board of directors. Ertegun, Stigwood, and Steve Ross—CEO, president, and chairman of Warner Communications—held a series of meetings in New York, Hamburg, London, and Paris.

'Steve Ross was incredibly seductive,' said Gershon, noting that the deal he offered was 'not unattractive'. Ross, however, wanted to buy the whole company. Stigwood was unsure about giving up his independence, and he worried that all his future movie projects would be tied to Warners. He turned Ross down. 'No matter how many millions they offered him to sweeten his personal pie,' said Gershon.

Siemens, the giant German-based multinational corporation that owned Polydor, was shocked to discover that Stigwood had been negotiating with Warners. Surely, as the major shareholders in RSO, they should have had first refusal? The company immediately began to offer a variety of alternative deals: Stigwood turned them all down. 'There's only one thing I'll do, and I'll do it with you or without you,' he declared. 'That is: to find a fair value for my shareholders and my insiders and start afresh.'

Under the name Polygram—a portmanteau of two of its labels,

Polydor and Phonogram, created as a parent company to oversee its expanding record division—Siemens bought up all the shares it did not already own in RSO. The price it paid for the company was said to be much larger than what Warners had offered, although the exact figure was not revealed. RSO was now private. Al Coury announced the worldwide distribution deal and marketing pact between RSO and Polygram Inc. to the press. David Shaw took his share of the money and left the company. Gershon became president, chief operating officer, and a partner in the Stigwood Group of Companies worldwide. He also represented RSO Records. Stigwood, with the massive financial backing of Polygram, retained a significant stake in his company, received a bonus of $145,000 a year for his services, and would continue to run the entire business. He was ready for a great expansion.

CHAPTER FOUR

SMOKE AND MIRRORS

ROBERT STIGWOOD
SOMEWHERE ALONG THE LINE
BARRY BECAME COMPLETELY IN TUNE
WITH THE TIMES.

At the beginning of January 1976, The Bee Gees reconvened at Criteria Studios in Miami to work on a new album. There was bad news. A disappointed Arif Mardin called to say he would be unable to produce the follow up to *Main Course*, blaming 'business and [record industry] politics'. 'That really broke us up,' said Maurice. 'We were upset because we'd just had out first successful album in years.'

Taking RSO private, The Bee Gees had been promised, would be financially rewarding. Barry, after all, had been the fourth largest shareholder in the company, and even before the deal was bragging about how all three brothers were 'dollar millionaires'. The deal Stigwood had struck with Polygram, however, was for the world, which meant that Atlantic Records had suddenly lost North American rights to RSO product, including The Bee Gees. Ertegun and the Warners hierarchy were smarting from losing out to Polygram, and Mardin had been told by Atlantic he could no longer work with the band. Barry desperately hoped to broker a solution—the band didn't want to lose Mardin. But it was impossible. He felt that Atlantic was using them to punish Stigwood. The sessions at Criteria were cancelled. 'We had to go with Robert because our loyalty said so,' said Barry.

Prior to Mardin taking over the band, Stigwood had approached Richard Perry, one of America's hottest producers. He returned to Perry now. The Brooklyn-born thirty-four-year-old had made his name producing Captain Beefheart and Fats Domino before moving to Los Angeles to work with Tiny Tim in the late 60s. He had gone on to produce a slew of huge acts, including Barbra Streisand, Carly Simon, Diana Ross, Harry Nilsson, and Ringo Starr. Recently, he had produced Art Garfunkel, Leo Sayer, and The Manhattan Transfer.

Perry agreed to take on the Bee Gees project. He worked out of Los Angeles, so Stigwood rented a huge Beverly Hills mansion for the band to stay in while they recorded in the city. It was a disaster. The band played Perry a handful of new tunes they had written, including 'You Should Be Dancing', but they left the producer unenthused. None of the songs sounded like hits, he said. There was talk of Robin being upset over a derogatory remark made about his voice, while Barry said he objected to Perry taking drugs in studio. He said the producer was either 'constantly out of it or constantly disturbing'. The Bee Gees walked out. All the material they recorded with Perry was scrapped. They begged Mardin to come back to work with them. 'You've got to do it yourself,' he said. 'You know what you want. You don't need anybody else. Go away and do it.'

The Bee Gees were back in Criteria at the beginning of March, determined to prove Mardin right. They were relying on the studio's chief engineer, Karl Richardson, who had worked on *Main Course*, for assistance. With his long hair and beard, he looked the archetypal dropout hippie, but *Rolling Stone* described him as 'more than a sound engineer', suggesting he 'works as an artist, gauging sound and effect for maximum efficiency and suggesting alterations'.

In Miami, the band settled into the familiar, laid-back groove. The weather was good, and there was plenty of time for the beach and sea. Barry was again listening to the radio to find out what was happening. 'FM, AM, black, MOR,' he said. 'You listen not to steal but to find out what little things are happening in songs and making hits.' The band had four finished songs, and Barry wanted to record them in what he called the 'what is happening now' framework. The Bee Gees intended, as usual, to write more songs in the studio, so the material was, Barry explained, 'really fresh'.

Richardson found the work challenging. The brothers never wrote anything down, nor could they communicate in clear musical terms what they wanted a song to sound like. They would indicate how they wanted a brass or string section to sound, for instance, by singing those parts. Richardson was overloaded. Handling the technical side of recording, the overall sound and balance, was demanding enough, but he also found himself attempting to work out the songs with the musicians. Robin, who did not play any instruments on Bee Gees records, was often only in the studio to sing his vocal parts, while Maurice's drinking was now becoming something of an embarrassment. Although he tried to hide it, cracking light-hearted jokes and quick one-liners, his consumption of vodka rendered him more of a nuisance than help.

With just the rudiments of two tracks recorded, Richardson introduced a new face to the studio: his best friend, twenty-nine-year-old Albhy Galuten. Richardson said what had caused him to call Galuten was an argument with the band's drummer Dennis Bryon about a hi-hat pattern that was 'too busy'. Richardson said he knew it was wrong but 'could not suggest an alternative drum pattern'. He introduced Galuten to the band as his 'music guru' and suggested he might become an 'advisor' on the album. He looked, to the band, like a tramp, arriving at the studio barefoot, with long hippie hair, a goatee, faded T-shirt, and scuzzy jeans.

Galuten had been living in Miami for some time and had strong links to Criteria as a musician and arranger, often helping out on producer Tom Dowd's sessions, including with Eric Clapton and The Allman Brothers. He referred to Dowd as his mentor, and sometimes referred to himself as an in-house producer at Atlantic, which is what Dowd was. Atlantic boss Jerry Wexler, however, would recall paying Galuten fifty dollars a week to 'hang around'. Nonetheless, he was plugged into the heart of the Miami disco scene via his links to the city's hip TK Records. He'd played keyboards on 'Rock Your Baby' and was pally with the KC & The Sunshine Band crowd.

The band members found Galuten objectionable. He lacked any diplomacy and grilled Bryon, insisting he play more like American session greats, dropping the names of men he felt could do a better job: Jeff Porcaro, Russ Kunkel, Steve Gad. The Bee Gees did not want to replace their drummer, however. 'He had fixation with drum loops, usually four bars repeated,' said Bryon. 'He wanted all the songs to be looped.'

Galuten had his most explosive arguments with Blue Weaver. He was a classically trained musician, and he wanted his vision for the songs executed correctly, right down to the last note, often showing Weaver the parts he wanted him to play. Mardin, Weaver complained, had encouraged the band to come up with ideas in the studio. 'Galuten told everybody exactly what they should be playing,' said Bryon. 'Nothing was good enough.'

Galuten would continue to criticise Bryon, Weaver, and guitarist Alan Kendall throughout the recording of the album. Barry watched intently as he worked on 'You Should Be Dancing'. He had hired a six-piece horn section and leading Miami drummer and percussionist

Joe Lala to play on the track, which would ultimately include eighteen separate tracks of various kinds of drums. It was, said Richardson, 'a wall of percussion'.

Stephen Stills played on 'You Should Be Dancing' too. The former Buffalo Springfield and Crosby, Stills, Nash & Young singer, multi-instrumentalist, and songwriter was recording a new solo album in another of Criteria's studios, with Lala a key part of his band. 'Barry is an old friend of mine, and I just sat in and played,' Stills said. 'I had a great time. I played on so many songs [on the album], I don't know which ones I played on and which I didn't.'

Barry decided he liked Galuten. 'He was a brilliant technical man, almost to the point of being a nuclear physicist,' he said. With Richardson, the three would remain a team for the next decade, producing not just The Bee Gees' biggest hits but also best-selling records for countless other acts. This unlikely alliance was to become one of the most successful production teams in music history.

'We had a vibe, very powerful and very creative,' said Galuten. The three men were of similar age; Barry was now twenty-nine, and Galuten and Richardson were simpatico with his heavy marijuana use, going through joints as regularly as the twenty cups of sweet milky tea he drank every day. All three loved nothing more than hunkering down in the studio to work. Barry began to refer to Galuten as his 'music interpreter'. He explained how, when the Gibbs wrote songs, they could 'hear the finished record in our minds' but would struggle to get the band to interpret it. 'We convey that to Albhy, who in musical terms conveys it to the band,' he said. 'The next step is that Albhy turns around to Karl and says, Get me this sound.' Galuten became indispensable to Barry on the record. As well as hiring musicians, he arranged the music, including the vocals, sometimes chose songs, and helped Richardson shape an overall sound for the new material.

Barry was singing lead on seven of the ten tracks, sharing vocals with Robin, who had co-written all the songs, on the rest. There was no doubt where the spotlight of the new record fell, with Barry's falsetto voice set to be the signature of the work. Although Galuten found Robin 'quiet', and an 'oddball', he recalled how his considered critiques of the recordings in progress were more often than not acted upon, improving the quality of the songs. This was in contrast to Maurice, who did not appreciate the level of control Galuten had suddenly acquired. His drunken outbursts were often self-defeating.

'Maurice's comments frequently were not helpful,' said Galuten. He could no longer be relied on to play bass guitar, either. 'He really was not paying attention and having difficulty with his alcohol problem,' said Galuten who simply hired another bass player, George 'Chocolate' Perry, to play Maurice's parts. Perry was a key part of Stephen Stills' backing band and a leading Miami session player who had played on many of TK Records' disco hits. Maurice, who was a new father, was less involved in these recordings than he had been at any time in the band's history, although he was credited as co-writer on eight of the tracks. He had, however, provided the crucial bass line to what was emerging as the key track on the new album. 'All Maurice,' said the band's keyboardist, Blue Weaver, of the driving bass line on 'You Should Be Dancing'. To others, it sounded as if it had been lifted from Sly & The Family Stone's classic 'Everyday People', which had provided a blueprint for many popular disco cuts—including those Perry had played on for TK.

As the album took shape, it was clear to those in the studio that 'You Be Should Be Dancing', credited to all three brothers, was the key track. It was full-on Miami disco: propulsive, rhythmic, repetitive, and beautifully constructed. 'Barry kept cranking the tempo, saying I want it faster than anything in popular music at the moment,' said Richardson. Much of the rest of the material struggled to rise above average, the weakness of the songs barely disguised beneath the contemporary sheen of the disco production: Barry's falsetto, bouncing basslines, generic disco funk guitar work, steady beats, cowbells, hi-hats, stabbing horns, big piano, and sweeping strings.

Stigwood arrived in Miami toward the end of the recording, in May 1976, to hear rough mixes. 'When he heard "You Should Be Dancing" he went crazy, slapping his hand on his leg and yelling, It's a fucking smash,' said Maurice. He also picked out two other tracks: the ballad 'Love So Right', sung in Barry's piercing falsetto, and 'Boogie Child', a track that eerily echoed the simple tropical disco funk of KC & The Sunshine Band. But he kept returning to 'You Should Be Dancing'. 'Somewhere along the line Barry became completely in tune with the times,' he later recalled. 'That's the phenomenon. It hasn't happened many times before but he has totally locked into what people are hearing. And what they want to hear.'

•

Stigwood had just returned from another trip to the Rio Carnival. He and Freddie Gershon had travelled to Brazil from Paris on the maiden voyage of Concorde. 'Rio was very rough and very exotic and the music never stopped,' said Gershon. The music in the clubs there was *all* disco. Stigwood had witnessed similarly wild scenes in clubs in England, France, and Germany. In Manhattan, where he regularly partied, disco was central to the fashionable and gay scenes he was familiar with. David Bowie had already spent time absorbing what he called Manhattan's 'great little disco scene' to help produce such monster hits as 'Fame'. Stigwood 'saw what was happening' around the world: that disco was 'going down the social strata', said Gershon. 'Five years earlier it would have been deemed effete for men to even be on the dance floor. Now men were becoming peacocks.'

Stigwood and the RSO crowd were often to be found at Regine's, a new disco club opened in May 1976 on Park Avenue in Manhattan. The chichi club, with dinner at a hundred dollars a head, attracted the hip in-crowd. Head of RSO Records Bill Oakes often went there with Nik Cohn. Champagne flowed freely, and cocaine was the drug du jour, although poppers, LSD, Quaaludes, MDA, and PCP were all being used freely. Disco music provided the soundtrack, but Regine's was more about posing than dancing.

Le Jardin was another exclusive club in Manhattan where the RSO crowd congregated. It was essentially an upmarket gay club, but there were some 'very pretty women there', according to Oakes. It welcomed fashionable straights and was popular with celebrities such as Andy Warhol and Diana Ross. 'Women could go dance without men hitting on them,' Oakes said. The DJ at Le Jardin, Bobby Guttadaro, was an influential figure in popularising disco. He had been handed gold records, in fact, for his contribution to making hits out of early disco cuts such 'Love Theme' by Love Unlimited Orchestra, and more recent hits such as 'Get Dancin'' by Disco Tex & The Sex-O-Lettes—records that broke in clubs instead of on the radio. (Monti Rock III of the latter group was a leading gay disco figure, and would later land the role of DJ in *Fever*.)

Le Jardin had been at the centre of much media attention when it opened but was now past its peak. Oakes recalled how he and Cohn quickly grew tired of the scene at the club and at Regine's, and that together they discovered 2001 Odyssey in Brooklyn: working class, straight, Italian. 'People went to Regine's in jeans,' said Oakes. 'The revelation we had in Brooklyn was finding that you had to wear proper clothes [to get in].' All those in the orbit of Cohn, including Stigwood, knew that he was writing a story for *New York* magazine about the club and disco. Cohn, a notorious self-mythologist, talked of little else for months. He had given an early draft of the story to Stigwood's long-time PA, Kevin McCormick, who in his early twenties had recently been promoted to become the head of the RSO film division, although he would describe his role as that of a 'glamorised gofer'.

'About six months before the story was published, Nik came to me,' said Stigwood. 'I'd known him from his days in England. He told me he wanted to write a movie, or write a story for a movie. So I said, OK, if you have an idea, come and see me again and we'll talk about it.' McCormick had lunch with Cohn three weeks before the article was published in *New York* magazine and made an offer to buy the rights for a film.

News travelled fast. 'Within three days everyone in the world was trying to buy it,' said McCormick. Ray Stark, one of the most successful and well-connected independent film producers in Hollywood, with hits such as *The Night Of The Iguana* and *Funny Lady* to his name, was also in the hunt. Stigwood acted quickly. 'I thought, This is a wonderful film subject,' he said. 'I thought it would be the perfect film, particularly with the disco craze starting to sweep the country. I felt sure that was going to build. So I called up Nik and said, You're crazy. You come to me about writing a story for a picture. This is it. And I made a deal with his agent in twenty-four hours to acquire the rights.' Stigwood had Freddie Gershon finalise the deal.

'I see a hundred-million-dollar-movie,' Stigwood told him.

'There are no hundred-million-dollar movies,' Gershon said. 'You are crazy.'

'This is a hundred-million-dollar movie,' said Stigwood. 'Get me the rights.'

'I seriously believed that disco would sweep the world,' Stigwood said. 'I am lucky. I just have a gut instinct with things.' Gershon said it was 'Robert's instinct that a Tony Manero'—the name given to Cohn's lead character in the film—'existed in every community in the world'. Gershon recalled negotiating an option on Cohn's article for $10,000;

in 2007, *Vanity Fair* reported that Cohn was paid $90,000 for the rights. With rivals circling, and bankrolled by Polygram, Stigwood, impatient to expand his RSO film division, sweetened the deal further, offering Cohn a first shot at writing the screenplay for a guaranteed $150,000, as well as percentage points on the soundtrack album.

The points were at Cohn's insistence: he knew the music would be an integral part of the film. Stigwood had already told RSO chief Al Coury to read the story. 'I'm going to take that story and make a movie and you are going to have the biggest soundtrack ever,' he told him. Coury had told RSO Records manager Bill Oakes of Stigwood's intentions, and he had, in turn, told his pal Cohn. Even so, Cohn remained unmoved by Stigwood's enthusiasm. 'I thought it was going to be a little film that might get made,' he said.

Stigwood was already thinking way ahead. He had just begun negotiating a huge deal with a young American actor called John Travolta to play the lead in his planned movie version of *Grease*. The co-producer on the movie, Allan Carr, had been thinking of casting Henry Winkler—The Fonz in *Happy Days*—but he was now ill, having recently had a heart bypass. It had been left to Stigwood to 'stand up and do the deal with Paramount to finance and distribute the picture'. Carr would later claim to have suggested Travolta for the lead role in *Grease* to Stigwood, telling him, 'This guy is beyond any male stereotypes. He bumps, he grinds. He's absolutely free on the screen.' Stigwood refuted the claim. 'I find that particularly irritating as I had to talk him out of using Donny Osmond in the part,' he said.

Securing Travolta was complicated—a major challenge. The twenty-two-year-old was a hot property, as the star of the hit TV American sitcom *Welcome Back, Kotter*, playing the swaggering, dumb but sexy Italian-American juvenile delinquent Vinnie Barbarino. The show was so popular that its theme tune had been a #1 hit in America in early

1976, and it had spawned a host of spin-off merchandise, with images of Vinnie Barbarino adorning everything from posters to lunch boxes. Travolta, a major teen heartthrob, had even scored himself a spin-off hit American album ['bland rock tailored to sub-teens', he called it] and a Top 10 single, 'Let Her In', that had sold more than 800,000 copies. ABC, the network that aired *Kotter*, was receiving 10,000 fan letters a week addressed to Travolta, and his public appearances were mobbed. ABC had asked him to star in his own show, based on the Barbarino character, but the ambitious Travolta turned it down, determined to land a major film role. He didn't want to hit it big, like David Cassidy, and then fade fast. And he had already had an eye-catching supporting role in hit horror movie *Carrie*.

ABC was protective of Travolta, who had signed a three-year deal to star *Kotter* in late 1975, and Stigwood needed to be at his most determined and ingenious to get him, despite the fact the actor was, in principal, keen to star in *Grease*, having got his acting break, aged eighteen, in the first national touring production of the Broadway show. Travolta had recently landed the lead role in Terrence Malick's *Days Of Heaven*, but ABC had refused to let him out of the *Kotter* production schedule, so Richard Gere had taken his place. The network instead made him the star of a TV movie it was making called *The Boy In The Plastic Bubble*, which would be aired later in the year.

Stigwood was staying at the luxurious Beverly Hills Hotel in Los Angeles while trying to conclude the deal with Travolta. The hotel provided privacy for many in Hollywood and the music business. It had twenty-three exclusive bungalows or cabanas. Stigwood was in bungalow five, in bed watching the TV, when Gershon arrived. Stigwood called him in. *Welcome Back, Kotter* was showing. Stigwood pointed out Travolta. 'That's Tony Manero,' he said.

Everything fell into place. In securing the film rights to *Grease*,

Stigwood had been forced to agree that the film could not be released until 1978—when the writers of the musical, which had been running on Broadway since 1972, felt the show would be nearing the end of its stellar run. In fact, the Broadway run of *Grease* would extend to 1980, becoming the longest running show in Broadway history. Now that he had secured the rights to Cohn's story, however, Stigwood had the perfect vehicle to keep Travolta occupied before making *Grease*. Typically, he gambled.

'I could see the momentum building for Travolta, and I did something the studios won't do,' he said. 'They love to work on an option basis and hedge their bets. I offered him a firm pay-or-play three-picture deal. Whether or not the movies were made, he got a million dollars [per movie].' Travolta was also offered a slice of profits. Stigwood guaranteed to ABC that Travolta would not break his obligations to *Kotter*, which would have virtually ended by the time *Grease* was released. The whole focus of the deal was on *Grease*. Travolta signed.

'Stigwood owned him the way old studios used to own an artist,' said Gershon. 'Like a chattel [a personal possession].' When the details of the deal were announced in September 1976 at a lavish press conference at the Beverly Hills Hotel, many in Hollywood thought that Stigwood had gone crazy. 'Everyone thought it was madness,' said Bill Oakes. 'Nobody had ever made the transition from television to movie stardom. So, a lot of us thought to pay a million dollars for Vinnie Barbarino is going to make us a laughing stock.'

Stigwood made a crack at the press reception that he had auditioned Travolta five years earlier, 'and I just heard back'. John T., as he called him, had tried out for a role in *Jesus Christ Superstar* on Broadway, he explained. 'We didn't use him because we thought he was too young to fit in with the rest of the cast,' he said. Stigwood had pencilled himself a note on a yellow pad, however: 'This kid will be a very big star.' He said he had 'remembered his name' and 'was intrigued a few years later to see him pop up on *Welcome Back, Kotter*'.

•

Meanwhile, at RSO Records, Bill Oakes was managing a run of spectacular hits. *Main Course* was followed by the *Bugsy Malone* soundtrack and another album from Eric Clapton, *No Reason To Cry*, a huge international success that hit the Top 30 in seven countries, peaking at #15 in America and #8 in the UK. The label had also scored a huge success with 'Disco Duck' by Rick Dees, a novelty disco track with Donald Duck-esque vocals. Al Coury had picked up the record for a measly $3,500, and it was now #1 in America, selling over four million copies and remaining in the Top 10 for ten weeks.

'Disco Duck' was a one-off for a label that kept the number of new acts it worked with to a minimum. Long-term, RSO hoped to develop Yvonne Elliman, who had been handed a track called 'Love Me' from the new Bee Gees recordings. Her version of the Barry and Robin song would peak at #14 on the US charts, acting as the title track to her second RSO album. The label was also planning another Bee Gees compilation album: an American-only release called *Gold* that would feature all their US Top 20 singles and within a year would sell a staggering 1.3 million copies.

RSO's limiting of the number of acts it worked with was a major benefit to The Bee Gees as the efforts of almost the entire workforce of 150 people were now focused on their new album, *Children Of The World*, scheduled for release in September 1976. Galuten and Richardson had moved quickly to secure a percentage share of the profits on the album, and were listed alongside the band as co-producers. Sensing the band's unease that the newcomers were on a percentage, Barry guaranteed Bryon, Weaver, and Kendall they would also be getting royalties on top of their wages. 'We're a unit now, it's the six of us,' he told them. There was a huge touring schedule ahead in support of the new album, too.

There was no need to hide the identity of The Bee Gees this time around, and lead single 'You Should Be Dancing' was picking up hugely positive responses across American radio on both pop music and R&B stations. In fact, Stigwood was a planning a publicity campaign in America that would see the group's profile significantly raised— one that was 'worthy of a presidential candidate', according to *Melody Maker*. While Atlantic had worried about putting the group's picture on the cover of *Main Course*, for fear of turning off the band's newfound black audience following the success of 'Jive Talkin'', Stigwood had been persuaded by Al Coury to make the group more visible. 'I felt we should at least give the audience interested in their music a chance to see what they looked like,' Coury said. 'I knew that since *Main Course* there was a new audience for their music, and it was our intention to exploit that.' So the band, tanned, hirsute, and handsome, wearing matching black leather jackets with white scarves tossed over their shoulders—Robin's hairy chest and medallion on show—featured on the new album cover.

'You Should Be Dancing' climbed to reach #1 on the American charts. Although it only stayed there for one week, the single was a huge dance hit, the band's biggest, topping the *Billboard* dance charts for seven weeks throughout August and September and also hitting the Top 5 on the *Billboard* soul charts. It was also a #1 in Canada. Alongside another huge commercial funky disco hit of the time, Wild Cherry's 'Play That Funky Music', it was one of the disco songs of the year.

With The Bee Gees' single blasting out in New York clubs and on the city's radio stations, Stigwood orchestrated a near riot in launching the band's new album while simultaneously unveiling their new shop. Dubbed the band's 'international headquarters', the store—on 57th Street, a busy midtown thoroughfare—was to sell gig tickets, albums, posters, photos, T-shirts, and other related Bee Gees product. The band knew little about it, expressing surprise at these plans when they turned up at the opening of the New York shop. They were surrounded by hundreds of screaming teenage girls as they jumped through a six-foot-high replica of their new album cover, for the cameras.

The Bee Gees spent the better part of a month in New York promoting the new album and upcoming tour. In interviews, they were quick to praise Arif Mardin for their current success. 'Arif did 50 percent of groundwork for the hits we have today,' said Maurice. 'We've learned to write our music more like he would produce it.' They used the Sheraton Hotel on 7th Avenue as a base, and as well as conducting countless interviews, they had a taste of the hedonism of the city's disco scene as the RSO staff continued to party hard. (Barry admitted to trying cocaine but disliking it.)

Thanks to the huge success of 'You Should Be Dancing' and the Stigwood hype, *Children Of The World* proved to be the band's best-selling album to date, racking up two-and-a-half-million sales and peaking at #8 on the US charts. Stigwood organised a show-stopping party for the band at the opulent and historic Gracie Mansion, the official residence of the major of the city of New York. Major Abraham Beame was to act as host at what was billed as gala luncheon. 'It's hard to get 3,000 of the beautiful people out for a pop group, but an invitation from the major is an offer they can't refuse,' he said. Notable celebrities who attended the event, which cost Stigwood $15,000, included James Taylor, Carly Simon, and Andy Warhol.

A second single from the album, 'Love So Right', also released in September, was another huge success, peaking at #3 on the American charts while also making the Top 40 of the *Billboard* black singles chart, the newly transparent promotion of the group clearly having had no significant impact on their black audience. This slick, smooth soul ballad, a showcase for Barry's confident falsetto, did nothing, however, to waylay the image the group now had among the general public: that they were a disco band.

'We're not just a disco group,' Barry said. He described 'Love So Right' as an 'R&B ballad' and insisted 'you certainly couldn't dance to it'. Maurice told the press the band would not be continuing with disco for 'the rest of our lives just because we've clicked again with it'. Barry added that for their next album, the band intended to 'add a little more melody', and 'place more importance on lyrics'. While their earlier career had been influenced by first Neil Sedaka and then The Beatles, he said, they now 'let Stevie Wonder influence us'.

'We're becoming bigger now than we ever were before,' said Robin. 'No one would ever have thought it would happen.' However, despite the #1 hit and the publicity blitz, tickets for the dates on the band's upcoming American tour were not moving as fast as expected, even in New York, where a looming gig at the 20,000-capacity Madison Square Garden was far from sold out. The band had turned down a lucrative two-week slot in Las Vegas, thinking it a retrograde move that would put them back into a cabaret style. They had been working hard on rehearsing their tight, modern band sound in the Isle of Man, and they wanted to prove themselves a serious live act.

Sensing the potential for embarrassment, Stigwood acted quickly, announcing that the band were donating the proceeds of the Madison Square Garden gig to New York's Police Athletic League, inviting the charity—that provided sporting facilities for underprivileged children via police-sponsored youth clubs—to bring 10,000 inner-city school kids to the concert free of charge. According to Freddie Gershon, Stigwood made the Police Athletic League a 'donation' of $50,000 to smooth the arrangements. The Bee Gees played at the prestigious venue to an appreciative audience, most of who had never been to a live gig before. The reviews were positive, too, with The Bee Gees able to announce that they had raised $31,000 for the charity. Stigwood also took ads in the entertainment press congratulating the band on there being standing room only at the show. 'With smoke and mirrors,' Gershon said, 'he reinvented them.'

The American tour was widely regarded in the business and among the wider public as the band's most successful yet, with the empty seats in places such as New Orleans and San Francisco going unreported. A final date on December 20, at the 17,500-capacity Forum in Los Angeles, was also patchy. The show was being filmed for an intended TV special, but the idea was sacked due to the underwhelming images of empty seats aplenty. Instead, RSO intended to rescue the audio from the show for a live album. Around the same time, a third single from the new studio album, 'Boogie Child', climbed to #12 in the US charts.

'We're fully aware that our music is almost totally commercial,' said Barry. 'We write for the present.' Even so, the band did little to promote the single. During the long tour, many of the familiar arguments between the brothers had resurfaced. Maurice had been desperate to get back onstage, but his drinking made him a liability. Barry said he would get so drunk before gigs he'd have to feel his way along the wall to get to the stage. The two had grown close as neighbours on the Isle of Man, spending time making home movies, acting out loose plots with Hugh often behind the camera and friends, family, and associates all inveigled into taking part. Now Barry was exasperated by Maurice's drinking, particularly as his brother was a now a father. The emotional distance between the pair grew greater when Barry decided to leave the Isle of Man, having recently bought a mansion in Miami. It was he said, 'a lovely peaceful spot away from showbiz crowd'.

Hugh and Barbara also made plans to relocate to Miami, with Maurice remaining on the Isle of Man for now. Robin was happy to keep his distance from his family, remaining in Surrey, where he bought a new £150,000 mansion with a pool, where he lived with Molly and their two young children. On the recent tour, his resentment toward Barry had simmered. Small things had aggravated him: how Barry always had the biggest hotel suite and tended to be at the centre of everything, especially now onstage, with his newfound falsetto dominating the shows. The same tensions that caused the band's split in 1969 were re-emerging. Robin felt he was being eclipsed and not getting the acclaim he served.

Back in the UK, Robin aimed barbed digs at his brother. 'I'm prepared to sacrifice some income as a price for staying in country I regard as home,' he said. 'Molly and I refuse to become tax exiles.' There was, he said, 'no better place to raise children' than England. Life was also less fraught in the UK. Although 'You Should Be Dancing' had been a hit in the country, reaching #5, it had not triggered significant sales of the *Children Of The World* album, which, like *Main Course* before it, did not break into the UK Top 40. 'Love So Right' also failed to make the Top 40 in the UK. The band's profile was much lower in Britain than it was in American and Canada. In fact, 'Jive Talkin'' and 'You Should Be Dancing' aside, The Bee Gees had failed to make any significant impact anywhere in Europe.

●

In Miami, Barry headed straight back into the studio, hooking up with Richardson and Galuten at Criteria to begin recording an album with his brother Andy, who was now eighteen. There had long been plans to incorporate Andy into The Bee Gees, but now it had been decided that he should be a solo star. He had signed a recording and management contract with Stigwood, who envisaged launching Andy as a teen-pop star in the mould of Donnie Osmond or David Cassidy. He was good-looking, like a miniature Barry, with blue eyes and blonde hair.

Barry took almost total control of Andy's career and the running of his life. He had spent the past few years living in Australia, and only six months ago, in July 1976, had married a sixteen-year-old called Kim. Andy talked about becoming a pilot and said he enjoyed being part of a 'normal family'—Kim's dad was a bricklayer and her mum worked in a factory. But there was nothing normal about the Gibbs. Barry had arranged for Andy and Kim to honeymoon at Stigwood's newly acquired luxury mansion on a twenty-six-acre estate in Bermuda. Stigwood and Barry were there too, and it was while on the honeymoon Andy had inked the deal that would bring him to America to be a superstar. In fact, on the honeymoon he had been flown from Bermuda to Miami to record demos of two of Barry's songs, both of which would become future singles: 'I Just Want To Be Your Everything' and '(Love Is) Thicker Than Water'.

Andy had now left Kim and Australia to live on a luxury houseboat in Miami, and Stigwood and RSO were gearing up to launch his career. 'In a way he didn't really want to do it, but he knew he had to,' said Kim. 'Barry instigated it,' said Andy. The two had a special bond. 'My parents had two sets of twins,' Barry said. 'One separated by twelve years. We were very close, as Robin and Maurice were very close as twins.' Interviewed as a nine-year-old, Andy had told the press that Barry, 'kind and generous', was his favourite brother. 'I hope when I grow up I'm like him,' he said. 'I don't like Robin, he doesn't talk to me.'

Andy had been a lonely child. Other kids had always treated him differently, the brother of the famous Bee Gees. 'I never had a good day at school ever in my life,' he said. He was forever in the back of a limousine or Rolls-Royce, or staying in plush hotels on the road. He watched his brothers on TV, grew accustomed to having 500 screaming girls outside his front door. The family moved around a lot. Before returning to Australia, Andy had lived in Manchester, London, the Isle

Leedon

BARRY GIBB &
THE BEE GEE'S

THE BEE GEE's SING & PLAY
14 BARRY GIBB SONGS

FEATURING:
I WAS A LOVER, A LEADER OF MEN
+ WINE & WOMEN

Nigel Dempster, the World's Boldest Gossip
Governor Carey Hits Rock Bottom, by Ken Auletta
The Mid-Life Crises of 'Time' and 'Newsweek'

NEW YORK

Tribal Rites of the New Saturday Night
By Nik Cohn

ABOVE Robin (*centre*) and Barry Gibb with Barry's wife Linda at London Airport, March 1971. **RIGHT** A promotional photo of Nik Cohn, issued around the same time.

OPPOSITE The fresh-faced Gibb brothers look out from the cover of their debut album, released in 1965; rehearsing for a 1968 television performance in Brussels, Belgium; the front cover of the 1976 issue of *New York* magazine featuring Nik Cohn's story about the 'Tribal Rites Of The New Saturday Night'.

ABOVE Barry Gibb at Criteria Studios with co-producers Karl Richardson (*left*) and Albhy Galuten (*centre*). RIGHT Barry, Maurice, and Robin celebrate the twentieth anniversary of The Bee Gees with manager Robert Stigwood (*centre*) and Atlantic Records boss Ahmet Ertegun (*right*).

LEFT Producer Arif Mardin at Atlantic Studios, New York, in the late 70s. OPPOSITE The Bee Gees in Central Park, New York City, 1975.

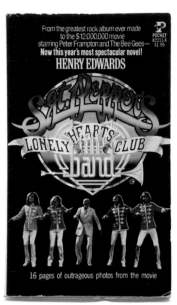

ABOVE Dancers at 2001 Odyssey, Brooklyn, New York, in 1978.
LEFT A series of promotional stills of John Travolta in *Saturday Night Fever*.
OPPOSITE A 'novelisation' of the *Sgt. Pepper's* movie; the *Saturday Night Fever* soundtrack LP; RSO impresario Robert Stigwood, late 60s.

LEFT The Gibb brothers and their parents, Hugh and Barbara, at the Waldorf Astoria, New York, 1978.
BELOW A poster for *Staying Alive*, the 1983 follow-up to *Saturday Night Fever*; Andy Gibb and his mum in Miami, 1978.

of Man, and Ibiza, where, aged thirteen, he had first started to perform. By then, he had been allowed to slip out of the education system, with Hugh and Barbara convinced he was set for a career in showbusiness.

In Ibiza, Andy played the hits of the day on an acoustic guitar for the tourists, trading on his Bee Gee association by including songs such as 'Words' in his repertoire—the tourist girls loved him. When Barry, Maurice, and Lulu visited, they would sing with him. Andy did not seem to have the same innate drive of his elder brothers, having been spoiled from a young age. He 'only had to ask' for something and he got it. At one point, he had wanted to be a show jumper. So Barry bought him a horse.

Barry, who had bought Andy his first guitar, encouraged him to write his own songs, and Maurice helped him record demos of them. Although he was nothing like his brothers—he was a 'real sports freak', according to Hugh—ever since he could walk there had been talk of him joining The Bee Gees. When he was fifteen, he had moved with Hugh and Barbara to the Isle of Man, where he fell into a depression. Plans for him to join the band kept falling through. 'Twice I nearly joined The Bee Gees,' he said. 'We talked about it and started to work out on a few ideas but we could never really make the final plans. They were touring ten months of the year, it was ridiculous, and we could never get down to sorting anything out.' He began to hope one of them might leave so he could step in. 'I can do any of their voices,' he said.

Andy was lonely and lost. 'One night he was really crying,' said Barbara. She did what she thought best: bought him a band's worth of new equipment, hired players, and got him up onstage. She even chose the band's name, Melody Fayre, after a Bee Gees song. They began playing clubs and hotels on the island, with Andy advertised as 'the youngest brother of the famous Bee Gees'. Sometimes Hugh sat in on drums. Déjà vu. Barry took an active interest, choosing material for the band to play:

Neil Sedaka, Paul Anka, Neil Diamond, Leo Sayer, The Hollies, Bread, Harry Nilsson, Wings, Elton John, The Everly Brothers, plus a range of Bee Gees hits such as 'I've Gotta Get A Message To You' and 'How Can You Mend A Broken Heart?' It was a dated set list for a kid to be playing, but more than anything Andy wanted to be like Barry, to sing like him, even, he said, to 'hold his guitar like him'. As one member of Melody Fayre put it, Andy was 'besotted with Barry, absolutely worshipped him'.

The family next sent Andy to Australia to gain showbusiness experience, hooking him up with the men who had helped The Bee Gees in the early stages of their own career. Andy did not seem to have much say in the matter. 'They controlled my career,' he said, of Barry and Hugh. 'They were planning for me to come back to America. Even when I was young, they told me basically how they had it all worked out, and I let them do it.'

Barry referred to this period as Andy's 'performing apprenticeship'. He landed support slots in Australia with visiting UK teen acts, including The Bay City Rollers and The Sweet, performing to crowds of up to 5,000 and getting his first taste of adulation. 'Their hands were feeling me everywhere,' he said of his teenage fans. He appeared on TV and played the Sydney circuit of shopping centres and clubs, adding each new Bee Gees hit to his set. He released one single in Australia, a self-penned middle-of-the-road ballad, 'Words And Music', that didn't do much. Before being whisked away to America, his last engagement had been playing Buttons in a production of *Cinderella*.

Barry worked long and hard on recording Andy's debut single for RSO, 'I Just Want To Be Your Everything', even though Andy said he had watched Barry write the song in 'about twenty minutes'. At Criteria, an impressive cast of top session players cut a final version of the song, including in-demand session drummer Ron 'Tubby' Ziegler. There was even a guest appearance from superstar Joe Walsh, guitarist with The

Eagles, who were recording their *Hotel California* album in one of the other Criteria studios. The single also featured Barry's unmistakable vocals and harmonies. In fact, the song sounded incredibly like The Bee Gees, with Andy's vocals an identikit version of Barry's, leading some critics to suggest Andy was a projection of Barry's ego.

Stigwood loved 'I Just Want to Be Your Everything'. It was commercial, disco-lite, full of sentimentalism and sex; a perfect vehicle for a teen idol. RSO planned its release for April 1977 and began preparing the groundwork for Andy's big launch. Stigwood had a gut instinct that Andy, like John Travolta, would be a star, and he trusted others to carry through his vision. It was not just his good looks, famous name, and the backing of The Bee Gees writing and production team, there was a vulnerability and innocence to the clean-cut Andy—who didn't drink or smoke—that Stigwood felt was perfect pop titillation.

●

Stigwood was full of plans, telling the press to expect a 'controlled expansion policy' at RSO Records, as, alongside Andy, he eyed up other established acts, including The Rolling Stones and Peter Frampton. *Rolling Stone* magazine noted that 'the sun rarely set' on 'bachelor' Stigwood. 'He is a constant traveller … a power broker with a penchant for style and a fondness for life in the grand manner.' He explained to the magazine the philosophy of the company he ran. 'We believe in working hard and having fun at the same time. It's a way of life for me and I feel tremendous. I feel very lucky to have the freedom to do the things I want to do. And, as I say, my clients are all my friends as well.' Others saw him as a lonely figure, a multimillionaire who 'thinks he can buy anything'. He was forty-two, still single, and living as a tax exile, having sold his London home. He moved between the spread in Bermuda and sumptuous homes in New York and Los Angeles. There were personal chefs, valets, and assistants in each location. His main focus was on the film business, but he was also predicting major action for his television operation and talking up the possibility of another Broadway stage show.

Stigwood's pursuit of Peter Frampton, the twenty-six-year-old Englishman who was currently the biggest superstar in rock music, having scored the best-selling album of 1976 with *Frampton Comes Alive!*, was both audacious and wonderfully executed. The former Humble Pie singer and guitarist had sold over thirteen million copies of the album, which had also spawned several hit singles. The cute, blonde Frampton had emerged from several poor-selling solo albums to suddenly find himself the hottest star in the world, famously pictured topless on the cover of *Rolling Stone* magazine, playing to huge audiences—120,000 in Philadelphia!—and blurring the lines between rock music and pin-up teen idol.

There was no wrestling Frampton from his long-term contract with A&M Records, but Stigwood found something else to offer him: the starring role in a big budget Hollywood musical he intended to make based on songs from The Beatles album *Sgt. Pepper's Lonely Hearts Club Band*. Frampton, who had no acting experience, was flattered. The figure that Stigwood paid him to star in the film was not revealed, but news of the project made headlines around the world. Stigwood had made sure, of course, that RSO would be releasing the film's sure-to-be-massive soundtrack. It was another classic example of the synergy Stigwood was now working into almost every aspect of his business empire. Frampton's manager, Dee Anthony, a tough fifty-year-old New Yorker who also managed Tony Bennett, Jethro Tull, and Joe Cocker, and had won *Billboard*'s 'Manager of the Year' award for 1976, said he had 'every confidence in Mr Stigwood's artistic integrity, talent, and ability to make this an important milestone in Peter's career'.

Stigwood had long nurtured the idea for the *Sgt. Pepper's* movie, having presenting a stage play based around songs on the famous 1967 album in London in 1974. He had planned to tour the show in arenas and stadiums, but the production was a flop and the play folded after seven weeks. Despite this, Stigwood had noted that audiences had sung along with the Beatles tunes. He envisioned the movie, with its combination of The Beatles and Frampton, would become the biggest blockbuster the world had ever seen. 'For a long time, I looked at those long lines of people at rock concerts and wondered why you couldn't have the same crowd for a film,' he said.

For the script, Stigwood had chosen rock writer Henry Edwards, who said he was reaching back 'into the golden age of MGM musicals'— films like *Singin' In The Rain*—for inspiration. The movie had been slated to start filming in January 1977, but it was a complex project, not least due to the negotiations involved in securing the film rights to The Beatles songs Stigwood wanted to use. He had already fired one director, Australian-born TV whizz-kid Chris Beard, one of the creators of *The Gong Show*, replacing him with Michael Schultz who had directed the hit TV show *Starsky & Hutch* and the recent disco-inspired hit movie *Car Wash*.

The signing of Frampton annoyed Barry. He would later claim Stigwood had promised The Bee Gees leading roles in the *Sgt. Pepper's* movie before this 'red-hot young man came along'. Instead, Stigwood was telling the press that The Bee Gees would play a supporting role to Frampton, with a rescheduled start date for film of September 1977. He said there would also be roles in the movie for The Eagles, Perry Como, Frank Sinatra, John Lennon, Bing Crosby, Bette Midler, and KISS.

Sgt. Pepper's was one of four films Stigwood planned to produce in 1977, but its six-million-dollar budget far eclipsed the others. In early 1977, *Rolling Stone* gave updated information on the other three movies, listing their working titles and budgets: *Saturday Night* starring

John Travolta (three million dollars); *Grease*, number two in Travolta's three-picture deal with Stigwood (four million dollars), and *The Geller Effect*, not yet budgeted, a loosely autobiographical film starring controversial twenty-year-old psychic Uri Geller, who had risen to fame on the back of his spoon-bending tricks on TV. The four films, *Rolling Stone* noted, represented a sizable jump in film activity for Stigwood. 'It was a combination of good things coming up,' he said.

There was an urgency now to make the movie based on Cohn's article, the one *Rolling Stone* called *Saturday Night*. Travolta had to film it during a break in the schedule for *Welcome Back, Kotter*, and *Grease*, which Paramount had already invested in, was due to start filming in June 1977. Stigwood had hired director John Avildsen for the movie, having been impressed by a rough cut of a low-budget boxing movie Avildsen had just completed called *Rocky*. Avildsen had insisted on hiring the notorious Norman Wexler to write the script. Wexler was both a brilliant writer—twice nominated for Oscars for his work on *Joe* (which Avildsen had directed) and *Serpico*—and a wild man: a chain-smoking, manic-depressive known to carry a .32-caliber pistol who had once been jailed for threatening to kill President Nixon.

Stigwood liked Wexler, although he admitted to being unnerved on their first meeting, when he spied a gun in the writer's bag. When Wexler had delivered the first draft of the script in September 1976, Stigwood thought it perfect, even though it was soaked in profanities. 'I wouldn't touch it,' he said. 'You know I wouldn't water it down. Because he wrote *Serpico*, he knew it had to be gritty—you can't gloss over the way those kids talk.' Wexler was the person who 'did the most research', Stigwood said. 'He really did hang out at those clubs, the rhythm of the dialogue, he got it perfectly.' Cohn's version of the script was junked.

When Stigwood showed Travolta the new script, however, the actor baulked. He had got on board with the movie after reading Cohn's *New*

York piece, telling Cohn how authentic he felt the characters were. 'It had images and values that were very strong,' he said. The Wexler script called for a reality he had not signed up to, nor one he had ever attempted on screen before. He did not think he was a strong enough actor for the role or 'could give it enough dimension'.

Travolta's forty-year-old girlfriend, sitcom actress Diana Hyland, best known her role in *Peyton Place*, did her best to reassure him. She saw through the fighting, bad language, rape, homophobia, and racism. 'Baby, you are going to be great in this—great!' she told him. 'This Tony, he's got all the colours! First he's angry about something. He hates the trap that Brooklyn and his dumb job are. There's a whole glamorous world out there waiting for him, which he feels only when he dances. And he grows, he gets out of Brooklyn.'

'He's also king of the disco,' said Travolta. 'I'm not that good a dancer.'

'Baby,' Hyland said, 'you're going to learn!'

Travolta was now immersed in the character. He had spent time lurking, and sometimes dancing, at 2001 Odyssey with Wexler. When he was recognised, he noticed how the disco's alpha males kept their girls in line. 'Their girlfriends would come up, and they'd say, Hey, stay away from him, don't bug Travolta,' he said. 'They'd actually push the girls away. Tony Manero's whole male-chauvinist thing I got from watching those guys in the discos.' He had also been spending three hours a day learning dance moves with the New York City Ballet's principal dancer, Jacques D'Amboise.

Although he had a script, a director, and a star, Stigwood still did not have a backer for the movie. 'He was financing it himself with his new partners,' said the inexperienced Kevin McCormick, head of the RSO film division. McCormick was having 'stomach aches every day' as Stigwood assembled a production team from his triplex penthouse apartment in Manhattan. 'We literally put together the soundtrack in

Stigwood's living room,' he said. The film's female lead, Karen Gorney, a star of the ABC soap opera *All My Children*, auditioned for Stigwood at the apartment and recalled being impressed by a giant silk Chinese screen along the wall that displayed 'the whole history of China'. It was one of the biggest, most luxurious penthouses in all of Manhattan, with Italian marble floors and views of Central Park, in the famous San Remo apartment building on 135 Central Park West. Stigwood boasted of how the Duke and Duchess of Windsor had owned the apartment in the 1940s. (When he moved out of New York, he sold it to Bruce Willis.)

McCormick said Stigwood had a 'blithe confidence' that the movie was 'going to be up and ready to go'. He was confident that Paramount, the movie studio he had dealt with on *Survive!*, *Bugsy Malone*, and *Grease*, would strike a distribution deal for the film. 'I picked Paramount because it was doing badly at the time,' Stigwood said. 'They needed movies.' One of the so-called 'big six' film studios in America, Paramount had been struggling since Robert Evans quit the company in 1974. As head of production, Evans had famously revitalised the studio with massive hits including *The Godfather*, *Rosemary's Baby*, and *Chinatown*. Recently, Paramount had put a new television-trained team in place, headed by Barry Diller, hoping to revitalise the studio.

Stigwood was employing the same tactic he had used on *Tommy*: risking his own money to put the movie together—book, script, actors, director, production team, and schedule—and gambling on raising the budget from distributors paying for a percentage of the gross. If the plan was successful, it meant he would alleviate all financial risk, retain ownership of the movie rights, and be able to negotiate for himself a far higher percentage of the gross profits than if a studio had put up the money to get the movie rolling. The process was not actually much different to the one with which he had revolutionised the UK music business in the early 60s. Paramount was keen in principle to do a deal but Stigwood had not yet signed. He was insisting he retained control of the final cut of the movie.

Meanwhile, money was not the only thing troubling McCormick. In late 1976, Avildsen's million-dollar boxing movie, *Rocky*, had become an unexpected smash hit, grossing five million dollars on its opening weekend in the US and going on to take $225 million worldwide. The movie was also a critical hit, and Avildsen was suddenly the hottest director in America. By early 1977, he was demanding huge changes to the *Saturday Night* movie. He told McCormick that Travolta was 'too fat' and couldn't dance, and he wondered if maybe the main character 'shouldn't be a dancer—maybe he should be a painter'. He then hired ex-boxer Jimmy Gambina, who had worked with Sylvester Stallone on *Rocky*, to get Travolta into shape, and brought in new scriptwriters, who delivered a revised script in January 1977. 'It was just weird,' said McCormick. Travolta was equally unhappy. He felt Avildsen wanted to change the role, smooth off the rough edges, make him the kind of nice guy who carries groceries for old ladies in the neighbourhood—another Rocky Balboa. 'A dancing Rocky,' as McCormick put it.

●

The Bee Gees were in France, recording material for a new album and mixing the live album they'd recorded at their end-of-tour Los Angeles concert. The band had expected to find grandeur at the recording studio RSO had booked for them, the Château D'Herouville, just outside Paris. Pink Floyd, T.Rex, David Bowie, and Elton John had all recorded here—John had cut his eight-million-selling US #1 album *Goodbye Yellow Brick Road* at the studio and named another album *Honky Chateau* in homage to the place, which was located in a grand eighteenth-century manor house. Instead, the studio appeared run-down. Barry, who had left behind the sunshine of Miami, found the cold January weather depressing and the accommodation shocking. There was no TV, and there were only two working showers for the entire band. Maurice was fooling no one by hiding his vodka in Perrier bottles. Robin was downbeat about having to spend time away from his young children and wife so soon after the lengthy recording and touring schedule of 1976.

There was a sour atmosphere at the Château. All three Gibbs were still angry at Stigwood's downgrading of their roles in *Sgt. Pepper's*. They did not fully understand either the complex tax and work visa issues that had brought them here, to this dump, rather than their preferred Criteria Studios. At least Richardson and Galuten were here, Barry thought. RSO had scheduled the live album for release in May, and there was much technical work required to get the music up to scratch, including some re-recording of vocals and instrumental overdubs. There was less pressure on the new album that RSO planned for September release, which was lucky, as the band had no finished new songs and hoped to write in the studio.

Barry imagined the new material moving away from disco toward what he called a 'black blue-eyed soul' sound, name-checking The Stylistics and The Delfonics as key influences. 'People who sing in falsetto,' he noted. The Bee Gees equated much of their recent success to Barry's newfound voice.

Barry sat in with the band—Kendall, Bryon, and Weaver—hoping to find inspiration. Galuten said that Weaver had 'tremendous input' into the first new song recorded in France, a soft ballad called 'How Deep Is Your Love'. The song was written in an afternoon as Weaver and Barry jammed on electric piano and acoustic guitar. Weaver had helped create the structure of the song by playing chords to Barry's melody line. He later admitted he was trying to play the popular 60s US #1 hit 'Theme From A Summer Place' by The Percy Faith Orchestra.

Robin immediately spotted the potential in the song, and he and Barry worked on the lyrics. Maurice might join them to sing vocal lines. The brothers often gathered on the imposing stone stairwell in the creaking manor house to sing, utilising the natural echo there. 'How Deep Is Your Love' was recorded with just keyboards, Barry singing and playing guitar, and Maurice on bass.

Robin was excited, suggesting the song had 'universal appeal'. As before, he was only in the studio fleetingly, to sing vocals or offer his opinion on working recordings—the 'objective production ear', said Richardson. He might say a song needed more emotion or suggest a structural change, often attempting to simplify and bring clarity to the music. Richardson appreciated his input, noting how he, Galuten, and Barry were 'so close to the music' that they often couldn't tell what sounded good. 'Robin comes in and calls it in a moment, it doesn't work or it sounds great,' he said.

'Robin's opinion was very valuable,' Galuten added. 'The day-to-day in the trenches was me, Barry, and Karl. It was clearly Barry's vision. We were executing Barry's vision.' (As before, Maurice was a less reliable sounding board. 'He was not great in the studio,' said Galuten. 'More of a social entity than a musical entity.')

Two more new songs fell quickly into place, both soulful and melodramatic and almost equal to 'How Deep Is Your Love' in terms of commercial appeal: 'If I Can't Have You' and 'More Than A Woman'. The band's writing was better than ever. Barry put it down to a combination of bad weather outside and 'no television' at the studio, which he said was 'very conducive to songwriting'.

A fourth new track was so good it surprised even Barry. It had resulted from a jam with guitarist Kendall, who had locked into a groove on a strong guitar lick. Richardson said he distinctly remembered Barry saying, 'Boy, Karl, have I got a song for you' and sitting down to play the song to him on an acoustic. 'It was like a chant and it was unbelievable,' he said. 'I said, Barry don't forgot that rhythm, that's a number one record. I knew, five bars in, no questions asked. You couldn't get past the intro without knowing it was a smash.' This was the beginnings of 'Stayin' Alive', as yet untitled.

•

Stigwood happened to be in Paris on business in February. He and Freddie Gershon were entertaining Mick Jagger, making an audacious attempt to steal The Rolling Stones from Atlantic Records. The Stones' deal with Atlantic for American distribution had run down. The band were restructuring their business, having recently signed a six-album deal with EMI for Europe worth a reputed $1.7 million per album. Stigwood hoped RSO would be able to acquire the North American rights to the band's music. Atlantic, which had distributed the Stones' music in America since 1971, totting up six gold albums, was desperate to keep them.

The scenario pitted Stigwood against his old pal Ahmet Ertegun, RSO against Warners, Atlantic's owners, the memory of losing RSO to Polygram still fresh in the minds of the senior executives there. Stigwood and Gershon enjoyed Paris and the game, unrestrained in their pursuit of the Stones. Between dinners and nights out with Jagger, they kept busy with other RSO business. One of the most pressing issues for Stigwood was the soundtrack to the *Saturday Night* movie. Travolta was rehearsing his big dance scenes to Stevie Wonder and Boz Scaggs. 'The Bee Gees weren't even involved in the movie in the beginning,' said Travolta. Now there were problems. Scaggs had just backed out of deal to let Stigwood use 'Lowdown' from his 1976 disco album *Silk Degrees*. Stigwood called Château d'Herouville and spoke to Barry.

'We want songs for this film,' Stigwood said.

'No, can't do it,' said Barry. 'Haven't got time to sit down and write for a film.'

While Stigwood and Gershon were in Paris with Jagger, the Stones' business manager, Prince Rupert Lowenstein, was in Los Angeles, meeting with Ahmet Ertegun. Stigwood was being played. Lowenstein was simply using RSO's offers to improve the deal he was negotiating with Atlantic. Stigwood made a final bid for the Stones, offering seven million dollars for six albums—which is what he had decided was his limit on the deal. He said the Stones wanted more and were getting 'very, very, very greedy'. He decided to back out, and the Stones re-signed to Atlantic.

It was a short journey from Paris to Herouville to listen to The Bee Gees' demos and convince them to write songs for his new movie. 'Forget the new album,' he told them. 'Put it on the back burner.' Barry didn't want to. He was enthused by the material they had already recorded, arguing that they had the basis of a great new album. Stigwood sat down and listened to the tracks. 'Please don't make a new album,' he said, explaining to the band the basic idea of his *Saturday Night* movie—'it's about a bunch of guys that live in New York who love to dance'—and plans for the soundtrack album, how he envisaged the music being released ahead of the movie, prophesising huge no.1 hit singles. 'This will be your new album,' he said.

Stigwood talked up the opportunity further: the music would be central to the movie, and as The Bee Gees had never done songs for movies it would be an invaluable experience. Maurice was impressed. 'Back then, you'd pay people to get your songs in films,' he said. 'Wow! Movie music! We got caught up in the Robert Stigwood syndrome. Anyone he managed he also wanted involved in his film projects.' Barry suggested 'How Deep Is Your Love' would be ideal for Yvonne Elliman to sing. Stigwood shook his head. The band must keep it. 'It was one of the most moving ballads I ever heard,' he said.

Stigwood said he would use all four of the band's new songs in the movie if the band could make them 'more disco-y'. He also asked the group to write the movie's theme tune, elaborating on the plot without supplying them with a script. 'It was hard to get them to read anything,' Stigwood said. They still didn't write down their own lyrics.

'He explained to us the film was about this young guy, who every weekend, blows his wages at a disco in Brooklyn,' said Maurice. 'He's got a really truly Catholic family, and he's got a good job, but he blows his wages every Saturday night. He has his mates with him. Then he comes back and starts the week again, and this goes on every Saturday night. But it's just one Saturday night that's filmed. So that's all we knew, excerpt it was John Travolta playing the part.'

The Bee Gees saw the prospect of writing the film's theme tune as a challenge. 'They spent a lot of time thinking of titles that would be evocative and represent the street scene of New York,' said Galuten. 'That's where "Stayin' Alive" and "Night Fever" come from. They were both potential titles for the film, finely crafted to the meaning of the film.' The band, said Stigwood, 'finished up very quickly', and that 'writing to order' was where their real brilliance resided. 'Night Fever' was the fifth song the band recorded in France and the only one written purposefully with the film in mind—a concerted effort to write a good disco song, with Bryon keeping his drumming simple and danceable.

Despite the occasional clashes between the musicians and Galuten, a strong sense of camaraderie began to blossom in the studio. Barry had begun talking to them all, brothers and band, about moving to Miami to be closer to him, and discussing starting a production company. 'We can all work together on different projects,' he said. 'We'll start a record label just like Atlantic. We could even build our own studio.' All of them were convinced that 'Night Fever' was the perfect theme song for the movie and would make an excellent single.

'Everybody was happy with the way it turned out,' said Richardson. 'It had a spark.'

They played Stigwood 'Night Fever' and suggested he change the title of the movie to match the title of the song. 'No,' said Stigwood. 'That's too pornographic, too hot, we can't use that.' Stigwood also felt the track was too mellow, not strong enough to be a theme song. If he was going to hang the promotion of the movie on one piece of music, he wanted something stronger.

The band returned to Barry's demo of the untitled 'Stayin' Alive' which still only had loose ad-lib guide vocals, mostly consisting of Barry scatting. They inserted the phrase 'Saturday night' into the chant and Stigwood seemed keen. Then, unfortunately, in the middle of developing the track, the band's drummer, Bryon, left the Château D'Herouville suddenly, needing to fly back to Cardiff to be with his mother who suffered from dementia. She had developed pneumonia and was in coma. The doctors had warned him they didn't think she'd last the day.

In Bryon's absence, Galuten and Richardson began experimenting with drum loops on the track. They felt the drum part he had laid down was not steady enough. They took a few bars from 'Night Fever' and looped them to use as the propulsive beat for the new 'Saturday Night' song, giving it a classic disco feel. Galuten also developed Kendall's guitar part, finessing the distinctive guitar hook that would define the finished song. He said he had been inspired by the keyboard part in Stevie Wonder's 'Superstition', one of his favourite recordings. Galuten also developed the bass line Maurice had played on the demo.

The Gibb brothers finished the lyrics to the song in just two hours, sparked to life by a few scrawled words Robin had jotted down on a plane ticket. They felt using 'Saturday night' as the chorus was naff. Maurice thought it was too strongly associated with The Bay City Rollers, who had scored a huge 1976 American #1 with a song called

'Saturday Night' that was all about chanting the title. Now they were singing about 'staying alive', surviving in city: 'People crying out for help,' said Barry. 'Desperate songs: those are the ones that become giants. The minute you capture that on record, it's gold.'

With Barry singing lead in falsetto, the brothers sang endless backing harmonies until they were satisfied with the recording. When Bryon returned to the studio, Barry declared it the 'best song we've ever written' and 'perfect for the film'. Bryon added fills and cymbals to the loop, giving it more human feel.

Stigwood loved it. 'Robert said, You hit the nail right on the spot,' said Maurice. 'That's perfect. But why are you singing "Stayin' Alive, Stayin' Alive", when it should be "Saturday Night, Saturday Night"? We said because there are so many bloody records out called "Saturday Night". It's corny. It's a terrible title.' It was the title of the film, Stigwood reminded the band. 'It's "Stayin' Alive" or we'll keep the song,' said Barry. Stigwood said he did not want that as the title for his film. The band refused to budge. It was 'left in my lap' said Stigwood. 'Randomly, in the end I chose "Saturday" and "Night Fever" [for the title of the film] and that seemed to gel,' he added. For Robin, however, it still sounded like a 'sleazy little porno film'.

The Bee Gees completed the recordings at Criteria. Joe Lala would again add percussion, and Galuten also brought in a horn section, as well as the Miami Strings, who had worked extensively at TK Records, to augment the tracks. Members of the band stayed at a beautiful rental house on North Bay Road to overdub parts to finish the work. Even so, Barry said the songs were not awarded the same level of care they would have received had they been intended for a new band album. 'We didn't take as much trouble even as we did with *Main Course*, and nowhere near as long as we had with *Children Of The World*.'

CHAPTER FIVE
SOUNDTRACK TO THE 70S

SIR GEORGE MARTIN
MY GOD, I'VE NEVER
HEARD ANYTHING LIKE IT.

emos of the new Bee Gees songs reached John Avildsen in New York. Preliminary filming of *Saturday Night Fever* had begun in March, and the first few weeks had not gone well. The changes Avildsen had made to Wexler's script—sixteen pages of changes in total—hadn't pleased Stigwood. 'Bloody awful,' he'd said.

'Robert is almost religious about scripts,' said Kevin McCormick, who was busy putting out fires everywhere, 'and he thought the Wexler version of *Fever* was one of the best film scripts he had ever read.'

Avildsen was in an imperious mood, almost impossible to deal with. In early February, he was had been nominated for an Oscar for 'Best Director' for *Rocky*. The film was up for several other awards, including 'Best Picture', with Sylvester Stalone nominated tor 'Best Actor' and his co-star, Talia Shire, up for 'Best Actress'. Stalone's script was also up for 'Best Original Screenplay'. Paramount had still not come through with the finances for *Fever*, although a deal had been agreed in principal with the studio for distribution, and Travolta was in the middle of personal crisis that saw him frequently flying off to Los Angeles. His girlfriend, Diana Hyland, was dying from cancer. On set Travolta was in a state of constant jetlag and distress. In late March, Hyland died in his arms, and there was concern he may not complete the film.

There were also problems with The Bee Gees songs. Avildsen was unhappy about the music he was hearing. He had wanted the theme song to complement a rewritten key scene in the film where Travolta and Gorney first see each other on the dance floor. Avildsen was very much nudging the movie toward being a romantic love story. He asked Stigwood if The Bee Gees could provide a slower-tempo bridge section to 'Stayin' Alive'. Stigwood, for once, was in agreement with the director. He felt it was a good idea, one that would actually enhance the song. He called the band in Miami.

'Robert wanted a song that was eight minutes long,' Barry said. He explained to the band that 'Stayin' Alive' was to be used for the scene where Travolta and Gorney connect on the dance floor. He needed a romantic interlude. 'Give me eight minutes—three moods,' Stigwood said. 'I want frenzy at the beginning. Then I want some passion. And then I want some wild frenzy!'

Barry wasn't keen. 'Robert, that's crazy,' he said. 'We want to put this song out as a single, and we don't think the rhythm should break. It should go from beginning to end with the same rhythm, getting stronger all the way. To go into a lilting ballad just doesn't make sense.'

Stigwood was insistent. The band wrote and recorded a bridge for the track, a slow section dumped in the middle. 'We just ruined a hit record,' said Richardson.

'We called Stigwood to say, This is bogus, and we're not doing it,' said Barry. Avildsen was furious. He said he didn't want any of The Bee Gees' music used in the film. Stigwood saw red. The director had also recently upset Travolta, who had been rehearsing to 'You Should Be Dancing' for two months for a big solo number. Avildsen had told him there was not going to be a solo dance spot in the film. Stigwood fired him.

A few days later, on March 28, Avildsen was named 'Best Director' at the 49th Academy Awards. *Rocky* also won Best Picture. To Paramount, to almost everyone in the movie business, it seemed as if Stigwood had made colossal error of judgement. Avildsen told the *New York Times* he'd rather not dwell on the reasons for his firing, while Stigwood explained that the director had 'wanted to make a different movie to the one I intended to make, and different from the one John Travolta wanted to make'.

'He knew the energy of the picture was going to be the music, he wasn't interested in having some auteur direct the film,' said McCormick.

Stigwood turned to John Badham, who he had already considered to helm the *Sgt. Pepper's* film. Badham was free, at short notice, having just quit the musical adventure film *The Wiz*, a reimagining of *The Wizard of Oz* featuring an African-American cast, with Michael Jackson as the scarecrow. Badham had objected to the casting of Diana Ross as Dorothy, stating that at thirty-three she was too old to play a schoolgirl. He had directed an impressive list of films for TV, including *The Law*, but he was short of cinema credits, having only just finished directing his debut major movie, a Richard Prior comedy backed by Motown boss Berry Gordy, who was also behind the financing of *The Wiz*.

Stigwood's chief concern was that Badham could work fast—the film need to be wrapped up in just a few weeks. 'He didn't mess around and could keep to time so I arranged for him to fly to New York,' he said. 'I got someone to give him the [original Wexler] screenplay, put him on a plane that day, and I met him the next day. The only problem with the script was that it was slightly too long. I asked him where he thought the cuts should be, and they were exactly the ones I had in mind. I said, OK, you got it.'

Badham recalled Stigwood handing him a cassette with three Bee Gees songs on it. 'He said, Here are three #1s,' said Badham, who wondered how anyone could be so arrogant. 'How do you know?' he thought. When Travolta met his new director, he was surprised how little Badham knew about Brooklyn. 'I said, Let me be your guide. Let me take you by the hand and show you New York and its environs— the real New York. I know this town,' Travolta said. The star felt he was in control of the movie and his character again. Kevin McCormick continued to worry, however, noting that Badham knew very little about disco, calling him the 'the most unmusical guy in the world'.

To help with the disco scenes, Balham brought to the movie choreographer Lester Wilson, who he'd been working with on *The Wiz*. The black thirty-four-year-old Wilson, a legend in New York gay clubs, was very much in touch with disco, and was also one of the best-loved dancers in all showbusiness. He had worked with a long list of stars, such as Sammy Davis Jr, Diana Ross, Liza Minnelli, Barbra Streisand (choreographing her 1975 film *Funny Lady*), Ann-Margret, and Lola Falana, Sammy Davis's one-time dance partner, now an all-round entertainer and the highest paid female performer in Las Vegas. Wilson had recently won an Emmy for choreographing a Falana TV special.

Travolta had been working on his disco moves with a young, inexperienced twenty-five-year-old white disco dancer named Deney Terrio. Wilson was in a different class. Terrio would use his status as dance coach on *Saturday Night Fever*, once the film was a success, to land a role as host of the hit disco-dancing variety TV show *Dance Fever*, which ran for six years form 1979 to 1985. He also appeared in a number of films and guest-starred on TV shows such as *The Love Boat*. But it was Wilson—his personality, presence, confidence, and dancing moves—who breathed new life into the stalling *Saturday Night Fever*.

'Deney Terrio did show John the moves, and I give him credit for that,' said Paul Pape, who played Double J, the most aggressive member of Tony Manero's gang. 'But I don't think Lester Wilson got nearly the credit that he deserved. The movie was Lester.' Travolta also appreciated Wilson. 'I liked black dancing better than white dancing,' he said. 'I used to watch *Soul Train* [which primarily featured performances by black R&B, soul, and disco acts], and what I wanted to create was a *Soul Train* feel in *Saturday Night Fever*.'

The Bee Gees' music also had a galvanising effect on the shoot. Badham, unlike Avildsen, accepted Stigwood's idea that the band's music was to have a central role in the film. The band had sent new rough mixes of the material they were working on at Criteria, and the crew and cast got to hear the music for the first time. It had a profound effect on them all. 'We all thought we'd fallen into a bucket of shit,' one crew member recalled, 'and then we heard that music. It changed everything. We didn't hear the soundtrack until we were about three weeks into the movie. But once you heard it, you said, Whoa! An aura came over it.'

Travolta's co-star, Karen Gorney, whose father, the songwriter Jay Gorney, wrote such hits as 'Brother, Can You Spare A Dime' and 'You're My Thrill', had the same reaction. 'The first time I heard the music,' she recalled, 'I said, Those are monster hits.' After all the upheaval and uncertainty, a positive atmosphere began to develop on set. 'I never thought it would come together,' said Freddie Gershon. 'But as Robert played tapes [of the music] it was clear something special was happening. They were all hits. Robert has golden ear. He has a great sense of the hook, of the commercial.'

There was much debate over whether to use a real club for the disco scenes. An idea was floated that filming might take place at a new disco nearing competition, Studio 54, which would open in April 1977. It was close to Stigwood's New York apartment. Many other discos were considered, including the chic Manhattan club Les Mouches, before it was decided to go to the source and film at 2001 Odyssey, the one-storey club where Cohn had pitched his original story.

Chuck Rusinak, DJ and manager at 2001 Odyssey, recalled being approached by the filmmakers and offered a deal: one-tenth of one percent of the movie's profits, or a flat rate. 'We figured we would take a flat rate,' he said. The club's interior was uninspiring, with its beaten-up wooden dance floor and dated furnishings. 'You'd walk in and go down a couple of stairs,' Rusinak said. 'To the right was a small room with a big U-shaped bar and a pinball machine. There was a go-go dancer in that part of the bar. Some people would hang out there and never go into the disco. If you went straight when you walked down the stairs, it was like a little lobby. There were bathrooms and a coat check, and down the hall to the left was the disco. As soon as you opened the doors you saw the dance floor.'

The room seated about 750 people, but the dance floor was small, with room for about fifty. The club had been a hotspot in Brooklyn for well over a year now and often featured hit disco acts such as Harold Melvin & The Blue Notes, The Stylistics, and Gloria Gaynor. 'We used to book the acts for five days—Wednesday through Sunday,' Rusinak said, 'The Trammps were the big thing at the time. That was the hot band.' Sometimes it'd be so crowded that you couldn't get in. The crowd was young, ostentatious. 'The guys back in those days, even though they were broke, they were dripping with their gold chains,' said Rusinak, adding that the girls 'got decked … it was always heels and Lycra bodysuits with a skirt over it, or really tight dungarees.' The club hit its peak between midnight and closing time, 2:30am, but Rusinak said cocaine was not a part of the scene. 'Manhattan was a cocaine scene,' he said. 'That wasn't happening in Brooklyn.'

Stigwood spent $20,000 revamping the club, most significantly giving the OK to a new multi-coloured dance floor that had lights underneath, designed to pulsate to the music. Extra lighting was installed in the ceiling, and a custom-made mirror ball hung above the dance floor. Other details were done on the cheap or improvised: walls were covered with aluminium foil and draped with Christmas lights. A major plus of shooting at 2001 Odyssey were the club regulars, whom it was decided would be used as extras in the film. The men looked just right in their Huckapoo shirts, tight-fitting polyester with a busy pattern, and everyone inside was a dance floor natural.

There is a memorable example of club regulars dancing the hustle with Travolta in the film. These were the guys who lived the life described by Cohn: the guys with dead-end jobs who danced at weekends to escape. Badham even used the club's regular topless go-go dancer in the film. 'Fifty percent of the people in the dance scenes were club regulars,' said Rusinak. 'You'll see a girl being spun around like a top. That's Buttons. Her real name is Elizabeth Curcio. She and her brother were a dance team.' Another nineteen-year-old young man convinced Travolta that Cohn had based Tony Manero on him. 'A kid dressed in three-piece suit and high heels, a blonde Italian,' Travolta recalled. 'He was very cool. He was not like the other guys in the discotheque.'

The regulars were enthusiastic about the movie, and about the cast and crew getting it right. They didn't want Hollywood bullshit. The lifestyle was important to them. The clothes the actors wore were bought off the rack at the same stores the regulars shopped in. Costume designer Patrizia von Brandenstein, who would later win an Oscar for her art direction on *Amadeus*, picked up Travolta's famous white suit in a boutique in Bay Ridge.

There was much appreciation for Travolta's efforts on the dance floor. He nailed his solo to 'You Should Be Dancing'. The script had called for it to be to 'Night Fever', but Travolta had spent many months rehearsing to the former, and he didn't want to start again. Stigwood said it was OK and simply instructed Bill Oakes at RSO Records that the song needed to be included on the movie soundtrack.

The scenes shot at 2001 Odyssey were electric, the results bringing the cast and crew tighter together and inspiring them to redouble their efforts. McCormick called it 'the most exciting time' of his life. 'I couldn't get up early enough,' he said. 'And I couldn't wait to see the dailies every night.' Gorney said the decision to use real people in the club sequences gave the film a level of authenticity it otherwise would have lacked. 'We improvised for two weeks, so that by the time it came to filming, Badham just shot what was happening,' she said. 'It wasn't acting.'

Except for two days of filming in Manhattan, the movie was shot entirely in Brooklyn—Bay Ridge, Sunset Park, and Bensonhurst—and utilised real locations, such as a White Castle burger joint, the Phillips Dance Studios, a real paint store, and Lenny's Pizza. The managers of these places were only paid a few hundred dollars each, and the moviemaking took on a guerrilla feel. Not everyone in Brooklyn was happy to play along. A local Mafia guy tried to shake down the crew for protection money. A firebomb was thrown at 2001 Odyssey as a warning shot, but it didn't cause any serious damage. 'These two guys appeared on the set,' said McCormick. 'They pulled me off to the side: You're being disruptive to the neighbourhood. You might need some security. And if you want to put lights on the bowling alley across the street, Black Stan really wants seven grand.' Cash changed hands.

Of far greater disruption to the location shoots was Travolta. When word got out that the *Welcome Back, Kotter* star was in the area, scores of fans would soon appear. McCormick recalled a phone call from the production manager, informing him of 'chaos' outside Phillips Dance Studios. 'There were ten thousand kids on the streets, and we only had four security guys,' he said. 'So we had to shut down for a couple of hours while we just regrouped and tried to figure out a way to make it work. It was the first time that we actually had a sense of who John was.' Traffic on Eighth Avenue in Brooklyn could often be at a standstill as fans flocked to the area. The cast's trailers were surrounded and rocked violently by female fans screaming for 'Barbarino!' The production staff finally resorted to putting out fake call sheets and would often start filming at 5:30am in the morning so as to be able to shoot scenes without fans appearing in the shot.

Travolta had amazed everyone with his ability to commit so wholeheartedly to the movie when it was obvious he was in deep grief over the death of Hyland. He seemed to be pouring all his emotions into the role and the movie. Screen tears were real and impromptu, and Badham often took the brunt of hysterical rants from Travolta, as the actor grew more and more involved in the filmmaking process. He had only just turned twenty-three, and this was his first major movie role, but he seemed possessed, flying into a sudden rage when he first saw the way Badham had edited his dance solo as close-up, so that all his hard work—the knee drops and the splits that he had laboured over for months—was rendered almost invisible.

'I was crying and very angry because of the way the dance highlight was shot,' he recalled. 'I knew how it should appear on screen, and it wasn't shot that way. You couldn't even see my feet.' He demanded he be seen head to toe, so that no one would think someone else had done the dancing for him. 'I called Stigwood,' Travolta recalled. 'I was crying and furious. I said, Robert, I'm off the movie. I don't want to be a part of it anymore.' Stigwood backed Travolta over the thirty-five-year-old Badham and allowed the scene to be re-edited under Travolta's direction. The result, with all of Travolta's body in frame, remains one of the most famous dance numbers in the history of film.

There was another major clash between the director and actor when Travolta saw the rushes of the opening scene of the movie, in which a stand-in—shot from the knees down—takes that famous walk along Brooklyn's 86th Street to the beat of 'Stayin' Alive'. Travolta had been unavailable when the sequence was filmed. He insisted that his character wouldn't walk like that. Travolta demanded the scene be reshot with him doing the walk. 'It was the walk of coolness,' he said. 'I went to a school [in Englewood, Chicago] that was 50 percent black, and that's how the black kids walked through the hall.' Badham, however, said that the strutting feet in the finished film belonged to Travolta's double, Jeff Zinn, and had been choreographed by Lester Wilson.

Stigwood followed the project closely. He was happy with Badham's faithful translation of the script and felt The Bee Gees had delivered something truly special with the music. But as he watched the dailies, checking the rushes, it was obvious to him that Travolta was going to be a major movie star. One lovingly photographed scene made him smile broadly. In it, Travolta preened in front of the mirror in his bedroom in just his black bikini briefs, a gold chain nestled in his chest hair. It could almost be mistaken for soft-core gay porn.

Paramount had already flagged up the issue, the studio having now inked the deal to distribute the film. 'We got all kinds of hassle,' said Badham. 'We were letting some man walk around in his underwear, showing his body off.' The image had been so blatantly homoerotic that the production designer had put a Farrah Fawcett pin-up poster up in the background, just to cool things off. Stigwood knew he had something exceptional in the can, but Paramount was not convinced. The studio's focus remained on the next film Travolta was making, *Grease*, which was already in preproduction.

With the postproduction for *Saturday Night Fever* being handled at the Paramount studio in Los Angeles, Bill Oakes set up an office there to oversee the music that would feature in the film and on the soundtrack album. 'They gave us an office on the lot the size of a broom closet,' he said. 'They didn't believe in *Saturday Night Fever*. Only Stigwood knew it was going to be something big. It was just the studio's "little disco movie"—that was the phrase that haunted me: How's your little disco movie, Billy? They thought it was rather silly. The word was, people had had enough … disco had run its course. The Deadheads were coming back; heavy metal was making a run at it. These days, *Fever* is credited with kicking off the whole disco thing—it really didn't. Truth is, it breathed new life into a genre that was actually dying.'

●

The Bee Gees were neither thinking about *Saturday Night Fever* nor disco. They were in Nassau with Peter Frampton and producer George Martin, rehearsing material for the soundtrack album for the *Sgt. Pepper's* film. Getting movie rights for the twenty-nine Beatles songs he wanted to use in the movie—most of them taken from the *Sgt. Pepper's* album, but also including tracks from *Abbey Road* and *Let It Be*—had taken Stigwood a year of negotiating with music publishers. He had also had to work hard to convince Martin, the man often dubbed 'the fifth Beatle', to produce the soundtrack.

RSO was said to be investing an incredible twelve million dollars in the music for the film—with a further million set aside for promotion of the double album. Martin said he had been 'scared of the responsibility' of re-recording the famous Beatles songs that had made his name. 'Whichever way it turned out it would offend someone,' he said. But the knowledge that The Bee Gees would be involved had made his decision to commit 'much easier'.

Stigwood had also assured Martin that he would have complete artistic control of the project, although he was pressuring the fifty-year-old producer to give some of the songs a disco makeover. Martin said he recognised that the rhythm on the original tracks was 'dated' and intended to develop 'the beat' so that it became much 'more danceable'. Barry talked about a 'potential goldmine' and the 'great excitement' of re-recording Beatles songs with Martin. The Bee Gees played Martin an early version of 'Stayin' Alive' to illustrate how their new music was shaping up. He took two steps backward and said, 'My God, I've never heard anything like it.'

The producer and band quickly hit it off, bonding over conversations about Barry's falsetto and experimenting in the studio. Martin said the Gibbs' 'zany sense of humour' gave him an 'uncanny sense of déjà vu'. 'Kids today don't know Beatles,' Robin noted. 'It will be our version they relate to and remember. The Beatles will be secondary. You see there is no such thing as The Beatles now. They don't exist and never performed *Pepper's* live … when ours comes out it will be in effect as if theirs never existed.'

While The Bee Gees and Frampton were slated to record the bulk of the material—often together on the same track—other songs were intended to feature the movie's supporting cast, which now included rockers Alice Cooper and Aerosmith; black dance act Earth Wind & Fire; keyboard supremo Billy Preston; comedians George Burns, Frankie Howerd, and Steve Martin; and actor Paul Nicholas, whom RSO had recently signed to a recording contract. The handsome thirty-two-year-old had played the lead roles in several Stigwood musicals, including *Hair* and *Jesus Christ Superstar*, and made a strong impression on movie audiences as the antagonist Cousin Kevin in *Tommy*. Stigwood had of course tried to launch Nicholas as a pop star once already, in the 60s, under the name Oscar. Now he was on a run of three Top 20 UK singles for RSO—a wave of success that would be topped off with an American Top 5 single, 'Heaven On The Seventh Floor'. In the *Sgt. Pepper's* film,

Nicholas was to play the greedy stepbrother and manager of singer Billy Shears (Peter Frampton) and his band (The Bee Gees) as they searched for their stolen magical instruments which once belonged to Shears' grandfather, the legendary Sgt. Pepper, whose Lonely Hearts Club Band had brought peace and happiness through their music, even causing troops in World War I to stop fighting.

There would be a stellar cast of supporting musicians on the soundtrack recording, too, including guitarist Jeff Beck and drummer Jeff Porcaro, and many months of studio work ahead in Canada, London, Colorado, Los Angeles, and New York, but already in Nassau there were the warning signs that this was going to a difficult project for Martin to oversee. Frampton and The Bee Gees were not natural collaborators; both were wary about how their two distinct identities would come together on the project without one or the other being diluted. The Gibb brothers had argued endlessly between themselves about which tracks they wanted to sing lead on—Robin grabbed 'Oh! Darling' and Barry took 'A Day In The Life'—but they were instantly in agreement that they didn't want to be treated as Frampton's backing group. Frampton, meanwhile, had just released a follow-up album to *Frampton Comes Alive!* that had gone to #2 in America, with the title track, 'I'm In You', at #2 in the singles chart. He felt he had earned the right to be the star and voice of the soundtrack—in fact, he had it enshrined in his contract.

The complexity of the work, the heavy schedule—twenty-nine songs to record—and the clashes of egos, plus Martin's lingering doubts about his decision to be involved, would make for a fraught few months. Barry would find working with Martin frustrating. 'He's got real tight lines [on] the way he wants to go and he made that clear to everyone when we were doing it,' he said. 'He was religious with arrangements.' The Bee Gees allowed any doubts they had over the project to be brushed aside by the ebullient Stigwood. They were also being paid a reputed million dollars each for their parts in the movie.

Stigwood remained convinced that this would be his masterpiece and greatest triumph. During a production meeting in Acapulco, a beach resort in Mexico, there was talk of curtailing some of the excesses Stigwood planned for the musical that was scripted to have no dialogue, just elaborately staged performances of the songs telling the story. The budget had ballooned beyond the original six million dollars, but Stigwood didn't want to drop any scenes. 'Let's find a creative way to do it for less,' he suggested. The deals he needed to put together to finance the movie and soundtrack were complicated. He had made a deal with Universal to distribute the picture worldwide. One of America's oldest film studios, it was now primarily a TV studio, closely linked to the NBC network. The company's film studio had been reinvigorated by *Jaws*, but that was almost two years ago now. Outside of America and Canada, Universal's movies were distributed in partnership with Paramount. Stigwood was planning more than just a film: he discussed with Universal an amusement park based on *Sgt. Pepper's*, a television movie about the production of film, and a novel of the story.

●

RSO was now juggling a bewildering number of projects. The record division was busier than it had ever been. The *Sgt. Pepper's* soundtrack was just one project, with major releases by The Bee Gees and Clapton to co-ordinate, alongside the *Saturday Night Fever* soundtrack. There was also a focus now on developing others stars such as Nicholas, Yvonne Elliman, and Andy Gibb, whose debut single, 'I Just Want To Be Your Everything' was slowly picking up radio play as it began its slow climb up the American charts. *Grease* was about to start filming, and Stigwood was having continual battles with Paramount over *Saturday Night Fever*.

Barry Diller, the boss at Paramount studios, wanted the movie to be PG-rated and relentlessly harassed Stigwood to tone down the language used in the film. Stigwood thought the film would do fine with an R rating, meaning under-seventeens would require an accompanying parent or adult guardian to see the film. Diller would not give in. 'How are the kids going to get in?' he kept asking. 'There were many fights,' said Freddie Gershon.

To outsiders, it looked as if Stigwood was barely in control. His whole organisation seemed too wrapped up in hedonism, with Stigwood as ringleader. 'Everybody was so out of it,' said one insider. He often appeared shambolic, hesitant, and indecisive. 'The minute you think Robert doesn't know what's going on here, he does,' said Barry. 'He's a brilliant man who appears flawed, when he isn't.' Gershon recalled arriving at Stigwood's apartment in New York to discuss a huge list of important decisions that needed to be made, only to find himself whisked into a limo and flown to Bermuda for lunch. 'He said to me we'll eat and drink, you'll be away from the front line and we can think properly,' Gershon said. 'And we did. We sat on the edge of a cliff in the howling wind; with the trees bending and he said, OK let's get to work. We went through every permutation of every problem. He told me to look at all of them from above. Let's play God. And for months afterward we were prepared for anything that they threw at us.

'The real thinking goes on in Bermuda,' Gershon continued. 'That is where the money is made in the conception of an original thought. He'll look at all the record companies in America, all the motion picture companies in America, he'll look at who's running them, all their figures, who's performing how and where the weak points are. Then he'll go off, looking as though he's causally having lunch or a dinner with some studio head, but he's done his homework and not just on the value of the property that he's selling. It's who needs him, and who's looking to score some points with their own boss by saying they just saw Stiggy. It's who needs product. It's how to extract the best deal.' (According to Maurice, 'Stayin' Alive' was 'really born, I think, more in Bermuda than anywhere else. We finished it off in France'.)

Bermuda was not just where Stigwood did his best thinking, it was also where he allowed himself his greatest excesses. Having initially lived on the Palm Grove estate in Devonshire, he had now purchased the lavish Wreck Hill estate. Here, visitors recalled decadent parties for 200, with invitations written on scrolls inserted into antique bottles and delivered by men on horseback dressed in eighteenth-century gear. The main house, where Stigwood stayed, was white, colonial, and dominated a whole hill above coral sand. There were catamarans, big-game fishing, five-course dinners, and lavish picnics. Stigwood imported nothing but the best. He had also acquired two yachts.

Eric Clapton, who was back in the US Top 20 in May with 'Wonderful Tonight', recalled visiting Stigwood in Bermuda to discuss his new album, *Slowhand*, titled after his nickname. He later said it was with Stigwood in Bermuda that he had 'some of the best times I ever had in my drinking years'. He took Ahmet Ertegun along with him—Stigwood having made up with the Atlantic boss after losing out on the Stones, sending Ertegun a bottle of expensive champagne and his congratulations. Clapton said they trashed the entire place 'like kids'. Preceded by another smash-hit single, the million-selling US #3 'Lay Down Sally', *Slowhand* was Clapton's biggest hit in years, reaching US #2 in late 1977 and selling over three million copies in America alone.

In May, The Bee Gees' live album was released. *Here At Last ... Bee Gees ... Live* was a double album, clocking in at over eighty minutes. The live recording had been revamped at the Château D'Herouville, and Galuten and Richardson had finished mixing the work at Criteria in Miami. 'I couldn't believe the sound,' said Maurice. 'We sound like that!' Although the release illustrated how much the band, live, still relied on their 1960s material—punctuated by famous ballads such as 'Words', 'To Love Somebody', and 'I've Gotta Get A Message To You'— it also showcased their new funky band sound, especially on recent hits such as 'You Should Be Dancing' and 'Jive Talkin'. It was no *Frampton Comes Alive!*, but it did good business for the band, reaching the US Top 40 by June, ultimately peaking at #8, and selling in excess of four million copies worldwide.

Here At Last also scored the group their first cover of *Rolling Stone* magazine. The shot of the three Gibbs was taken by acclaimed fashion photographer Francesco Scavullo, and was set to be iconic. It shows all three dressed in white satin and silk outfits, tight trousers, long coiffed hair, tanned faces, clipped beards, broad smiles revealing white teeth. Barry is at the centre, being leaned on by Robin and Maurice on either shoulder, with his shirt undone to his navel, flaunting an expensive gold medallion, a heavy gold bracelet dangling from one wrist, and a selection of gold rings.

Above all, it was the matching white outfits—which deliberately echoed the famous white suit Travolta was to sport in *Saturday Night Fever*—that grabbed the attention. 'The photographer brought the clothes,' said Barry. 'Suddenly there we were looking like Abba. It was just a bit of fun.' Scavullo had recently been working with disco queen Donna Summer, shooting two album covers with her; he had also controversially shot Burt Reynolds nude and framed a seemingly nude Barbra Streisand and Kris Kristofferson for the sensual kiss that adorned the poster of their 1976 film *A Star Is Born*.

Stigwood loved the *Rolling Stone* cover photograph and used it for the cover of both *Saturday Night Fever* and the 'Stayin' Alive' and 'Night Fever' singles. It would become the most identifiable image of the band during this period of their career. The *Rolling Stone* article offered an overview of the band's recent comeback from apparent oblivion, its headline reading, 'How Can You Mend A Broken Group? Answer: The Bee Gees Did It With Disco.' The interview had taken place chiefly in London earlier in the year, with Robin the sole representative of the group. Barry was back in Miami; he is quoted in the article, but barely. Robin dominates the piece. 'Show business is something you have to have in you when you're born,' he is quoted as saying. Asked about the group's songwriting—Candi Staton's version of 'Nights On Broadway' was in the UK Top 10 at the time—he said, indignantly, 'No one has ever talked to us about our songwriting! That's always amazed me. I don't think people even realise that we write our own songs. I call it musical ignorance!'

Barry was furious with the article, and deeply irritated at the way Robin had presented himself as the frontman of the group. 'It became important for Robin to give every interview, to grab every spotlight,' he said. 'That's how the battle raged for us.' Stigwood had been interviewed for the article, too, and used the opportunity to talk up *Saturday Night Fever*. *Rolling Stone* reported that the band had written four tunes for the film. 'Quite staggering,' said Stigwood, 'particularly as they did it all in a week.'

•

By June, it was apparent that RSO had another huge star on its hands. Andy Gibb's debut single was heading to #1 in on the American charts. Not only was it smash on pop radio, it had also been picked up by black stations, and was a hit on the *Billboard* soul charts, too. Andy's face began to appear on the cover of teen magazines such as *16* and *TigerBeat*. He told interviewers he wasn't 'a very typical rock and roll star' and relied on his famous brothers to point him in the right direction. 'Any mistake they made I make sure I don't repeat,' he said. 'If I need anything or if I've got problems, they're right there.' He was portrayed as clean-cut in the classic mould of 70s teen idols like David Cassidy and The Osmonds, and talked up his fellow Gibbs as 'like a slightly cool Osmond family'. He said they were all 'very close' and 'don't go out that often', describing how they 'basically all sit at home with cups of tea and watch television'.

'I Just Want To Be Your Everything' hit the top spot in July and stayed there for five weeks, spending a remarkable sixteen weeks in the Top 10 and remaining in the Top 40 for thirty-one weeks in total. It was the second-biggest-selling single of 1977 in America, with over half a million copies sold. Andy was suddenly one of America's biggest pop attractions—a major teen heartthrob. It overawed him. In interviews he said he owed the success 'chiefly' to Barry, while also thanking Stigwood. 'I know they did it all,' he said. His young wife Kim was pregnant, and even with his family all around him in Miami (Hugh and Barbara having bought a home close to Barry's), he was unprepared for the level of fame he had suddenly acquired. 'I Just Want To Be Your Everything' went to #1 in Australia and Canada, too.

Barry completed the recording of Andy's debut album at Criteria in between commitments to the recording of the *Sgt. Pepper's* soundtrack, assisted by Richardson and Galuten. Andy, keen to score himself some musical credibility, had declared himself a fan of Randy Newman, Don McLean, The Eagles, and The Allman Brothers. Galuten was a constant presence in the studio, with a sizeable budget at his disposal. He assembled some of the best session players in America, including Clapton's guitarist George Terry and the heavyweight rhythm section of Ron Ziegler on drums and Harold 'Hog' Cowart on bass. Ziegler and Cowart were favourites of Jerry Wexler at Atlantic Records and had backed stars such Aretha Franklin and Stephen Stills. Galuten played keyboards across the album and developed the songs Andy had written for it—he 'turned them around', as Andy put it. He would be rewarded with co-writing credits on two of the songs. Andy's voice was not strong, and when Barry was unavailable to sing backing and harmony vocals, Galuten had brought in a top session vocalist Johnne Sambataro, who like Ziegler and Cowart was a Criteria stalwart.

Often, Andy was a bystander to the making of the album. Credited to the Gibb-Galuten-Richardson production team, the record sounded like a Bee Gees side project and was seen as a cash-in for RSO. It had already been decided that none of Andy's songs were good enough to follow 'I Just Want To Be Your Everything', so another Barry song, '(Love Is) Thicker Than Water' was readied as his second single. Andy was credited as co-writer, but all he had done was suggest the title 'thicker than water'. 'Even though it says B. & A. Gibb, it is really Barry's song,' he admitted.

For RSO Records, Andy was more of a moneymaking machine than a serious artist: a teen idol who could, for as long as the fad lasted, sell not just records but untold merchandise to young girls. The album, titled *Flowing Rivers*, and the new single were released in September as Andy took to the road, supporting Neil Sedaka, who was at the peak of his 70s comeback, in American and Canada. Andy's teenybopper fans, some as young as twelve, ate him up. His flawless, angelic face was spread across endless teen magazines. The album sold well, and would rise in the coming months to peak at #19 in the US, selling over a million copies. '(Love Is) Thicker Than Water', a mid-tempo mainstream romantic ballad, was all over the radio during the closing months of 1977 as it began another slow climb to the top of the American charts, eventually reaching #1 in March 1978 with sales of 500,000 copies.

Once Andy had completed the Sedaka tour, he and Kim moved to Los Angeles. The Bee Gees were already holed up there, living in a luxury Beverly Hills mansion, filming their roles in *Sgt. Pepper's*—a process expected to last three months. Andy was naïve, gullible, nineteen, and soon surrounded by a coterie of hangers-on. 'He got in with the wrong people,' said Barry, while Kim recalled, 'Cocaine became his first love.'

Andy started to make the wrong sort of headlines. He was caught partying in Hollywood with Brit actress Susan George, who had also dated Rod Stewart and Jimmy Conners and was seven years his senior. A heavily pregnant Kim left him and flew home to Australia. When he was not high, Andy was depressed. In interviews, he was forced to deny using drugs and warned others against doing so. He hid his drug use from his family, too. But it was hard to avoid cocaine. He was even offered the drug when he visited his brothers in October, on the set of *Sgt. Pepper's*. Maurice remembered there being an incredible amount of cocaine on the set. He said he arrived every day at 7am and was 'showered with loads of the stuff'.

Sgt. Pepper's was being shot at the MGM studios back lot in Culver City, Los Angeles, where such famous MGM musicals as *Singin' In The Rain* and *The Wizard Of Oz* had been filmed. Stigwood had overseen the construction of a surreal olden-days fantasy town called Heartland, supposed to represent a mythic American idyll. At its centre was bandstand topped with a twenty-five-foot effigy of a cheeseburger. It was the most expensive, elaborate set built for a movie to date, costing a reputed one million dollars. Over two hundred carpenters had been working twenty-four-hour shifts to complete it. 'It has the right feel to me,' said Stigwood, who referred to the movie as the 'ultimate fantasy'. Scriptwriter Henry Edwards said it was 'a fable about the redeeming power of music'.

The Gibbs and Frampton were kitted out in approximations of the famous candy-coloured military jackets The Beatles had worn on the cover of the *Sgt. Pepper's* album. Robin was missing home, abusing amphetamines by day and taking large doses of downers to get to sleep at night. Maurice was a full-blown alcoholic. Barry was distracted. Linda had given birth prematurely to their second son in September, and the baby was in special care. The band were often left perplexed by the huge song-and-dance routines that unfolded around them and the scores of extras, including clowns, dancing girls, and comic strongmen, that surrounded them.

The loose plot saw the Heartland band sign up to Big Deal records (whose logo imitated that of RSO, but a pig instead of a cow) and move to Los Angeles, where they were exploited and seduced into drugs, drink, and debauchery (cue outlandish silver costumes). Meanwhile, Heartland's magical instruments—which guarantee the town lives happily ever after—are stolen by a demented ex-real estate agent (Frankie Howerd), resulting in the town falling into a hotbed of vice. The band's money is stolen; there is a hot-air balloon chase and cameos from a crazed plastic surgeon (Steve Martin), a cult leader (Alice Cooper), wig-wearing robots, and a Future Villain Band who plan to take over the world, played by Aerosmith. All ends well, with the band retrieving the instruments and cleaning up Heartland, with even Frampton's fallen sweetheart, Strawberry Fields, being brought back to life by the town's weather vane come to life (Billy Preston). 'It's a send up of me, the whole rock business, and the idea that money is the essence of life,' said Frampton. Stigwood suggested it was about 'the end of decency'.

The Bee Gees were shuttled bemused between the MGM set and Universal studios in the San Fernando Valley region of Los Angeles, where the film's interiors were shot. 'The whole focus of the movie is on Peter,' said Robin. 'We're always turning around saving him from something. I hated doing the film. We didn't have the chance to act because we didn't talk.' George Burns, who played Heartland's elderly major, had the only speaking part, acting as narrator. Director Michael

Schultz praised the Gibbs' 'eagerness and willingness to do whatever was needed to make it work'. They spent their plentiful spare time between takes writing songs.

For the film's climax, shot in December, Stigwood planned a tribute to The Beatles' famous original album cover for *Sgt. Pepper's* and invited 400 celebrities from all over the world to a special party on set, followed by Gala dinner. Stigwood sent each of them a first class plane ticket and booked them at hotels of their choice, at a total cost of half a million dollars. For his 'grand finale sequence', the guests were lined up in a formation, imitating the album cover, while singing a reprise of the title track. Among the guest were Donovan, Leif Garrett, Eta James, Johnny Rivers, Del Shannon, Tina Turner, Frankie Valli, Bobby Womack, Curtis Mayfield, and Robert Palmer. The party afterward, spread across three soundstages, featured strolling violinists, a disco, lavish catering, and private tents for each star. The film's final budget was an eye-watering eighteen million dollars.

Stigwood was staying in his own Beverly Hills mansion while overseeing the making of *Sgt Pepper's* and *Grease*, which was also being shot in Los Angeles in late 1977. The mansion belonged to Hollywood producer Freddie Fields and came with a swimming pool and a private screening room. (Fields had just enjoyed huge success with *Looking For Mr Goodbar*, staring Diane Keaton, which used disco music for its soundtrack.) The Bee Gees saw *Saturday Night Fever* for the first time at the mansion when Stigwood showed a rough edit in the screening room. The band sat with Stigwood, Travolta, Travolta's *Grease* co-star Olivia Newton-John, and the film's director, John Badham.

Maurice recalled 'cringing' at the use of demo versions of their songs in the edit, since Bill Oakes was still putting the soundtrack together. 'The first thing "Stayin' Alive" is going and John's walking in tempo with it and the director is describing little things her and there,' said

Maurice. 'I thought it's not the greatest story in the world, but it's an exciting film. The language was quite good. It seemed like an X-rated film [the same rating given to movies such as *Midnight Cowboy* and *A Clockwork Orange*] … they wanted a PG but they got an R rating because of the swearing.'

Stigwood stood firm over the strong language used in the film even after audience members walked out at previews in Cincinnati and Columbus because of the language and sex scenes. Barry Diller at Paramount was still pressing for some censoring. 'It was a street movie,' said Stigwood, 'and I told them no kid going to see it would believe it if it was full of "goddamns". So I said to Barry Diller, right at the end of a very tense meeting, that I would "consider" taking out five "fucks" if they gave me another 5 percent. They said yes.'

Stigwood wound up with a reputed 45 percent of the gross profits from the film. He was actually in profit before the film was released. The movie was on budget, at $3.2 million, and Paramount Pictures had paid several million for distribution rights. Stigwood had driven such a hard deal that Diller latter admitted that the head of business affairs at Paramount had instructed, 'Never let Diller loose with Stigwood again.'

●

Bill Oakes mastered the film's soundtrack in early October. The Bee Gees had six tracks on the double album, four new songs: 'Stayin' Alive', 'How Deep Is Your Love', 'Night Fever', and 'More Than A Woman', plus 'You Should Be Dancing' and 'Jive Talkin''. Oakes stacked the new songs onto the A-side of the first disc, where they sat alongside Yvonne Elliman's version of another Gibb brothers song written in France, 'If I Can't Have You'. 'Those first five songs,' said Oakes, 'which I put on the first side of the soundtrack double album—that's the side you couldn't stop playing.'

The Bee Gees said they preferred Elliman's version of 'If I Can't Have You' to their own. Barry's falsetto remained a prominent feature on the recording, especially on the song's chorus. It was produced by Freddie Perren, the writer and producer behind many early-70s hits for The Jacksons who had become a king of the disco era. Perren had also produced the 1975 US #1 'Boogie Fever' by The Sylvers and the about-to-be-massive 1978 classic 'I Will Survive' by Gloria Gaynor. He was also working with the funk group Tavares—five brothers who were on a run of major disco hits with cuts such as 'It Only Takes A Minute' and 'Heaven Must Be Missing An Angel' (the latter co-written by Perren)— and he got them to cut a version of 'More Than A Woman'. It sounded fantastic, and the band, signed to Capitol Records, planned to release it as a single. In an unusual move, Oakes put the Tavares version of the song on the soundtrack alongside The Bee Gees' original version.

Oakes went after the biggest and best in disco to make up the rest of the soundtrack. It meant The Bee Gees were pitched alongside an almost exclusive cast of the most happening black groups in America. The Trammps, the 2001 Odyssey regulars, newly signed to Atlantic Records, had been making disco tunes since 1973. They had scored a number of dance hits in the past year, including 'That's Where The Happy People Go' and 'Disco Party', and were about to be voted 'Top Disco Group' by *Billboard* magazine for the third year in a row. Oakes heard a ten-minute-plus version of 'Disco Inferno', a track planned as the lead single of their new album. The extended track had been created by Tom Moulton, a legend on the club scene famed for producing, in 1975, one of disco's defining hits, Gloria Gaynor's version of 'Never Can Say Goodbye'. Moulton was a pioneer of long, radical dance mixes, an idea that had become a club staple as 12-inch singles gained popularity. Oakes grabbed the Trammps cut. Atlantic would release it as a single in December 1977; it became a Top 10 hit on the R&B charts but failed to cross over into the Top 40, although it did hit the UK Top 20. Once *Saturday Night Fever* took off, Atlantic re-issued the single. It would peak at #11 in the US charts in the spring of 1978.

MFSB were another legendary black funk band. They had performed on a slew of hits for Philadelphia International Records, the label that had dominated the black music scene of the early 70s, grossing a remarkable twenty-five million dollars annually. MFSB were also the band behind what was widely credited as the first disco hit, The O'Jays' 'Love Train', and had also backed The Stylistics, Harold Melvin & The Blue Notes, Teddy Pendergrass, and The Delfonics, becoming crucial to originating the smooth 'Philly soul' sound. Although primarily a studio outfit, they had scored a huge 1974 #1 hit with the instrumental 'TSOP (The Sound Of Philadelphia)', the theme to the hit TV show *Soul Train* and a track credited with establishing the American disco sound. Although the band's own recordings were faltering commercially they were seen as key disco touchstone, tracks of theirs such as 'Love Is The Message' were hugely popular in New York clubs. Oakes picked up one of their big 1975 dance hits, 'K-Jee', a cover version of The Nite-Liters 1971 song that had reached #2 on the *Billboard* dance charts. Like 'TSOP', it was an instrumental.

Kool & The Gang were another seminal funk band and key act on the disco scene, best known for their 1973 Top 5 hit 'Jungle Boogie'. The band had been operating since the late 60s and were regulars on the R&B charts, although they had not scored a US Top 10 hit for a few years. The band's record label, De-Lite, had just been taken over by Polygram, the owners of RSO Records, which made the licensing of their track 'Open Sesame' for the soundtrack a relatively simple process for Oakes. The song had featured as the title track on the band's recently released eighth album and had made the Top 10 on the US dance charts.

The Bee Gees' close relationship with the Miami dance scene meant that Oakes found it easy to negotiate with the city's TK Records, picking up two more huge dance hits from the dominant disco label of the era. Miami's KC & The Sunshine Band were the most famous of all the disco acts to be included on the soundtrack. Their huge success in 1975 had continued with two more massive US #1 singles, 'Shake Your Booty' and the recent 'I'm Your Boogie Man'. Oakes settled for 'Boogie Shoes', taken from their biggest selling album to date, their eponymous 1975 triple-platinum second album.

TK also supplied 'Calypso Breakdown' by Ralph McDonald. McDonald was a producer and songwriter best known for writing 'Where Is The Love', a 1972 US Top 5 for Robert Flack and Donny Hathaway. As a musician he was one of the most in-demand percussionists in the industry, playing steel pan for the Harry Belafonte band before backing superstars such as Carole King and George Benson. 'Calypso Breakdown' had featured on his debut 1976 album *Sound Of A Drum*, while the 12-inch version of the song was an underground club hit in Miami and New York but was as yet unknown to mainstream audiences.

The best-known song Oakes picked up for the soundtrack was one that had gone to #1 in America in late 1976, 'A Fifth Of Beethoven' by Walter Murphy. When people spoke about disco having run its course, it was this track, alongside RSO's own novelty cut 'Disco Duck', that they were thinking of. Although 1977 had produced some huge disco classics that had all sold in huge quantities, such as Thelma Houston's 'Don't Leave Me This Way' and 'Best Of My Love' by The Emotions, disco was not the dominant sound it had been in 1975 and 1976. Soft-rock and pop/rock by acts such as James Taylor, Meatloaf, Steely Dan, ELO, The Eagles, Billy Joel, Rod Stewart, Foreigner, and Fleetwood Mac were all scoring with huge albums, while a new musical movement, punk, was being championed in the media. For many, 'A Fifth Of Beethoven', a pulsating disco instrumental based on the first movement of Beethoven's Fifth Symphony that had sold two million copies, was the point where disco reached saturation point. Certainly Oakes had now had enough. 'I had been listening to disco for so long, I never wanted to hear the stuff again,' he said. 'I just wanted to get it [the production of the soundtrack] over with.'

The remaining three tracks on the album were by forty-year-old TV and film composer David Shire. He had scored endless TV shows and films, many for his bother-in-law Francis Ford Coppola, such as *The Conversation*, as well as the recent hit *All The President's Men*. He was hired to provide orchestral pieces for the film score, recording the music in a single day. Oakes used the music as soundtrack filler. He was delighted to finally finish the project but full of doubts that the double album, which had cost a small fortune to compile, would be a hit. He recalled being stuck in traffic in Los Angeles, shortly after signing off the record, and the car in front had a bumper sticker reading 'Death To Disco'. Oakes had just put together the year's most unconcealed disco music album, featuring a front cover dominated by a still from *Saturday Night Fever* of John Travolta posing in his white suit on a lit-up disco dance-floor with a glitter ball overhead. 'I was sitting there thinking, Perhaps it's too late! It's too boring,' he recalled.

●

RSO was already pushing 'How Deep Is Your Love' as the album's lead single. Stigwood had chosen to use the track as his preliminary promotional tool for *Saturday Night Fever*. It had been sent to radio stations in September. Stigwood had told Al Coury that he wanted the single to hit #1 a week before the film came out in December. 'So I counted back eight weeks,' Coury said. Eight weeks was the average length of time it took a single to climb to #1 following its actual release in America.

'How Deep Is Your Love' was a risky first release to promote a disco movie: a slow ballad with only subtle disco overtures. It was, however, a highly anticipated release. It had been over a year since The Bee Gees' best-selling *Children Of The World* album and their massive hit 'You Should Be Dancing'. The recent *Rolling Stone* cover, the well-publicised filming of *Sgt. Pepper's*, and imminent release of the *Saturday Night Fever* album and movie ramped up the anticipation. Radio stations across America began playing the single immediately. Stigwood backed the release with massive billboards and a TV ad campaign that sold the single and upcoming soundtrack album. In total, RSO had budgeted seven million dollars toward promoting the movie and album—a promotional budget said to eclipse any other in the film and music industries, and far beyond what might be considered typical marketing. For the album, released in November, there was a deluxe advertising campaign scheduled for all American print media and extraordinary special promotions planned for shops, TV, and radio.

Choosing 'How Deep Is Your Love' as a lead single proved to be a masterstroke by Stigwood. It was a standout hit, a super-slick, sensual, suggestive yet romantic ballad that had mass appeal, and it quickly hit the American Top 40. Barry's falsetto was restrained, beautifully counterbalanced by Robin's deeper voice and the brothers' rich harmony singing. Each time the single was played on the radio, the soundtrack album was mentioned, and each time the album was mentioned there was talk of the movie. '[Stigwood] basically pioneered an entirely new way of doing business in the distribution of films, records, stage, and television,' Bill Oakes said. 'I think his being from Australia had a lot to do with it—that sort of buccaneering adventurism, that entrepreneurship. I don't think he would have been as successful if he'd been English.'

By December the single was at #1 in the American charts. It would remain in the Top Ten for a then-record seventeen weeks, selling over a million copies. Stigwood's gut instinct had told him the song would be a hit but its phenomenal success could not have been predicted, as it eclipsed 'You Should Be Dancing' to become The Bee Gees' biggest-ever single. After America, 'How Deep Is Your Love' conquered the world, reaching #1 in a remarkable list of countries such as Canada, France, Chile, and Brazil. In the UK it reached #3—the band's highest chart position since 1969. 'With all the new wave and punk rock out, I would have thought something like "How Deep Is Your Love" wouldn't have a chance,' said Barry. 'We always kept going forward and we're getting stronger every day.'

The *Saturday Night Fever* soundtrack album shipped gold in America, meaning RSO had sent out 500,000 copies to the shops, sale or return. The label scrambled to make enough copies to supply demand for the double album around the world. Its release in America coincided with the film's trailer being heavily promoted in cinemas and on TV. The trailer featured the opening shots of the movie: Travolta, hair sculpted perfectly, strutting down the street to the sound of 'Stayin' Alive'. Travolta's huge teen fan-base was mobilised, and a huge buzz built up around the film as the image seared into the public consciousness.

The mental picture was accompanied always by the sound of the song. 'Stayin' Alive' was impossible to shake, becoming a jingle almost for the strut and the film. RSO Records was deluged with calls from radio stations demanding to know when the song would be released as a single. The stations themselves had been besieged by callers wanting to hear the song. RSO rush-released 'Stayin' Alive', and the single was being given blanket airtime on America radio the very week 'How Deep Is Your Love' reached #1. It was difficult not to hear either one or the other song on the radio. The 70s had seen a flood of falsetto-voiced dance hits, and stars such as Marvin Gaye and Mick Jagger had all used the voice. 'Stayin' Alive' took it to another level, almost comically. The song was shrill, piercing, manic, excessive—and unforgettable. *Rolling Stone* wrote that the vocals sounded like 'mechanical mice with an unnatural sense of rhythm'.

Everything was lined up: *Saturday Night Fever* was the most talked-about film in America. There was already a frenzy among Travolta's fans, and now a palpable sense that the broader public was buying into the picture. Stigwood hyped up his star, calling Travolta 'the new Robert Redford, the new Rudolph Valentino'. There were battalions of paparazzi and reporters at the film's LA premiere, held at Mann's Chinese Theatre on Friday December 16. TV cameras beamed the excitement across America, showing queues a mile long outside the cinema, and the crowd screaming as celebrities such as Hugh Hefner, Peter Frampton, and Andy Gibb arrived and were interviewed on the red carpet.

The Bee Gees arrived from the set of *Sgt. Pepper's*, filming having coincidentally finished that same day. With the movie over, there was a show-stopping after-party that cost RSO $150,000 to host and saw a jubilant Stigwood take to the dance floor with Travolta's mum. The party continued for the film's opening in New York, where Stigwood hosted a lavish event at Studio 54, the glitziest, most decadent, and most exclusive of Manhattan's disco clubs. It was the hottest ticket in town. Before any reviews were published, the film was a major story on TV news and chat shows and in all the major gossip and entertainment columns. In Brooklyn, audiences were reportedly talking back to the screen and screaming and yelling, 'You nailed it!' Elsewhere, audiences were said to be dancing in the aisles.

In its first eleven days of release in America, *Saturday Night Fever* grossed more than eleven million dollars. Only Steven Spielberg's sci-fi blockbuster *Close Encounters Of The Third Kind* was doing better at the box office. Barry Diller at Paramount could not believe the figures. He was taken aback by the success of the film, but not dumbstruck.

He finally got his way and played his part in making the movie even more successful, talking the actors, who pressganged Stigwood into submission, into making a PG cut of the movie. Diller told the cast that if they wanted to make further earnings down the line they needed a version that could be shown on TV. 'Ruined the film,' grumbled Stigwood. 'Doesn't have the power.'

Stigwood needn't have worried about the reviews. His original cut was and still is gritty and gripping viewing. More than the swearing, it was the scenes of rape, racist gang violence, dysfunctional family life, teenage pregnancy, and suicide that made *Saturday Night Fever* more than just a cash-in disco flick. The film even tackles faith, but more than anything it is about working-class America as the country verged on the brink of recession. Tony Manero's macho posturing is ripped open to reveal boredom, alienation, and dead-end prospects. It was a theme that chimed with punk's 'blank generation', 'no future' sloganeering, but Travolta offered up something much grander than nihilism. His grace under pressure on the dance floor made him a true hero, and his character remains not just the most revealing but the most compelling and popular working-class figure of 70s America.

Although some American critics took offence at the racism and homophobia on display—the popular trade magazine *Variety* called the film a 'piece of trash' and 'vulgar'—many others in the media were instantly enraptured. The most influential film critic of the day, Pauline Kael of the *New Yorker*, loved Travolta: '[He] acts like someone who loves to dance. And, more than that, he acts like someone who loves to act. … He expresses shades of emotion that aren't set down in scripts, and he knows how to show us the decency and intelligence under Tony's uncouthness … he isn't just a good actor, he's a generous-hearted actor.'

Kael's review was one that Travolta treasured. He was stunned by the popularity of the film. He told interviewers he thought he was just 'doing a little art film in Brooklyn'. Now he found himself the hottest teen idol since Elvis; a Marlon Brando and James Dean for the 70s. 'I had the field to myself,' he said. 'A few years later, Cruise would come along, and Tom Hanks, and Mel Gibson, but for a long time there was no one else out there. It was like Valentino-style popularity, an unimaginable pinnacle of fame.'

Stigwood and Diller at Paramount were already counting the millions as they anticipated the upcoming release of *Grease*, Travolta's next film. Nik Cohn, who had attended the *Saturday Night Fever* premiere in Los Angeles, arriving by limousine with Yvonne Elliman on his arm, was in thrall to the actor. 'The whole phenomenon was just Travolta, because his particular gift is sympathy,' he said. 'There's something about those puppy-dog eyes and the wetness around the mouth. And the other ingredients—my character, The Bee Gees' music, Wexler's script—they all had their function. But it would not have been a touchstone, it wouldn't have worked with anybody else—nobody else could have done it.'

While other heavyweight American publication also singled out Travolta, with *Time* magazine praising his 'carnal presence', there were plenty of positive mentions for The Bee Gees' music. The *New York Times* named the band as the film's 'most influential principals, although they never appear on screen' and their songs the 'most important parts of its score'. *Rolling Stone* was also full of praise for the movie's music, concluding that 'Stayin' Alive' 'not only provides the disco pulse of this blockbuster, it also communicates the spirit of the film … it's the band's movie too, right there from the start, their songs define, explain and heighten action'.

'Without the Gibb brothers' music the movie could have been just another film that lacked a real hook,' Kevin McCormick told *Billboard*. 'The Bee Gees provided us with the means to break *Saturday Night Fever*

out and to make it available and interesting to millions in America. The
score opened it up 35 percent. It opened it up for people in the suburbs
who didn't know disco and who do now.' Stigwood called The Bee Gees
'co-creators' of the movie.

After the film's release, sales of the double-album soundtrack were
sent soaring. Al Coury said RSO 'sold 750,000 copies of the album
in four days between Christmas and New Year'. By January 1978, the
soundtrack was #1 in America, replacing Fleetwood Mac's *Rumours*,
which had been holding the top spot for almost six months. The film
grew more popular, grossing more than eighty-one million dollars in its
first sixteen weeks—eleven times it's break-even figure—on its way to
grossing $350 million worldwide. Stigwood was estimated to have made
one hundred million dollars from the movie. By February 4, 'Stayin'
Alive' was #1 on the American charts, outstripping 'How Deep Is Your
Love', with sales of two million copies in America and three million
worldwide. It would stay at #1 for four weeks. The single was also #1
in Australia, Canada, Italy, Mexico, Holland, New Zealand, and South
Africa, and #2 in France, Germany, Spain, Austria, Belgium, Finland,
and Switzerland. It peaked at #4 in the UK.

In February, The Bee Gees won their first ever Grammy for
'How Deep Is Your Love' in the category of 'Best Pop Performance
by a Group'. The glitzy event was broadcast live on US TV from the
Shrine Auditorium in LA. Fleetwood Mac's *Rumours*, The Eagles' *Hotel
California*, and Barbra Streisand's 'Evergreen (Love Theme From *A Star
Is Born*)' were named album, record, and song of the year; the *Saturday
Night Fever* soundtrack and 'Stayin' Alive' had been released too late
for 1978's Grammy nominations but would be recognised at the 1979
awards show.

Fevermania, as it had been dubbed, was reaching a crescendo in
America. With 'Stayin' Alive' at #1, RSO released a third single from

the soundtrack album, 'Night Fever', and it was selling faster than any other Bee Gees single. The demand was so strong in the UK that RSO was forced to import hundreds of thousands of records from America and Europe to keep it in stock.

The film's premiere in London was another huge media event, attended by Stigwood, Travolta, and Robin and attracting screaming throngs of fans. The *NME*'s Nick Kent wrote that 'Stayin' Alive' sounded 'astonishing within context'. For the party afterward, Stigwood had spent £30,000 on revamping a club to look like 2001 Odyssey. Robin told the press that critics who said The Bees Gees had jumped on the disco bandwagon were 'damned ignorant and stupid'.

The band picked up more awards for 'How Deep Is Your Love' in London when the song was named 'Best Pop Song' and 'Best Film Music' at the 23rd Ivor Novello Awards, the prestigious annual UK songwriting event, beating off competition from Paul McCartney's 'Mull Of Kintyre' and Andrew Lloyd Webber and Tim Rice's 'Don't Cry For Me, Argentina', from their 1976 rock-opera concept album *Evita*. (Although the pair were still managed by Stigwood, MCA, not RSO, had released the album and single, which went to #1 in the UK. The album had done well in the UK and Europe—exceeding sales of their *Jesus Christ Superstar* album—but had failed so far to make significant inroads in America.) Stigwood was in the late stages of preparing the work's transition onto the West End stage for a musical of the same name due to open in June 1978.

Sales of the *Fever* soundtrack kept on growing. It would stay at #1 in the UK for eighteen weeks. 'Being accepted again is the biggest kick I've ever had,' said Maurice. In America, the soundtrack was selling a rate of 200,000 tapes and albums a day. 'You couldn't keep them in stock,' said Freddie Gershon. 'Shops put up signs: Yes, We'll have more *Fever* by this afternoon … Yes, We'll have more *Fever* by tomorrow.'

The album would remain at #1 in America for twenty-four consecutive weeks, becoming the best-selling movie soundtrack album of all time, beating *The Sound Of Music* into second place. It went to #1 in every country it was put on sale: Australia, Canada, Austria, Holland, France, Italy, Japan, Germany, Norway, and Sweden, to name just a few.

Not only was the album popular, it was hugely profitable. '*Rumours* sold between nine and ten million units at $7.98,' said Coury. 'Before that the big album was Frampton's *Comes Alive!*, seven-to-eight million at $6.98 originally, and then $7.98. Before that it was Carole King's *Tapestry*, which did ten-to-twelve million, with most of the sales at $5.98. *Saturday Night Fever* became the top-grossing album of all time when it hit eight million units, retailing at $12.98.'

At its peak, global sales of the album hit one million copies a week. RSO was predicting that the soundtrack would gross one hundred million dollars, with The Bee Gees themselves set to net between twelve and fifteen million. 'It made us all a bit crazy,' said Barry. '*Fever* was #1 every week. It wasn't just like a hit album. It was #1 every single week for twenty-five weeks. It was just an amazing, crazy, extraordinary time.'

March 1978 would be a month Robin would never forget. He had been obsessed by charts positions since he was a teenager. At the start of the month, in America, 'Stayin' Alive' was superseded at #1 by Andy Gibb's '(Love Is) Thicker Than Water', his second consecutive chart-topper in America. The single stayed at #1 for two weeks before it was replaced by 'Night Fever', which would stay at the top for an incredible eight weeks, selling in excess of two and a half million copies in the US alone. It was the band's third consecutive #1 single in America. It also went to #1 in the UK, giving the band their first #1 in their home country in almost a decade, since 'I've Gotta To Get A Message To You' in 1968. It was also a #1 hit in Brazil, Canada, and

Spain, and #2 in Germany, Japan, Belgium, Mexico, Norway, New Zealand, and South Africa.

'Stayin' Alive' refused to die in America, and with 'Night Fever' at #1 it rose back to #2 in the charts. The Bee Gees were the first act since The Beatles to hold the top two positions on the US charts. RSO had also, in February, released a fourth single from the soundtrack, Yvonne Elliman's version of 'If I Can't Have You', and by the end of March that was also in the US Top 10. It was joined there by another song Barry had written (with Robin) and another Gibb-Galuten-Richardson production: 'Emotion' by the Australian singer Samantha Sang, the former child star, now twenty-five, whom Barry had produced in the late 60s.

Recorded at Criteria, 'Emotion' had been intended for the *Saturday Night Fever* soundtrack but was not completed in time. Released in December as single by Larry Utal's Private Stock label—the record company behind Walter Murphy's 'A Fifth Of Beethoven'—it was now at #3 in the American charts (as well as #1 in Canada and Australia and #11 in the UK), selling over a million copies. Like the current Yvonne Elliman and Andy Gibb hits, it heavily featured Barry's distinctive falsetto vocals and could virtually have been a Bee Gees track. There were even rumours circulating that Sang did not exist and the track was by the band under a pseudonym. (The track would feature in the hit 1978 disco/soft-core porn film *The Stud*, while an album by Sang, also called *Emotion*, made #29 in the US charts, selling 500,000 copies. It was a high point for a singer whose career quickly evaporated.)

It meant that there were now five songs written by the Gibbs in America's Top 10: 'Night Fever', 'Stayin' Alive', 'If I Can't Have You', 'Emotion', and '(Love Is) Thicker Than Water', four of them performed by Gibbs. They were the first group since The Beatles to achieve this. They were also #1 in the album charts. Huge advertisement boards in

Times Square in New York crowed, 'Bee Gees have the #1 single and #1 album in *Billboard, Cashbox*, and *Record World*. Congratulations! 5 hits in the Top 10!'

Stigwood could not be prouder. 'We weren't on the charts,' said Maurice, 'we were the charts.' When 'If I Can't Have You' replaced 'Night Fever' at the top of the US charts (while also going to #1 in Canada and #4 in the UK), it meant that five songs written by Barry, Robin, and Maurice had been at #1 in America for eighteen consecutive weeks. They would by denied a sixth consecutive #1 by American rock band Player, whose 'Baby Come Back' was, remarkably, released by RSO. With that, Stigwood's label had notched up a run of six consecutive US chart-toppers—an unequalled record—with a combined total of twenty-one weeks at #1 … almost as long as *Saturday Night Fever* spent at the top of the American albums charts that year.

'I think we've cracked it,' said Robin.

CHAPTER SIX

DEATH
OF DISCO

KEVIN McCORMICK
I KNEW I'D WORKED FOR A
MAGICIAN—AN ALCHEMIST.

aturday Night Fever was more than a film. 'It gave the decade its cultural identity,' said Travolta. The impact was being felt the world over. At the place where it had all started, 2001 Odyssey, DJ and manager Chuck Rusinak became a mini-celebrity. The club was 'packed beyond belief ... you couldn't move,' he said. 'At one point it was so busy that people would come in for three hours, we'd empty the club and then line everybody up again.' One of the club's regulars tried to sue Paramount, saying he was the real Tony Manero. 'He walked around the club with a lawyer and a white suit,' said Rusinak.

Incredibly, 2001 Odyssey now rivalled the super-hip Manhattan hotspot Studio 54 as America's most famous disco club. Famed for its strict door policy, high celebrity count, and even higher quotient of cocaine use and debauchery, Studio 54's reputation would ultimately outstrip the rough, backwater club Cohn had stumbled across in suburban Bay Ridge and, like *Saturday Night Fever*, become forever synonymous with the disco era. In 1978 the club released an album on Neil Bogart's quintessential disco label Casablanca Records, and launched a brand of jeans and even a franchise, with Studio 54s opening in London, Munich, and Tokyo. 2001 Odyssey, however, could lay claim to starting the first ever kiddie disco, on Saturdays from twelve to five.

Discomania and Fevermania were interchangeable words to describe the same thing. America was disco crazy. The movie and The Bee Gees' music had seduced 'Middle America back on the dance floor', said *Rolling Stone*. In New York, AOR rock station WKTU switched to disco and became the city's number-one station. Rock stations in Los Angeles, Boston, and Detroit followed suit. By the end of 1978 there would be 200 all-disco radio stations in America. In Manhattan, more huge disco super-clubs opened to rival Studio 54, such as Xenon and New York New York. There were soon, it was estimated, more than twenty thousand discotheques in America and thirty-seven million Americans on the dance floor.

It was boom time for all things disco: clubs, sound systems, dance floors that lit up, mirror balls for clubs, homes, and cars, and dance lessons. Disco-dancing schools opened up everywhere in America. Companies started to sell disco pizzas, disco jeans, disco haircuts, and disco drinks. There was a *Night Fever* pinball machine. The kids TV show *Sesame Street* released a disco album, *Sesame Street Fever*, which went gold. Mickey Mouse released a disco album, *Mickey Mouse Disco*. RSO released a disco version of 'Bridge Over Troubled Water'. There were disco versions of everything—even weddings—and a massive shift in the way people dressed. 'Thousands of shaggy-haired, blue-jean-clad youngsters are suddenly putting on suits and vests, combing their hair and learning to dance with partners,' wrote *Newsweek*. Fashion labels such as Fiorucci became must-haves, the Italian brand's flagship New York stores blasting out disco. The Abraham & Straus department store in Brooklyn even opened a 'Night Fever' menswear boutique. John Travolta lookalike contests were popular.

NBC launched a Brooklyn-based disco sitcom, *Joe & Valerie*, there were scores of disco dance shows on TV, and disco was featured heavily on all the major mainstream music shows, including *American Bandstand*, *Soul Train*, and *Solid Gold*. Even rock shows such as *Midnight Special* were featuring disco. Casablanca Records made its own disco movie in conjunction with Motown, *Thank God It's Friday*, a modest hit at the box office with a Top 10 soundtrack album. Roller-discos—disco on roller-skates—took off and inspired films such as *Roller Boogie*. There was even an Icecoteque—disco on ice skates.

A slew of *Saturday Night Fever* rip-off films appeared, mainly Italian ventures such as *Disco Delirio* and *American Fever* but also the German *Disco Fever*. There was a Dracula meets disco movie, *Love At First Bite*, and a porno, *Saturday Night Beaver*. Disco, it was estimated, was generating revenues in excess of four billion dollars in America— two-thirds the combined gross of the recording and movie industries. *LIFE* magazine ran a cover story on the phenomenon with the headline 'DISCO! Hottest Trend in Entertainment'. Respected business magazine *Fortune* ran a disco feature too and put The Bee Gees on the cover. Travolta was featured on the cover of *Time* magazine alongside the words 'Travolta Fever'.

Saturday Night Fever 'institutionalised disco', according to Kevin McCormick. It was not just in America—similar things were happening around the world. The number of discos in France jumped to a number in excess of 3,500. In the UK, outré disco acts such as Boney M would enjoy a huge upsurge in popularity. In Brazil, *Saturday Night Fever* had such an impact that a word was invented to describe the condition of disco fever—*travolter*, meaning 'to travolt'.

The soundtrack album was a phenomenon, too. It would not stop selling. The Tavares version of 'More Than A Woman' was the latest hit single to be taken from it, becoming another American Top 40 hit and peaking at #7 in UK in May. The *Saturday Night Fever* soundtrack was now eclipsing all predictions, having racked up sales of eighteen million, with RSO calculating that sales would approach twenty-seven million by the end of 1978—more than the total sales of the three previous biggest selling albums in chart history combined. It was now expected to generate a quarter of a billion dollars in sales revenue.

Each track on the album was said to earn ten cents for the performer per record sold. A lot of people, not just The Bee Gees, were getting rich. *Record World* reckoned 'one out of every seven families in America' owned the soundtrack. 'All the black people in America had the Bee Gees records,' said Nile Rodgers of Chic, the most prominent new band capitalising on the disco revival in America, hitting #1 with 'Le Freak' (Atlantic Records' best-selling single of all time). 'I just think *Saturday Night Fever* is genius,' Rodgers added. 'Disco has been the one source of music where everyone is equal, where you can have a good white disco group and a good black disco group and people who come to see you don't care less.'

The Bee Gees were in a state of shock. Barry's Biscayne Bay home on Miami Beach was besieged. 'I remember not being able to answer the phone, and I remember people climbing over my walls,' he said. He was happiest in the studio, at Criteria. 'The studio is my spaceship,' he said. 'I lose all sense of the outside world.' He described making and writing music as like 'the sex force', and he had several projects on the go, not least a new Bee Gees album. It would soon be two years since the release of *Children Of The World*. The *Washington Post* had recently pointed out the band had, with *Saturday Night Fever*, 'rocked to fame on less than one full side of one record'. Barry felt he still had much to prove and was driven to achieve more success.

Maurice too was now living in Miami permanently with his wife, son, and in-laws, having bought a Georgian-style mansion just six blocks away from Barry's home. His wife's brother had also moved to Miami. Maurice drank whiskey for breakfast and hid liquor bottles around the Criteria studios. If he was awake, he drank. He would take little part in the music on the new Bee Gees album. Instead he invested his time and money in a speedboat and a Falcon 20 jet.

With Hugh and Barbara, and Andy, back from Hollywood, living close by in Miami, it left only Robin as the odd man out. Even the band's drummer, Dennis Bryon, had moved to Miami, purchasing a Spanish mansion on North Bay Road with sea views. He said he paid in cash, having just received his first royalty statement from RSO for the *Fever* soundtrack—for $200,000. It was quickly followed by a second royalty cheque for $220,000 that he used to renovate his new home, installing a Jacuzzi in the courtyard and a brand new pool overlooking the bay, and also investing in toys such as a twenty-four-foot fishing boat and a Baldwin Grand piano.

Robin did now own a house in Miami but would not commit to living there full-time. The idea of being so close to the other Gibbs did not appeal to his wife, Molly. The new Bee Gees album would take eight months to complete, on and off, and the time Robin spent in Miami away from his family put a strain on his relationship with Molly. In fact, he almost died in Miami while out cruising on a thirty-one-foot boat he had bought. He lost two engines and the steering apparatus during a storm, and with the boat heading for a bridge he jumped in the water. The boat was demolished, and Robin managed to swim to shore half a mile away. His addiction to stimulants had not abated. He was also, and had long been, cheating on Molly.

Barry tended to dominate not just work in the studio but life. His Spanish-style villa worth £300,000 and located on Miami's 'Millionaire

Row', boasted a pool and tennis courts. Stars of the magnitude of Willie Nelson and Glen Campbell visited to jam with him. Linda's parents resided in attached living quarters, as did her brothers. Barry still smoked marijuana but preferred tea to alcohol and avoided the limelight, preferring to watch movies or play snooker at home or take trips on one of the six boats the family owned. He was still having RSO ship out from London home comforts such as baked beans, processed peas, Bovril, and Yorkshire pudding mix.

With the media glare upon them and hedonism a big part of the disco movement, Barry put the emphasis on portraying the band as devoted family men, espousing old-fashioned family values and clean living. 'They are all family people, which is very strange in this business,' Stigwood said. 'They don't create scandals just to see their names in print.' Mum Barbara even denied Maurice had a drink problem, claiming he had beaten his addiction and was now just having 'a beer after work'. But life was not that simple. Tour boats sailed past Barry's waterfront home several times a day, the passengers equipped with cameras and binoculars. There was also a tour bus that regularly drove past his home, the *Miami Herald* having printed his address. And there were always scores of screaming girl fans outside his home and outside Criteria Studios, too.

'I remember death threats ... crazy fans driving past the house, playing "Stayin' Alive" at 120 decibels,' said Barry. 'Everything seemed out of control. It was just unbelievable.' He had his home fortified: nine-foot-high fences were erected, guard dogs, electronic wrought-iron gates, and a security force employed. He already had two full-time assistants living in his home. Trips to the cinema and restaurants became impossible. Now even plane journeys were problematic, with Maurice noting that the band members could no longer take commercial flights.

'We were suddenly living in a goldfish bowl,' said Barry. It was, he said, 'starting to feel like '67 and '68' again. 'We lost all sense of reality. Everybody's running your life. Your wife ends up a distant friend, passing in the corridor between appointments.' He retreated, more and more, to the studio. In Criteria, life was normal, the team of Richardson and Galuten a foundation stone for whatever the future might bring. The studio was his drug. 'I was aggressive about making records,' he said. 'There was a time when I would spend eighteen hours a day in the studio, with my brothers or not.' He worked on new songs that he, Maurice, and Robin had written on the set of *Sgt. Pepper's*. They included 'Tragedy', 'Too Much Heaven', and 'Shadow Dancing'—three songs Maurice would claim were written in a single day. 'The drugs must have been good that day,' he said.

'We're trying just a little to avoid disco,' Barry said. 'We're keeping the solid rhythms but we're not saying hey, you have to dance to this song. We can write all kinds of songs, some call it selling out, but if you're adaptable you stay, if not you go when the crowd changes its mind.' He said he had 'a complete picture, like Technicolor, of how the record should be'. He understood what makes a hit: 'where it goes up, where it goes down, where you put the colours'.

The band said they had turned down offers for their own weekly TV series in America, talking instead of writing their own TV shows and films. Barry said they were thinking about a film linked to the new album, where 'each of the band will die in hysterical ways, ascend to heaven, and be sent back to earth to fulfil their destinies'. He said they were looking for someone like Woody Allen to write a 'mature' screenplay.

There was no great sense of urgency toward finishing the new album, although a number of songs, including 'Tragedy' and 'Too Much Heaven', had been recorded in a raw state. Barry would grow obsessed with new technical developments that allowed him to overdub onto the songs endlessly. Galuten was his equal in studio tinkering, seeing technology as a way to precision brilliance, with drum loops and drum machines used tirelessly. 'I had to fight just to play anything live,' said Bryon. It would take six more months to complete the album, which would end up costing a significant $700,000 in recording costs.

●

'Shadow Dancing' was destined not for the new Bee Gees album but for Andy Gibb, who would be credited as co-writer alongside Barry, Maurice, and Robin. The Gibb-Galuten-Richardson production team took control of the song in Criteria as they recorded a second Andy Gibb album. It was a string-drenched, easy-on-the-ear disco tune underpinned by a taught propulsive rhythm courtesy of Ziegler and Cowart. It could easily have been mistaken for The Bee Gees, as a follow-up to 'Night Fever', with Andy's vocals sounding disconcertingly like Barry, whose own falsetto vocals were all over the chorus. The video for the single saw Andy trussed up in a white disco outfit to echo Travolta and The Bee Gees. He even wore a gold medallion with a diamond in its centre, a gift from Stigwood. He too was caught up in the *Fever* phenomena.

Fresh from his second American #1 single with '(Love Is) Thicker Than Water', Andy was now living aboard an opulent cruiser in Miami with three staterooms, three bedrooms, and a grand piano in the main lounge. The boat had previously belonged to a Miami drug lord who had reputedly been shot to death in one of the bedrooms.

Andy was twenty now, and his fame continued to disorient him. He was reputedly worth two million dollars. His cocaine habit raged. He felt he had not earned his success. 'My brothers handed it down to me on a silver platter,' he said. 'I didn't have any confidence. I always thought that people were buying my records as an extension to The Bee Gees and I never thought their was an individual thing in there they liked.' Critics had attacked his music as banal, the *New York Times* calling it 'an old man's idea of what a young man's music should be'. His inner turmoil often resulted in childish fits of temperament. He threw tantrums at his mum now when he saw himself being advertised as the 'younger brother of The Bee Gees' and told teen magazines that he hated being called 'the fourth Bee Gee'.

Andy's private life was mess. He had got a quickie divorce from Kim, filing divorce papers two weeks before she gave birth to their daughter. The divorce cost him a reputed $225,000. He did not attend the birth of his child as he promised he would and made no effort to see his daughter after the event. Kim told the *News Of The World* that Andy had changed as soon as he hit the big time, that 'he was dazzled by the limelight', and she talked openly about his cocaine habit. 'If I couldn't get him off drugs, no one could,' she said. 'He was self-destructing.' The press was now linking Andy to eighteen-year-old Marie Osmond, whom he had met while filming a slot on the *Donny & Marie* TV series. He seemed obsessed. Marie was a Mormon, and her family did not take kindly to Andy's pursuit. 'He was doing tons of drugs and she did not even drink Coca-Cola,' said Galuten. When Andy flew out to surprise her in Hawaii, where she was filming, he was asked to leave.

'Shadow Dancing' was his biggest hit yet, at #1 in the US charts by June 1978, making Andy the first solo artist in history to have topped the American charts with his first three singles. The single stayed at #1 for an impressive seven weeks, selling two and a half million copies. His debut album had now sold over one million copies. The level of success and fame Andy had achieved in just under a year had taken everyone by surprise. He was America's biggest teen idol—a position that came with a clear sell-by date—but Andy, looking to his celebrated brothers, saw more for himself. He wanted credibility. He said he liked the classic rock of The Steve Miller Band, and that was 'where I'm trying to go now'.

Such delusions were the result of excessive cocaine use and the coterie of fast friends he had surrounded himself with. For Al Coury, the president of RSO Records, 'He was treated like a superstar from day one, paid very well, lived like a king, private planes. You had to worry about him because you knew some day the hits were going to stop.' Barry was also apprehensive. 'We're concerned for the boy,' he said. There's a lot of heavy drugs around, a lot of shady characters, and he's not always within the realms of family.'

On his giant circular bed in his bedroom on his luxury boat, Andy looked at himself in the mirrored ceiling. On the bed beside him were two semi-automatic machine guns, a .357 magnum and a riot gun—he was paranoid about Caribbean pirates. Prowling the room was a pet lion cub called Samantha that he had bought at auction. He couldn't get enough of buying things—a Ferrari, a collection of motorbikes, a fifty-eight-foot cruiser he named Shadow Dancer, a thirty-one-foot Bertram sports fishing vessel, and a sixty-four-foot luxury Hatteras yacht, moored at the trendy expensive marina next to downtown Miami. He enjoyed cruising to Nassau and other easy to reach spots in the Bahamas, sometimes by himself.

Andy was sent out on a mammoth forty-four-city tour of America, taking in such huge venues as the Nassau Coliseum in New York, where he played to fifteen thousand fans. At a concert in Miami, his brothers joined him to sing 'Words' and 'Shadow Dancing'. It was the 'proudest moment of my life', said Hugh, whose ambition had been to see all four of his sons perform together. In total, Andy would play to almost a quarter of a million fans on the tour. His success rivalled that of The Bee Gees.

'We're both peaking,' said Andy. 'I couldn't think of anything nicer than this forever. A lot of people thought I was going to join them when I grew up. I'm happy to stay as I am. But on the other hand, if they did ask me, I would probably jump at it.' Hugh, who was also alarmed by Andy's erratic behaviour—the tour finished him off, essentially—said that this would not be happening. There was too 'too much of an age difference', he said, for Andy and Barry to play together. 'Besides, Andy has his own fans.'

Andy was now out of control. He was ordered to stop phoning Marie Osmond. Lawyers were involved. 'I have it from Marie's lips that this has to be nipped in the bud for Andy's sake,' her attorney said.

For his second album he had hoped to work with other songwriters to broaden his horizons, but Stigwood had not wanted to alter a winning formula. Andy had written six forgettable songs for the record, which would coast on the back of the hit single and was predictably titled *Shadow Dancing*. Produced by the Gibb-Galuten-Richardson team it had been put together with many of the same session players that appeared on Andy's first album—and in a similar way with little contribution from Andy.

The vocals on *Shadow Dancing* often sounded as if Barry had actually recorded them—and he had. Andy was frequently absent from recordings, unfit or unwell. 'On a couple of my albums you can hear Barry singing,' Andy said later. 'People thought it was me but it was him.' The album would reach #7 in the US, selling a million copies. The one track Barry had written, 'Everlasting Love', a romantic disco track, was released as the follow-up single to 'Shadow Dancing' and would reach US #5. Barry's vocals were all over it. The track took off in Britain, too, peaking at #10 and selling 250,000 copies, helping the *Shadow Dancing* album reach the UK Top 20. A European promotional tour had to be cut short, however. Andy fell asleep in an interview and couldn't finish a photo shoot. It was not just the drugs and self-doubt.

RSO had worked him incredibly hard for months. 'I broke down,' he said. 'Not mental, a physical collapse.'

●

As well as writing and producing Andy's solo material, Barry, with Richardson and Galuten, had also written and produced a song for Teri DeSario, a singer Galuten had heard in a Miami club. The disco pop track, 'Ain't Nothing Gonna Keep Me From You', credited just to Barry, peaked at #43 in America. Stigwood had also asked Barry to write the theme tune for Travolta's new movie, *Grease*. Stigwood was in a hurry and wanted it quick. 'I had finished the film and thought, who can work fast?' he said. 'Barry! I said this is fairly instant and he said, I understand, and about ten minutes later the phone rang and a word had stuck in his mind and he translated that into "Grease is the word".'

Barry said he had sketched song out while he watched TV, explaining his inner monologue as:

> *How can anybody write a song about grease?*
> *How can you make that romantic?*
> *If you write a song about the word 'grease' it could work.*

'And that's all I did,' he said. It didn't take long, and he didn't think much of it. Stigwood asked former Four Seasons vocalist Frankie Valli to sing the song. It was 'real smart casting', said Barry: Valli had 'one of the hallmark voices of our generation', one that had been a key influence on his own falsetto sound. 'He created a style that we all still strive to emulate,' Barry said.

Barry, Richardson, and Galuten produced the track, which featured Peter Frampton on guitar. Valli said it was an 'extraordinary pleasure' to work with Barry, and described the chemistry between the team of Gibb-

Richardson-Galuten as 'perfect'. The single was rush-released and rose to #1 in America, selling two million copies, while also peaking at #1 in Canada, #3 in the UK, and #2 in Germany. Before the movie premiered, RSO released a second single from the upcoming *Grease* soundtrack album, 'You're The One That I Want', a duet between Travolta and female lead Olivia Newton-John. 'One of the fastest selling records I have been associated with in the past five years,' said Al Coury. It shot to #1 in America, selling two million copies on its way to becoming one of the Top 20 best-selling singles of the year, and topped the charts in the UK for nine weeks, where it remains one of the best-selling singles of all time, with sales of over two million copies. It was also a #2 hit in Canada and Australia.

In a moment of carefully controlled hype, it was suggested Travolta and Newton-John, aged twenty-nine and managed by Allan Carr, who had co-produced *Grease*, were an item. Born in England, Newton-John had grown up in Australia, where she had worked similar TV and radio shows to The Bee Gees. Her career had taken off in the early 1970s with a slew of Top 10 hits in America and the UK. She'd had two US #1 albums in 1974 and 1975, as well as two huge #1 singles, including her best-known tune, 'I Honestly Love You', and had won several Grammy awards. *Grease* was her first major movie role, although she had recently starred in her own hour-long NBC TV special, *Olivia!* (Andy Gibb had appeared with her, singing a medley of ABBA hits.)

In almost identical circumstances to those surrounding the success of *Saturday Night Fever*, by the time *Grease* was released in theatres, on June 16 1978, the hit singles from the film's soundtrack had created huge interest in the movie. Although Stigwood had allowed the budget for the movie to rise to six million dollars, the kitsch 1950s-set musical grossed almost nine million on its first weekend. It went on to become the biggest box-office hit of 1978, grossing $394 million worldwide.

There was a near riot when thousands of fans turned up to the film's premiere in London. The *Grease* soundtrack album, another double, was #1 in America by August and spent twelve weeks at the top spot.

Al Coury was furious with The Rolling Stones, whose *Some Girls* album had recently replaced *Saturday Night Fever* at the top of the US album charts. It stayed there for one week before *Grease* knocked it off the spot. 'My fucking plan was to be number one all year!' Coury said. In the UK, the *Grease* soundtrack album spent thirteen weeks at #1. It was a hit around the world, quickly amassing sales of eight million and ultimately selling an incredible forty-four million copies. The soundtrack yielded two more huge hits in 1978: 'Summer Nights', another Travolta/Newton-John duet, became a second UK #1 and peaked at #5 in the US; 'Hopelessly Devoted To You', sung by Newton-John, reached #2 in the UK and #7 in America.

Even Stigwood found it hard to comprehend the success he was having. The two RSO soundtrack albums, *Grease* and *Saturday Night Fever*, would account for almost 10 percent of *all* record sales in America in 1978. RSO was awarded more platinum single records [awarded for sales of over one million] for 1978 in America than the entire record industry had received the year before. Freddie Gershon estimated the company made half a billion dollars *just from records* in 1978.

Stigwood bought The Bee Gees each a Cadillac with platinum metallic finish and partied harder than ever. One close friend said he 'had never seen anyone dole out such a staggering degree of punishment to his or her body in the pursuit of such an astonishing degree of fun'. An English journalist recalled attending a cocaine, marijuana, and champagne-fuelled party at Stigwood's New York apartment and being proposition by him. The journalist said he told Stigwood he was straight, so Stigwood led him to a bedroom with a woman waiting on the bed, suggesting that he would watch.

'He was a hedonist,' an old associate said. 'He did everything—and I mean everything.' Neighbours in New York complained to the co-op board about afternoon male orgies on his penthouse balcony. He spent weekends out in the Hamptons on Long Island with gaggles of men. He enjoyed long nights at Studio 54, drank through much of the day, and travelled with a pack of handsome young men. 'I remember meeting him once at 7:30 in the morning, and he was drinking a beer,' Andrew Lloyd Webber recalled. 'I said, Really, Robert, don't you think it's a bit early? And he said [it was] for the vitamin B.' For Tim Rice, Stigwood had the 'constitution of an ox on steroids'.

In the same month as the New York premiere for *Grease*, for which he threw a party at Studio 54, Stigwood hosted an opening-night party for *Evita* in London, with eight hundred guests invited to a boat off the Victoria Embankment. 'I'm in the lucky position where my work is my hobby,' he said. 'I'm very thankful I have that opportunity in life. I really do things I enjoy doing but I take the commercial approach. I'm not a great believer in subsidised art.'

In London, Stigwood rode around in his white Rolls-Royce with its floor covered in furs and holed up in his usual vast suite at the Dorchester. The Webber and Rice musical rode on the back of the successful album of the same name (and its hot singles) and was a massive success in the West End, picking up numerous awards. It would run for an incredible eight years and 3,176 performances, transferring to Broadway in 1979. Stigwood even had hip disco producer Boris Midney remix the *Evita* album for the disco market. Adaptations of *Evita* were staged around the world, making it one of the most successful and profitable musicals of all time. 'Robert never thought big, he thought massive,' Rice said.

Stigwood immediately talked of turning the hit show into a movie, with Barry tipped for a lead role alongside Barbra Streisand, who had invited Barry to produce her next album. 'This is about the biggest and best thing that's ever happened to me,' Barry said. 'Barbra is the greatest. There's no one in the world I'd rather work with. I'm just knocked out by it.' Robin and Maurice less so: Barry's success with Andy and the *Grease* theme tune, plus the fact he was now the undisputed voice and star of The Bee Gees, had reopened old wounds, exacerbated by their respective addiction to barbiturates and alcohol. The fact Barry was being lined up to produce Streisand without them rankled. 'They see that I get more attention and there's nothing they can do,' Barry said. 'They know it gives me more opportunities.'

American gossip magazine *People* suggested The Bee Gees were splitting up. 'Everyone is jealous of Barry,' it wrote. 'He writes the stuff, produces the albums, the big lead vocalist; all the girls think he's the sexiest one. It's really too much for Robin and Maurice.' Maurice told *Rolling Stone* that he 'hated and resented' the impression that had been created that Barry did more on The Bee Gees records than he or Robin. 'It's a load of shit,' he said. 'People get the impression because Barry's out front a lot and gets quite a bit of attention for his work with Karl and Albhy on other people's songs and for his work with Andy. But as far as our records are concerned we all contribute equally and produce equally.' Called upon for a comment, Stigwood said, 'Rapport within The Bee Gees had never been better. They're working together better than they've ever done.'

●

In late July The Bee Gees came together as a group for the premiere of *Sgt Pepper's*. There had been innumerable delays in recording the soundtrack album. Frampton had struggled to cope with the overwhelming fame the success of the *Frampton Comes Alive!* album had bestowed on him and was drinking and drugging hard. 'I felt scared because I was too big,' he said. Two further singles form his 1977 album *I'm In You* had performed poorly. There was a sense he had blown up too big, too fast.

Frampton's manager, Dee Anthony, had also clashed with Stigwood, who planned to imitate the sort of synergy that had made *Saturday Night Fever* and *Grease* such huge successes at the box office and in record stores. Since it was now The Bee Gees who were the significantly bigger act, he wanted to use their name to promote the project in advertising posters for the film and soundtrack. Anthony had objected, claiming he had been promised top billing for his client. Stigwood stood firm and Anthony took the matter to court, seeking an injunction against RSO to prevent them from reducing Frampton's star billing. He found a judge to rule in his favour. An RSO spokesman said it was 'a silly little case really', but the legal wrangling meant that the label was unable to agree on the release of a lead single from the soundtrack. Then, in June, Frampton was involved in a near-fatal car accident in the Bahamas. He had been up all night and fell asleep at the wheel, crashing into a wall and suffering concussion, multiple broken bones, and muscle damage. It was feared he might lose his arm. He was subsequently absent from all promotion for the film and soundtrack. The dramas prevented RSO from running the same sort of music-led campaign that had proved a success with *Saturday Night Fever* and *Grease*. The *Sgt. Pepper's* film and soundtrack were now being released almost simultaneously.

Stigwood had still managed to create significant hype around the film's release. 'This is my dream,' he told the press, describing it as 'the ultimate rock'n'roll movie'. The Bee Gees gave countless interviews to promote the film; they were on the cover of *Rolling Stone* again and in a multitude of other magazine features, but privately they were unsure about not just the music they had made for the soundtrack but the film they had seen at a pre-release screening. 'We asked Robert to take us out of the film,' Barry said.

The press descended on the premiere in Los Angeles, which was attended by all four Gibb brothers and two of The Beatles, Paul McCartney and Ringo Starr, and followed by an extravagant party for over a thousand people. Al Coury predicted the soundtrack album 'could make *Saturday Night Fever* look like a punk album, like a test run for the main event'. Stigwood was so confident of the film's success that RSO had shipped out three million copies of the album in America on sale or return and allocated a million-dollar budget to promotion. It was a lavishly packaged double album that came with a free poster for a retail price of $15.98 and debuted at #5 in the American charts in its first week.

In scattergun fashion, four singles were released simultaneously from the soundtrack in America—none by The Bee Gees or Frampton, and none hugely successful. 'Come Together' by Aerosmith peaked at #23, 'Get Back' by Billy Preston stiffed at #86, and 'Oh! Darling' (from *Abbey Road*), attributed to Robin Gibb, peaked at #15. In the video, an edit from the film, his strained-local vocals take a back seat to close-ups of his brothers and Frampton backing him and action from the movie. The biggest hit from the album was by Earth Wind & Fire, whose version of 'Got To Get You Into My Life' made #9 in the US Top 40 and #1 on the R&B chart.

Reviews for the film, which was almost two hours in length, were routinely appalling. Janet Maslin of the *New York Times* wrote that film's 'musical numbers are strung together so mindlessly that the movie has the feel of an interminable variety show'. *Rolling Stone* called it 'inane', stating that Frampton had 'absolutely no future in Hollywood' and the film was 'a fiasco so unique it should win some kind of award for ineptness ... you keep laughing and thinking it can't get any worse. But it does.' The soundtrack, the review added, was 'excremental'. *Newsweek* reckoned it had a 'dangerous resemblance to wallpaper'. There was almost nothing good written about it.

The Beatles were not happy, either. McCartney and Starr shunned the film after seeing it, while John Lennon and George Harrison had refused to view the film altogether. 'I feel sorry for Robert Stigwood, The Bee Gees, and Peter Frampton,' said Harrison, 'because they had established themselves as decent artists, and suddenly it's the classic thing of greed. The more you make the more you want to make, until you become so greedy that ultimately you put a foot wrong. It's damaged their images, their careers, and they didn't need to do it.' The film still managed to attract audiences—ultimately grossing twenty million dollars at the box office to just recoup its budget—but most were puzzled rather than impressed: this was not the Frampton or The Bee Gees they had bought into.

'It was the best of times, we had the worst of films,' said Robin.

'You don't watch it,' Barry said, 'You tolerate it.' He would later call the film 'the biggest load of shit ever'.

Stigwood appeared with the band to promoting the movie on American TV. Speaking on *The Merv Griffin Show*, he skilfully steered the conversation away from the wreckage of the film to the new album The Bee Gees were making. He declared it 'two-thirds finished' and said it was 'going to surprise the world'. He turned to the Gibb brothers and said, 'Not only do I think it's the best album you've ever done, but I think it's the best album I've ever heard.' He singled out 'Too Much Heaven', calling it 'one of the most beautiful songs The Bee Gees have ever written'.

Stigwood was happier still to talk about *Saturday Night Fever*. He said he was amazed that the film had not been recognised at that year's Oscars, which had taken place in April. The only recognition the film received was for John Travolta, who had been nominated in the 'Best Actor' category but did not win. Stigwood felt the soundtrack album should have been nominated for 'Best Original Score', a category won by John Williams's music for *Star Wars*. Stigwood had actually filed a formal complaint about its omission, milking the ensuing publicity, and, on the night of the Oscars, he had thrown a massive 'anti-Academy Awards party' at his mansion in Beverly Hills, with a guest list that included actor Anthony Perkins, writer Christopher Isherwood, and Hollywood legend Ava Gardner. He told Griffin that there should at least have been an Academy Award nomination for 'Stayin' Alive' in the 'Best Original Song' category. 'There's never been a more perfect marriage of movie and music,' he said. 'I think the popular consensus is The Bee Gees won the Academy Award.'

The bad stink over *Sgt. Pepper*'s was something the band were keen to distance themselves from—and quickly. They were in the final stages now of completing their new album, preparing for another huge promotional push and massive world tour. Maurice told the press that making the film had been 'exciting and educational', while Robin said he wanted to do another film. 'Not a musical but an adventure drama,' he said. 'We've written a screenplay.' He also talked about The Bee Gees starting their own production company and record label.

This was met with a strong rebuff from RSO when it was interpreted that, like Eric Clapton, who was now in dispute with Stigwood, the band were keen to severe ties with their long-term manager. 'There is no question of the group splitting from Robert Stigwood,' said a spokesman. 'But if, for example, they discovered an act they wanted to produce, they could do so on their own label.' The ending of Clapton and Stigwood's relationship, stretching back over a decade of mammoth success, was messy, with their entangled business arrangement taking years to resolve. At the time, Stigwood was also contending with another potential absconder from his management clutches as Andrew Lloyd Webber aggravated to take control of his own finances and future. Webber would not write another musical for Stigwood after *Evita*.

Reviews of the *Sgt Pepper's* soundtrack album were as damning as those for the film. *Rolling Stone* called it the 'worst album of the year'. With the film a critical disaster, sales of the underwhelming and often embarrassing album took a nosedive. It fell out of the Top 100 after only six weeks and, like the film, made little impression around the world, peaking at #35 in the UK. Al Coury had boasted that by shipping three million copies of the album he had grossed forty million dollars, but now retailers began to return their unsold stock. 'We shipped triple platinum,' said Freddie Gershon. 'That was unheard of, and then lo and behold the movie stiffed and then the album stiffed. The assumption was it would be another huge hit.' It quickly became infamous in the music industry as one of the first albums to 'return platinum', meaning over one million copies came back to RSO unsold, with hundreds of thousands ending up being destroyed.

In fact, RSO hid the real amount of returned copies of the *Sgt. Pepper's* album. 'We sent out three million albums and we probably had to take back more than four million,' said Gershon. The Mafia had moved in and begun bootlegging RSO product. They had seen the success of the *Fever* and *Grease* soundtracks and wanted a piece. The bootlegs the Mafia was producing were so good that RSO could not identify the fakes by eye. 'The artwork was fabulous.' said Gershon. 'Under a spectroscope you could see the quality of vinyl, which was cheaper than our vinyl.'

An FBI investigation discovered a major record-pressing operation in the Midwest. 'The FBI told us that the word got out to the guys driving a convoy of trucks that the *Pepper's* albums were valueless,' said Gershon. 'They found them all dumped on the side of some road in Southern California.' This meant that not only did RSO had to contend with its own miscalculations over *Pepper's*, it had to shoulder the miscalculations of the Mafia, too. Four million unsold albums would likely have sunk RSO Records but for the success it was having with *Fever* and *Grease*. But it was still a substantial blow. The news that the Mafia was taking an interest in the company's affairs was also a worry. Still, the label turned a huge profit in 1978, and there was another Bee Gees record on the way to boost profits even further, with plans to press a remarkable five million copies of the album.

●

Records were only one part of RSO, and the company's film and publishing operations were delivering even more profit than the record division. Al Coury said that over five years the Stigwood Group of Companies had made fifty-six million dollars after expenses and tax— the equivalent of around four times that amount in today's money— with the record label responsible for less than half that amount. Stigwood was now thinking about protecting his share, getting out, and slowing down. He had recently initiated a profit-sharing plan at RSO, applicable to all his staff, from managing director to office boy. It was one of his last significant acts at the company—a reward for the staff's loyalty as he began his retreat from the front line.

Stigwood was not superhuman after all. The eighteen-hour days and constant travelling had finally caught up with the forty-four-year-old. He had made so much money over the past year it was mind-blowing. His achievements had been so colossal that nobody could ever dream of repeating them—not even, he realised, himself. He wanted to enjoy himself in other ways, to take a break from the day-to-day management of his company—to become a man no longer available to talk business twenty-four-hours a day. He would be missed.

'I knew I'd worked for a magician—an alchemist,' said Kevin

McCormick, one of just four men, most of them still in their twenties, who constituted the entire staff at RSO Films and were responsible for producing almost as many films as MGM in 1978. 'But after *Saturday Night Fever* you could never get him interested in anything again. He really had no serious desire. He wanted to be safe. And all that money went offshore to Bermuda.'

'He removed himself from everyday life, almost like Howard Hughes,' Bill Oakes, at RSO Records, said. 'He was literally on his yacht, or in a suite somewhere. To get him to go out was a major achievement.' Stigwood still had things he wanted to do, but they were less urgent. The Uri Geller movie would be shelved, but he talked of making a thriller based on Bob Randall's book *The Fan*.

Travolta left Stigwood after completing the third picture in his deal with him, a romantic drama called *Moment By Moment*. He had formed his own production company and arranged a two-picture deal with Orion for a million dollars per movie. 'The big difference between me and Stigwood was, when something is that big, people feel in a way that they'd rather get out if they can't replicate that incredible success,' Travolta said. 'He pulled up his ladder, moved to Bermuda, decided to get out of the game.'

Although *Moment By Moment* would be viewed as a critical and commercial failure, the way Stigwood had approached the financing of the movie with distributors Universal was a lasting testament to the way he operated—the sort of hard-fought success he now needn't trifle himself with. 'I said when I deliver the picture, you, the studio, will pay me ten million dollars,' he recalled. 'That's what it would cost you to do it yourselves. It just so happens I took all the risks in commissioning, and that's my price. Then, when you break even, we'll split the gross. They couldn't see why I thought I was entitled to make three million to four million dollars on delivery of the picture.'

Released in December 1978, *Moment By Moment* received a spate of terrible reviews, with one wit suggesting the film would be better titled 'hour by hour'. It took only ten million dollars at the box office and the soundtrack album was a dismal failure, not even making the Top 100 in America. Stigwood had tried and failed to get The Bee Gees interested in the project, wanting 'Too Much Heaven' as the movie's theme tune. Despite protests to the contrary, however, the relationship between the band and Stigwood was under great strain, and Barry, particularly, was keen to take control of his own career and the band's finances. There was much emotion here, with Stigwood's absence from the frontline aggravating Barry. He found it frustrating dealing with Stigwood's lieutenants and the black type of legal documents. He missed those mischievous blue eyes and the speed and certainty with which Stigwood had always got things done.

•

Still reeling from the catastrophic *Sgt. Pepper's* album, RSO released a new Bee Gees single in October. 'Too Much Heaven' was the song Stigwood had loved upon first hearing. In fact, he had also laid the groundwork for much of the promotion due to accompany the band's re-emergence. The slow, sensual, super-slick song showcased Barry's falsetto at its best. The brothers' harmonies had been worked to perfection, and the strings were subdued in their swooning, so it sounded less like a full-on disco cut.

'There are so many new directions to take our music that we refuse to stay in one place,' said Barry. 'If you try to repeat or hold on to a successful formula you die. We are always changing.' The band appeared unfazed by the critical mauling of their film debut, echoing the philosophy of positive thinking that Stigwood had always tried to instil in them. 'I imagine by my belief and actions I communicated the positive action to them,' Stigwood had once revealed to *Playboy*.

'Positive thinking means success,' Barry said now. 'You say to yourself while you're doing it, this is going to be successful and when you tell it to other people they believe you.'

'Positive thinking is electric,' Robin added.

The new single picked up airplay on both pop and black radio stations and began its climb up the charts to #1 as the band reaped the accolades from their success earlier in the year with a shower of prestigious year-end awards from *Billboard*, *Cashbox*, and *Record World* for single, album, band, and producers of the year. Barry had a hand in writing eight of the twenty best-selling American singles of 1978, including 'Shadow Dancing' and 'Night Fever' (#1 and #2, respectively), 'Stayin' Alive' (#4), 'How Deep Is Your Love' (#6), and '(Love Is) Thicker Than Water' (#8).

In January 1979, The Bee Gees' star on the Hollywood Walk of Fame in Los Angeles was unveiled in front of 5,000 fans—'the largest crowd they've ever had', according to Robin. Shortly after that, the nominations for the 1979 Grammy awards were unveiled, with the band up for six awards. 'Too Much Heaven' was now top of the charts in America, becoming the band's fourth consecutive American #1 and selling in excess of two million copies. It was their first single since 'Night Fever', over ten months old now, and demand for new material around the world was at an all-time high, with 'Too Much Heaven' going to #1 in bewildering list of countries: Argentina, Brazil, Canada, Chile, Italy, New Zealand, Norway, South Africa, Spain, Sweden, and Switzerland. It peaked at #3 in the UK.

Stigwood had organised for The Bee Gees to play live for the first time in over a year on January 9 at a high-profile charity concert in aid of UNICEF—the United Nations International Children's Emergency Fund—at the General Assembly Hall of the United Nations in New York. The event was set to raise money for the UNICEF world hunger programme and mark the beginning of the International Year of the Child. It was being televised in seventy countries, and the band headlined a list of acts that included Olivia Newton-John, Rod Stewart, Donna Summer, ABBA, John Denver, and Earth Wind & Fire. Stigwood had dreamed up the event in early 1978 with heavyweight TV personality David Frost, who acted as compere for the concert. He wanted to 'give something back', said Barry.

In America the ninety-minute extravaganza was shown on NBC and billed as 'the greatest pop show seen on television'. Most of the acts played live, but The Bee Gees clearly lip-synched 'Too Much Heaven' at the concert's finale. Also on the bill was Andy Gibb, back in the US Top 10 with a third single from his *Shadow Dancing* album, '(Our Love) Don't Throw It Away'. The song, written by Barry and Blue Weaver during the *Saturday Night Fever* sessions in France, was a tender ballad with Barry's vocals all over it. Attempts to keep Andy sober were ongoing. He had sold fifteen million records to date and had just received a royalty cheque for one million dollars. His addiction to cocaine was crippling him, however, and Miami was awash with the drug. Maurice warned his younger brother that his career would soon be over and all his riches would disappear if he kept doing what he was doing. Andy was not listening. On top of the cocaine, he'd also started drinking more heavily and downing pills, chiefly Quaaludes.

For the UNICEF concert Andy played two songs, which was just about all he was capable of: 'I Go For You', from *Shadow Dancing*, and 'Rest You Love On Me', a country ballad on which he duetted with Olivia Newton-John, whom he was rumoured to be dating. The song—an unreleased Bee Gees track from their 1976 *Children Of The World* sessions—was intended as a potential single to be included on his next album, and the rumours of a romance were intended to stir up publicity. Barry, Richardson, and Galuten would struggle to get Andy into the studio, however, and spent the rest of the year, on and off, trying to complete the album. When Andy did show up he was often incapable of singing in any meaningful way.

Newton-John ended up duetting with Barry when she came to record her parts at Criteria. 'It was magical,' said Galuten—but not so magical when they had to try to replace Barry's vocals with Andy's drug-ravaged voice. In fact, Barry had ended up singing vocals on all of the album tracks, with Andy merely singing over them when he showed up. 'Andy was in bad shape,' said Galuten. 'He was a basket case. It wasn't an Andy album any more, it was a contractual obligation.' Barry regretted pushing Andy into the business. 'He would have been better off finding something else,' he said. 'He was most insecure man in the world. Even when he had hit records he felt it was still not good enough.'

Andy's life spiralled out of control. He met his daughter for the first and only time in Los Angeles in early 1979, spending a few short hours with her. 'He was clearly not well,' said his ex-wife Kim, who had arranged the visit. 'I didn't know who I was anymore,' he said. His pet lion cub had grown bigger and now clawed at and bit anyone who visited him, while Andy slept with a gun under his pillow. He was careless with the gun, and with money. He bought a private jet in partnership with the actor Robert Redford and rented a mansion in the hills overlooking Los Angeles, and another on Malibu Beach overlooking the Pacific Ocean, where he could escape his family and take cocaine freely. He was still a star, but one that was burning out rapidly. Stigwood was forced to step in, but Andy thought he was interfering. 'You become the enemy,' Stigwood said. 'He knew how to spend, both on drugs and in countless other ways. He blew millions. He got paranoid; he couldn't fly on public planes. He had to have private planes.'

The UNICEF concert was seen by an estimated three hundred million people worldwide and raised one million dollars at the time for the charity, with the performers donating their performance royalties and those from one song each to UNICEF. Polydor released a recording of the concert as an album. Some artists released the royalties for only a limited time, but The Bee Gees donated all earnings from 'Too Much Heaven' in perpetuity. The song would go on to raise seven million dollars for UNICEF. Later in the year, The Bee Gees would be invited to the White House by President Carter, who congratulated them for their work with the charity. It had been another sublimely planned and orchestrated Stigwood promotion for the group.

At the beginning of February, RSO released their new album, *Spirits Having Flown*, with expectations and pre-sales high. All ten tracks were credited to Barry, Robin, and Maurice, even though Maurice had contributed very little; many of his bass parts were replaced without his knowledge. Barry dominated the record, singing lead, almost exclusively in falsetto, on nine of the tracks, and even did many of the backing and harmony vocals himself. Alongside The Bee Gees' regular band—Bryon, Kendall, and Weaver—the album used a long list of the best in American session players, many who had played on Andy Gibb's material as well. There was even a guest spot from the American rock band Chicago, who had scored five successive #1 albums in the mid 70s and had been recording in Criteria while *Spirits Having Flown* was being put together.

'I think we will surprise a lot of people with the new album,' said Barry. RSO gave it a huge promotional push, with a second single, 'Tragedy', released to radio. Although the album showcased the band's divergent styles—a mix of ballads, soul, straight pop, and R&B—'Tragedy' was the album's most overt disco track. It was another single picked by Stigwood, and another instant hit, rocketing to the top of the America charts, knocking 'I Will Survive' by Gloria Gaynor from its perch to become the band's fifth consecutive US #1. 'Tragedy' would also go to #1 across Europe, including in the UK, selling in excess of three million copies worldwide. It was the single that cemented the band's reputation as the preeminent disco act of the era.

Disco was at its peak in America, with nine of the Top 10 singles on the charts being disco cuts. Earth Wind & Fire were back on top with 'Boogie Wonderland' and 'After The Love Has Gone', and Donna Summer was enjoying her best year yet with 'Bad Girls' and 'Hot Stuff'. Also in the charts were the unforgettable 'You Can Ring My Bell' by Anita Ward, 'Knock On Wood' by Amii Stewart, and Sister Sledge's 'He's The Greatest Dancer' and 'We Are Family'. Two of the hottest new bands in America were Chic and The Village People. The latter act made their live debut at 2001 Odyssey before hitting with their singles 'Y.M.C.A.' and 'In The Navy'. *Newsweek* ran a disco cover story with the headline, 'Disco Takes Over', calling the music 'thumpus uninterruptus'.

The Bee Gees were back on US TV on February 15 for the 1979 Grammy Awards broadcast. The *Saturday Night Fever* album won 'Album of the Year', with The Bee Gees picking up awards for 'Best Arrangement for Voices' for 'Stayin' Alive' and 'Best Pop Vocal Performance by a Group' for the *Fever* soundtrack. The Bee Gees, Albhy Galuten, and Karl Richardson also won the award for 'Producer of the Year'. For Barry, the accolades were 'like a dream come true'. *Spirits Having Flown* was #1 on the album charts in America by March, selling four million copies. It also went to #1 in the UK, Canada, and a glut of other countries, ultimately selling twenty million copies worldwide. RSO continued to have problems with bootleggers, however, with reports of perfect counterfeit copies flooding the UK, where the press reported that it could be 'the first million-pound rip-off in British pop history'. With 'Tragedy' and *Spirits Having Flown* at #1 in the UK, The Bee Gees were back at the very pinnacle in their home country, their success recognised at the 1979 Ivor Novello Awards in London. They won the 'International Hit of the Year' award for 'Stayin' Alive' with 'Night Fever' picking up two awards, for 'Most Performed Work' and 'Best Selling A-Side'.

A third single from *Spirits Have Flown* was released in April: the disco-tinged, slow funk pop of 'Love You Inside Out'. The band had sent Stigwood a version of the song on which they sang the words 'backwards and forwards with my cock hanging out'. They were having trouble now getting his attention. The finished version replaced 'cock' with 'heart'. *Billboard* called it one of the best cuts from the album, Barry's falsetto range a delight. It would be #1 in America by June— their sixth consecutive #1 single in the country, equalling a record set by The Beatles. No other band, however, had ever had three consecutive number one singles from two successive albums. Although it didn't sell as well as previous singles, 'Love You Inside Out' stayed at the top in America for two weeks. It also went to #1 in Canada, peaking at #13 in the UK. As if further evidence of the band's incredible popularity in America was needed, all forty-one dates on their recently announced American tour had now sold out. The gigs were all in huge arenas and stadiums with vast capacities. There were three consecutive nights at shows Madison Square Garden in New York. In total they had sold 800,000 tickets, generating ten million dollars. Merchandise sales was expected to double that figure.

●

The Bee Gees had never attempted such a huge tour—this one taking place from June until October, with a three week break scheduled for August—and never would again. Not only did the three Gibb brothers find choreographing a stage show and agreeing on its logistics troublesome, they would not be able to withstand long months on the road together. It was only four years since Batley and the hatred they had felt for one another there. The bewildering success they had achieved was a salve, but the relationships between the three remained full of torment. For twins Maurice and Robin, particularly, the fame and riches—the houses, boats, and cars—had not brought any real sense of contentment or fulfilment. Alcoholism had made Maurice a mess. He was in denial about his drinking and concerned about both his hair loss and his role in the band.

During rehearsals for the tour, which took place over three weeks in May 1979, in a vast warehouse near Miami Beach that was owned by KC & The Sunshine Band and TK Records, Maurice had to accept that a session bass player was required to play the parts onstage. All he had left were his backing vocals, his daft little comedy moments—he was still checking his watch while Barry sang 'Words'—and a guitar he played to little effect. He was suffering from profound depression. 'Every day I didn't want to get up,' he said. 'I had all these beautiful things around me and I didn't appreciate a damn thing. I wasn't happy with me. It was the boozing. I was totally unhappy. I just didn't feel worthy of what I was doing, or my contribution.'

Robin was, if anything, even more messed up. He was insisting that there would be no drugs on the tour while hooked on an array of uppers and downers, a fragile being who wanted to be the band's frontman but had been reduced to a bit part. Even the one song he sang on the new album had been done in falsetto, and Barry had drenched the chorus with his own vocals. For the tour, Barry had hired an all-female group of backing vocalists, The Sweet Inspirations, who were newly signed to RSO and had worked with Elvis in the past, which only further reduced Robin's sense of worth. He had a starring role on the medley of old hits the band stuck into the middle of their set, including 'I Started A Joke', but when the band moved up the gears he was really a superfluous figure, there, like Maurice, as a refraction of the show's star: Barry.

Robin recalled the time, almost ten years ago now, when he'd walked out on the band, fed up with standing in his elder brother's shadows. Hadn't Barry said back then that he, Robin, had one of the 'greatest voices' he'd ever heard? 'He has a far better voice than I have,' Barry had said. Now Robin was made to feel like a circus freak, his plaintive warble no longer suited to the sleek and sexy disco hits. He was often up all night, unable to stop his mind whirring, indulging in debauchery. It was not only drugs that he filled his emptiness with. Fame had opened many doors and sex had also become if not an addiction, an indulgence. He was often away from his English home, his wife Molly, and his young children, and his womanising was relentless. Even when he was in the UK, he was said to spend evenings in London, where he owned a beautiful Georgian house near Harrods in Knightsbridge, entertaining women—friends said his favourite sexual pastime was watching two women get it on.

Before the tour started, Molly told Robin she would not be coming with him and wanted a divorce. Barry and Maurice would have their wives and children with them on the road, while mum and dad, Barbara and Hugh, also planned on being on the tour. Robin was distraught—horrified by his own moral collapse and the thought of how a divorce would affect his children. He and Molly entered a period of intense acrimony.

Barry was in charge; of that there was no doubt. The warehouse they rehearsed in was big enough for a full-size stage, lighting rig, and sound system. The stage set he had helped create, designed to replicate 2001 Odyssey—with the central feature being a copy of the dance floor that lit up—was also installed. Richardson and Galuten helped him get the sound he wanted, with the band augmented by a large brass section. Barry agreed on a wardrobe, too: the Gibbs would be dressed in identical white satin outfits, tight flared trousers, white scarves, and spangled jackets open to the navel to reveal hairy chests and medallions.

The set list was finalised: the band would open with 'Tragedy' and a firework display and climax, as mirror balls magically descended, with a run of disco classics: 'Nights On Broadway', 'Stayin' Alive', 'Jive Talkin'', and 'You Should Be Dancing', the song *Saturday Night Fever* had revitalised. With Stigwood now a distant figure, Barry, soon to turn thirty-two, had it all to do, and he wanted everything to be perfect, as stress free as possible. He pored over every detail. Security was a priority: all three Gibbs had attracted stalkers, and fans had recently broken into their mansions in Miami. He picked out a number of luxury hotels to use as bases for the tour and hired a private jet, a luxury fifty-five-seater Boeing 707, for the band to use to travel between them at a cost of one million dollars. It was painted black and emblazoned with the band's logo.

The plane was also segregated. The front half—equipped with four TV screens and the facilities to serve gourmet meals—was cordoned off for the Gibbs and guests, with the touring musicians put in the back. It wasn't the only notable division on the tour. The Gibbs travelled to and from airports in limousines while the musicians were packed onto a bus, and no one was allowed on the plane before the Gibbs.

Despite the extensive planning, the mood on tour was often tense. The fans were unbelievably frenzied. In Los Angeles, for the gig at the 60,000-capacity Dodger Stadium, touts were selling $15 tickets for $700, and it was calculated the band were making $3,000 a minute on merchandise. And there was always drama. Maurice was often passed out from booze and carried comatose to his room; Robin was testy, rebelling. 'Like being in prison,' he said of the tour. 'To go out and buy a shirt takes two hours planning for logistics and security.'

Even Barry, still smoking marijuana prodigiously, struggled to cope. 'I found myself either on top of the world or totally depressed,' he said. As the weeks piled up, the exhaustion, pressure, and unnatural environment—'It's like Presley,' Barry said—took their toll. 'A couple of times I was at the point of bursting into tears,' he said. 'Being The Bee Gees is like three people being one person. It's impossible. We are each of us having an identity crisis. It could drive us all crazy.'

Offstage, the brothers did their best to avoid one another. There was an overwhelming sense that this was a farewell tour for the band—they would not be unable to repeat such a schedule. The state Maurice was in was a constant worry. Robin was hyper from lack of sleep. Barry hit the cocaine. 'You've got to do it every half hour,' he said, declaring a preference for speed. 'Amphetamines last four-to-six hours. And in those days there were some great amphetamines.'

After shows, in his luxury hotel suite, Barry entertained. Barbra Streisand visited him to discuss their upcoming project together; Michael Jackson, who would become a close friend of his, seemed star-struck when he dropped by. He told Barry he loved *Saturday Night Fever*. 'I knew every note, every instrument on the record,' he said. 'I cried listening to their music.' Jackson would later say the *Fever* soundtrack had inspired him to make his record-breaking 1982 album *Thriller*. More immediately, it was easy to hear the influence of Barry on his late 1979 disco-funk single 'Don't Stop 'Til You Get Enough', an American #1 and Jackson's first attempt at using his own falsetto voice.

Robin watched them come and go—Karen Carpenter, Cary Grant, Rod Stewart, Olivia Newton-John, Diana Ross, Al Pacino, Billy Joel, and Jimmy Connors—all seeking out Barry. It was the same with John Travolta, who joined the band onstage at a 40,000-seat stadium gig in Houston, Texas, busting some disco moves to 'You Should Be Dancing'. Even his own brother, Andy, who appeared onstage with the band at the 60,000-capacity Oakland Coliseum in California, also to perform 'You Should Be Dancing', saw Barry as the band's star. David Frost, who joined the tour temporarily to record material for a documentary on the band that he was co-producing with Stigwood, gravitated toward Barry, too. Robin fumed. The brothers were back to hating one another. Barry blamed 'drink, pills, the scene, egos'.

●

There were still moments of levity. Maurice had got hold of a T-shirt that said 'Shoot The Bee Gees' across the chest. There had been an almost suffocating, unspoken sense of paranoia on the tour that despite the tight security the band might fall prey to a crazed attacker amid the fan hysteria. The T-shirt deflated that fear and had the Gibbs in fits of giggles. It was being advertised for sale in a number of American music magazines at the time, alongside another that read: 'Death To Disco'. Not everyone, clearly, was a disco fan—or a Bee Gees fan.

The band also had a chuckle when they heard that some of their records had been set on fire at a recent 'anti-disco' event in Chicago that had made the news when it exploded into violence. The event, held at the city's baseball stadium on July 12, had been hosted by WLUP personality DJ Steve Dahl and his sidekick, Garry Meier, who had built up a local following by constantly disparaging disco records on air and pretending to blow them up. Dahl, a shock jock, always pronounced the word 'disco' with a camp lisp and had destroyed a copy of 'The Hustle' on the day Van McCoy died of a heart attack. He and Meier would also do impressions of The Bee Gees on the show, after first inhaling helium.

Dahl referred to his listeners as the 'anti-disco army', 'dedicated to the eradication of the dreaded musical disease known as disco'. He had organised it so that anyone attending a particular Red Sox baseball game would be admitted to the stadium for a reduced fee of 98 cents if they brought with them a disco record he could destroy. The Red Sox had been averaging home crowds of 15,000 in a stadium that seated 45,000. Dahl advertised the promotion exhaustively on his radio show, billing it as a 'disco demolition'. Everyone had a disco record and 98 cents was a snip for a baseball game. On the night, the stadium was full, and there was at least 10,000 more people milling around outside the stadium, trying to gain entrance.

Before the game, Dahl and Meier had taken to the field to lead the crowd in chants of 'disco sucks'. Dahl told the crowd, 'This is now officially the world's largest anti-disco rally!' There was a huge box on the field filled with approximately 10,000 disco records, some of them Bee Gees records. Dahl lit a fuse and blew up the box. He then encouraged the crowd to throw onto the filed any remaining disco records. Thousands were thrown like Frisbees; a melee ensued where hundreds of people invaded the field and, inspired by Dahl, gathered piles of disco records to set on fire. Mob rule had taken over, and the crowd tore out seats from the stands to throw on the bonfires.

Eventually, police on horseback intervened. Thirty-nine fans were arrested on charges of disorderly conduct. When Dahl showed up at the studio the next day to do his show, he found the American media waiting. His anti-disco message was transmitted around the country, coagulating around the phrase 'disco sucks'. Just as Dahl's shtick had been a hit in Chicago, it also appealed, all over the country, to vast swathes of a similar demographic to that of his local 'anti-disco army', chiefly white rock fans, aged eighteen to thirty-four, who had felt excluded, and even threatened, by the disco scene. Dahl had given them something to rally around—a reason why they didn't like to sway to the music du jour—disco was 'gay'. The phrase 'disco sucks' was a clear pejorative term.

Dahl had detonated more than a few records. The anti-disco

movement spread rapidly, and soon disco records were being destroyed by DJs on radio stations in other major cities across America—in Los Angeles, Seattle, Portland, and Cleveland. The records were either scratched, sped up, or cut short, to be followed by the sound of flushing toilet noises or vomiting, sometimes chainsaws. They were even mock burials. Such skits would routinely be followed by the opening guitar chords of a bombastic Van Halen or AC/DC track. In Detroit, it was noted there were two anti-disco vigilante groups: the Disco Ducks Klan and DREAD (Detroit Rockers Engaged in the Abolition of Disco). The Christian right also got involved in the 'disco sucks' movement, too, and in much the same way as rap music would be attacked in the 80s, they fermented a sense of moral outrage that disco—the music of gays, blacks, and Latinos, and the soundtrack to drug use and casual sex—had corrupted white American youth culture. There was a word for all this—'discophobia'—and The Bee Gees, the most famous disco group in America, were prime targets with their 'gay' falsetto voices, disco music, and carefully sculpted 'gay' disco image.

'Our father always said, Look, no one ever criticises you when you're down, you only get the criticism when you're up, so shut up,' said Barry. While on tour, the band gave little thought to the 'disco sucks' movement, the evangelicals, or rock DJs as crowds of 30,000-plus screamed their names across America, from New York to Cleveland, Chicago, Cincinnati, Philadelphia, Pontiac, and Providence. Dahl had tapped into something with 'disco sucks', however. As reactionary and ridiculous as it was, it resonated deeply and captured the zeitgeist perfectly. The Bee Gees would be shocked to discover that after the last date of their *Spirits* tour—at the Miami Stadium, where they played to 60,000 people—they were no longer the band they thought they were. They had gone from being the hottest band in the world to laughing stock in just a matter of weeks. It was an unprecedented turn of events.

Disco had essentially become a victim of its own success. Everyone was at it: one of the best-selling American singles of the year was Rod Stewart's 'Do Ya Think I'm Sexy', and acts such as Elton John, KISS, the Stones, and Barry Manilow had all jumped on the bandwagon. There were clear signs the public's appetite was waning: the Broadway musical *Got Tu Go Disco* closed after just nine days, and Allan Carr's film starring The Village People, *Can't Stop The Music*, was on its way to being a box-office disaster. There were other portents that the excesses of the disco era were coming to an end. The owners of Studio 54 were charged with tax evasion (and would soon be jailed) after a raid on the club, with *New York* magazine running a cover story about the bust under the headline 'The Party's Over'. The reign of disco at 2001 Odyssey was also over: the club was now hiring male strippers to fill certain nights and even booked glam heavy-metal act Twisted Sister, who took twenty copies of *Saturday Night Fever* onstage with them and set fire to the lot.

Serious critics took pot shots, with disco attacked for its political apathy, and for what it had once been celebrated for: its escapism and hedonism. The riot in Chicago would become known as the 'The Night Disco Died', but it had been living on borrowed time ever since *Saturday Night Fever* blew up. More than anything, it had been the movie and the music of The Bee Gees that had created disco's *annus mirabilis* of 1978, in America and around the world.

Disco had dominated for most of 1979, too—until August, every American #1 record had been a disco record. In September, 'My Sharona' by The Knack hit #1. It was seen as an emblem of a 'new wave' of American rock that included bands such as The Cars: bands who wore skinny ties and black jeans and returned to 60s guitar music for inspiration. 'My Sharona' had also knocked Chic's disco classic 'Good Times' off the top spot, a symbolic act that also heralded a seismic shift in America's musical tastes. By the end of September there were no disco songs in the US Top 10, with many critics declaring the genre 'dead'. The Knack, Led Zeppelin, and The Eagles topped the American album charts for the final four months of 1979.

The Bee Gees were suddenly out of fashion, trapped by their phenomenal disco success and association with *Saturday Night Fever*. They were confused and beleaguered. 'The exhaustion of being The Bee Gees set in and we couldn't see what tomorrow was going to bring,' said Barry. With Maurice admitted to a private clinic in London to treat his alcoholism after the *Spirits* tour ended, Barry and Robin spent time writing songs for the Barbra Streisand album that Barry was due to produce in early 1980. The celebrated singer and actress had demanded, Barry said, 'contemporary' material—not her usual Broadway musical-style songs. The pair had imagined 'writing a screenplay for her', Barry said. The Gibb brothers also negotiated the purchase of the Miami Beach warehouse where they had rehearsed the tour. The owners, renowned disco label TK Records, were suffering badly from the disco backlash and would soon enter administration. The warehouse was close to their homes, and they planned to convert it into a recording studio and band offices. It was an expensive process, but when complete it would allow them almost complete autonomy to record who and when they wanted.

Barry was also growing increasingly frustrated with Stigwood's lack of communication and apparent disinterest in the band's future. Their manager now seemed intent on derailing the Streisand project, having baulked when Streisand's manager asked for a cut of the publishing on the Gibb songs intended for the album and countered with a demand for three-quarters of all royalties and advances from Streisand's record label, Columbia. Stigwood had figured he owned three of the four participants in the project (Barry, Robin, and Maurice), and as ever he wanted to maximise the percentage he could take out of the project as his management fee.

Streisand did not want The Bee Gees or Stigwood, Barry argued. She wanted him and his songs. RSO responded by stating that Barry was under contract and was unable to work with Streisand, or take on *any* work, without the label's consent. The situation ignited a battle that had been brewing for some time. Al Coury, the president of RSO Records, believed the acrimony went back to the *Fever* album, for which the band had demanded such a high royalty for the tracks they supplied that RSO, if they had agreed, would have lost 'approximately 15 cents per album'. The Bee Gees 'still wound up with an excessively high royalty' Coury said, and he believed that Stigwood 'even give them a percentage of the film'.

The Bee Gees had two albums to deliver on their current deal with RSO, and Barry had wanted to increase the advances and royalties on those, too. 'It seems that they have forgotten the costs involved in selling records and are asking for even more than what has already been given,' Coury said. 'It is impossible for us to be more generous without putting ourselves out of business.' Barry had also annoyed Stigwood by commissioning an independent audit of RSO Records to find out if the band had been paid all the money they were owed under existing deals. The relationship between Stigwood and the band was described as 'frozen'.

In late 1979, RSO issued a cash-in hits package called *Bee Gees Greatest*, compiling the band's best songs from 1975–79. It was aimed squarely at the Christmas market. The band did not support the release; they were 'suffering from burn out', as Robin put it. The album mopped up the last of The Bee Gees' popularity and was propelled by the hastily completed Frost/Stigwood documentary broadcast by American network NBC in late November, on the night before Thanksgiving— one of most sought-after slots on American TV. The documentary was basically an elongated advertorial and featured Frost's interviews with the band intercut with footage of them on the *Spirits* tour and in the studio. The double album would be the band's last hurrah of the era, reaching #1 in America in January 1980 and selling in excess of two million copies in America and another 600,000 worldwide (peaking at #6 in the UK). After one week at the top in America, the album was replaced by Pink Floyd's album *The Wall*, which stayed at #1 for three months—a period when disco was definitively buried.

By February 1980, *Billboard* reported that American radio had adopted a 'virtual ban' on disco as a format. Barry called it 'evil' and 'censorship'. 'A segment of the industry wanted to shed the whole disco movement, and we were the heads they put on a stick,' he said. It was also increasingly apparent that the mood of pop culture, and the general public at large, had turned against them. They were becoming less a band and more a punch line, the butt of endless comedy sketches— the falsetto, the white outfits, hairy chests, big teeth, and medallions all mercilessly sent up. In the UK, a gang of comedians calling themselves The Hee Bee Gee Bees released a parody song called 'Meaningless Songs (In Very High Voices)', while *Saturday Night Fever* was spoofed in the hit American comedy film *Airplane!*

Barry tried to protest that The Bee Gees were more than just a disco act, but it was no use: they were irredeemably typecast. '*Saturday Night Fever* became our albatross,' said Maurice. 'Before the film we were called blue-eyed soul but after we were Kings of Disco. "How Deep" was an R&B ballad but after the film came out it was a disco ballad. The *Fever* period was such a saturation that people got bored with us.' Robin was equally pragmatic. 'The public had OD'd,' he said.

The group who had scored more US #1s during the 1970s than any other (nine, with their nearest rivals, Elton John and Stevie Wonder, stuck at five each), spent more weeks at #1 in America than any other act (twenty-seven, ahead of Rod Stewart and Paul McCartney), and who had written five of the ten best-selling singles of the decade ('Stayin' Alive', 'Night Fever', 'How Deep Is Your Love', 'I Just Want To Be Your Everything', and 'Shadow Dancing') were now thrown onto the cultural bonfire like flotsam.

'It was almost like people were angry with us and it was more interesting to make fun of us than to actually try and understand or appreciate what we had actually done,' said Barry. 'It became trendy to laugh at us. *Saturday Night Fever* was such a really huge social phenomenon that it created an image for us that was out of control.'

It was rumoured that the band might split. 'It looks like we can't go on being The Bee Gees,' Barry said. He found it almost impossible to cope with the backlash against the band. 'Everyone hated us,' he said. 'It wasn't cool to even be seen with The Bee Gees.'

AFTERMATH

I WANT TO SEE THE BEE GEES WHERE
THEY ARE NOT MADE FUN OF. IT MAY
NEVER HAPPEN BUT I AM PREPARED
FOR THE FIGHT.

The production team of Gibb-Galuten-Richardson began work with Barbra Streisand in March 1980, recording in Los Angeles and at The Bee Gees' own studio in Miami Beach, newly completed and named Middle Ear. 'Basically, she became The Bee Gees,' said Barry. 'A different instrument to play with.'

A first single from the project, 'Woman In Love', continued the phenomenal streak Barry was on as a writer/producer. Released in August 1980, it went to #1 on the American charts and stayed there for three weeks, selling two and a half million copies. The single also went to #1 in the UK (where it sold over half a million copies on the way to becoming one of the Top 30 best-selling singles of all time in the country), Australia, Canada, and across Europe, in Germany, Spain, and France (where it sold over a million copies to become one of the Top 30 best-selling singles of all time in that country, too). In total, 'Woman In Love' sold five million copies worldwide, becoming

Streisand's biggest international hit. It would win another Ivor Novello for Barry and Robin (who had written the song), picking up the 'Best Song Musically and Lyrically' award in May 1981.

'We gave out best songs to other people to secure our reputation as songwriters,' said Robin. 'The ability and opportunity to write for other people was a saving grace for us.' Barry suggested the transformation from band to songwriters-for-hire had been his idea, with Maurice and Robin keener to continue The Bee Gees. 'Radio wouldn't touch us and we were censored,' said Barry. 'I had to convince my brothers: Stop trying to get on the radio, change course, because we're walking into a shit storm here,' he said. 'If we continue to make these kinds of [disco] records [as The Bee Gees], we're condemned with everyone else. Let's write for other people.'

The cover of the Streisand album, *Guilty*, predominantly featured a photograph of a groomed and bearded Barry in white silk shirt and slacks. He looked tanned and handsome, his eyes laughing as he hugs Streisand, who was also dressed in white. The photograph was a clear echo of the famous cover shot of *Saturday Night Fever*, and suggested this was Barry's album as much as Streisand's—a first solo album, and not on RSO but Columbia. It was to become Streisand's best-selling album ever, a phenomenal success: a #1 in America, the UK, and around the world, topping the charts in fifteen countries, with sales of over twenty million copies.

A second single from the album, the title track—a duet between Barry and Streisand—was an instant hit, peaking at #3 in the US. The only track on the album to be credited to all three Gibb brothers, the song would win a Grammy Award in 1981, but only for Barry and Streisand for 'Best Pop Vocal Performance'.

The award did little to ease the jealousies brewing again between the brothers. Maurice, Barry said, had 'reached the razor's edge'. Rehab had failed, and he'd been booted off a Concorde flight while drunk. Robin again felt his own work was being overlooked. The success of the Streisand project—a third single from the album, another duet between Barry and Streisand, 'What Kind Of Fool', reached #10 in America—had eclipsed his own production work. He and Blue Weaver had produced an album for RSO with soul singer Jimmy Ruffin, best known for his 1966 hit 'What Becomes Of The Broken Hearted'. The album had been cut in New York in late 1979, close to Robin's home in Long Island, where he was now living, alone, as a tax exile. The project had produced a hit single written by Robin and Weaver, 'Hold On (To My Love)', which put Ruffin back in the US Top 10 for the first time in over a decade and was also a Top 10 hit in the UK.

Stigwood had indicated that he wanted to slowly wind down his record company operations, but the Ruffin project was just one of many significant successes for RSO Records in 1980. The Gibb-Galuten-Richardson team had finally completing the stilted recording of Andy Gibb's third album, *After Dark*, and the lead single, from it, 'Desire', written by Barry, Robin, and Maurice, released in January 1980, was a major hit, peaking at #4 in America. The second single from the album, Barry's 'I Can't Help It', a duet between Andy and Olivia Newton-John, was also a hit, reaching US #12. Andy was not fit for touring or prolonged promotion, however; the album peaked at a disappointing #21 in the US charts and quickly disappeared. It did nothing in any other country.

Stigwood announced he would not be renewing Andy's contract with the label and could no longer manage him. In private, he tried to address Andy's cocaine addiction and behavioural problems. 'I tried and tried and tried and it broke my heart,' said Stigwood. 'He got devoured because he was the current celebrity.' RSO released a compilation album, *Andy Gibb's Greatest Hits,* in September 1980 and it faltered at #46 in the

US despite a new single included on the album, 'Time Is Time', written by Andy and Barry, peaking at #15.

In April 1980, RSO also released a live double album by Eric Clapton, *Just One Night*. The guitarist was now a chronic alcoholic and, he later confessed, suicidal. Since the huge success of *Slowhand* in 1977, Clapton had recorded two albums for Polydor that had sold well but not achieved anywhere close to the same impact, commercially or critically, as his 70s work on RSO. Although they had been involved in a legal dispute, now that Clapton's deal with Polydor was at an end, Stigwood was considering re-signing him to RSO. *Just One Night* proved to be a one-off, however. Recorded in Tokyo the previous year, the record did well for all parties, reaching #2 in the US and #3 in the UK. It was unclear if Stigwood had done Clapton a favour or if the album was a contractual obligation. Either way, Clapton entered rehab and signed a new long-term deal with Warner Bros Records soon after.

The other major hits for RSO in 1980 were both soundtrack albums. The most successful was the soundtrack to the teen musical film *Fame*—a box-office success that spawned a TV series and a stage musical. The album sold around the world, propelled by the title song, sung by the film's lead actor, Irene Cara, which went to #4 in the US charts and #1 in the UK. In March 1981, 'Fame' won the Academy Award for 'Best Original Song'. A second single from the soundtrack, 'Out Here On My Own', another Top 20 hit in America, was also nominated for an Oscar—the first time in history that two songs from one film were nominated in the same category. The film's score (essentially the soundtrack) also won the award for 'Best Original Score'. (Both the 'Fame' single and the film score also won Golden Globes.)

RSO had also secured the rights to the soundtrack to the *Star Wars* sequel *The Empire Strikes Back*, the highest-grossing film of 1980. Composed and conducted by John Williams and performed by the

London Symphony Orchestra at a cost of about $250,000, RSO released the film's original musical score as a double album. It was nominated in the same 'Best Original Score' category as *Fame* at the 1981 Oscars.

Like *Fame*, *The Empire Strikes Back* soundtrack album sold well around the world and had a significant shelf life and cultural impact.

Less successful for RSO was the soundtrack to a film Stigwood produced himself, *Times Square*. Released in October 1980, the film, about a group of female teenage runaways, had cost six million dollars to make. Stigwood had great hopes for it, calling the fifteen-year-old lead, Robin Johnson, 'the female John Travolta'. The soundtrack, another double album, featured new wave cuts from acts such as The Ramones, Talking Heads, Lou Reed, The Pretenders, and Patti Smith. The film bombed, grossing $1.4 million, and the soundtrack, while generating some media interest, sold poorly. (Thanks largely to its lesbian love theme, the film is now considered a cult classic.)

Stigwood backed away from business, spending time on his two luxury yachts, Sarina and Jezebel, the latter described as 'a floating fantasy' by the *New York Times*. Both were familiar sights in Bermuda's waters for many years. He lived on board, irritating taxmen around the world while hosting famously decadent parties. The Bee Gees wanted to axe him as their manager—a decision said to be driven by Barry and his legal advisers. Robin and Maurice were not aware of the detail, since they were deep, at the time, into all-consuming private problems.

In the summer of 1980, the independent audit of RSO Records that Barry had commissioned had reputedly revealed that The Bee Gees were owed sixteen million dollars in unpaid royalties. In October of that year, the band filed a lawsuit against Stigwood and Polygram seeking seventy-five million dollars from each, plus fifty million in punitive damages. The press reported the details greedily. The band's lawyers claimed that Stigwood had 'treated the group as his own Fort

Knox', 'failed to offer the Gibbs services to bona fide third-party record companies or publishing firms and did not solicit offers from such firms', and 'fraudulently failed and refused to account properly to the Gibbs for royalties and other income payable to them and concealed the fact that substantial sums were owing to the Gibbs'. The band wanted to the cancel their 'many and tangled' contracts with Stigwood and were demanding the return of their master recordings and copyrights.

Al Coury, president of RSO Records, told the press that this was a 'betrayal' of Stigwood, who said he was 'angry, dismayed and revolted' by the lawsuit. Stigwood filed a countersuit a few weeks later and asked for $310 million for libel, extortion, corporate defamation, and breach of contract. He said he wanted to 'see the truth is told and that those responsible for this travesty are made to account for the misconduct'. He reminded the band, via the press, that he had transformed them from penniless youths into multimillionaires. Referring to the song 'Grease', Stigwood's countersuit alleged, 'Barry Gibb has earned more than three million dollars for writing and producing the recording of that one song. That is, to the defendant's belief, the most money ever paid to anybody to write one song and produce a single record.'

Stigwood's lawyers debunked the idea RSO was withholding royalties from the band, suggesting the Gibbs' claims were merely a bargaining tool in an attempt to gain 'even more concessions' from Stigwood and RSO. 'What you're dealing with is a bunch of guys who are trying to renegotiate their contracts through the press,' Freddie Gershon told *Rolling Stone*. 'The Bee Gees have reached a certain point in their careers, and they're trying to capitalise on it and they're frustrated because, for the last year and half, Robert has refused to renegotiate. I don't believe that The Bee Gees believe in this lawsuit. Barry Gibb looked at me in the eye and said, We have to start with a high number, so we can negotiate down to a new deal.'

An out-of-court settlement was reached in May 1981, and The Bee Gees withdrew their lawsuit. 'The Bee Gees deeply regret the distress caused by allegations made ostensibly in their name,' an RSO press statement announced. 'The Bee Gees and Robert Stigwood are delighted to continue their immensely successful long-term association.'

'If you've been in the business long enough,' Gershon told the press, 'you know that all artists go through periods of temporary insanity. The Bee Gees started investigating the facts, and they realised it wasn't worth it to go through several years of litigation only to have a judge or jury tell them the same thing they found out themselves; that Robert Stigwood has always treated them fairly and correctly. I believe they were embarrassed to find that out, and they dropped the suit and went away with their tails between their legs.'

'They had some mad, bad attorney who ended up costing them a fortune,' Stigwood said. 'If they have some crook bending their ear and the whole world is at their feet, it's hard for them. So there are no recriminations; it happened and we're the best of friends.'

In August 1981, The Bee Gees put their side of the story forward, buying full-page ads in *Rolling Stone* and *Variety* to issue a hard-hitting statement, asserting that, firstly, they had never apologised to Stigwood and never would. As part of the settlement, they asserted, they had won increased advances and royalties for the two albums they still owed RSO, and after that would be free to sign to whomever they wanted. They claimed they had also improved the royalty rates on all the records they had made for RSO since 1975. 'Substantial arrears' in royalties, totalling millions, had also been paid to The Bee Gees, and further audits were taking place.

The statement went on to outline that Stigwood was no longer The Bee Gees' manager, and that RSO now had 'no say over or participation in' any future projects. The band also stated that their publishing deal with Stigwood's RSO company Abigail Music had been prohibitive and was now terminated, citing a draconian clause whereby RSO had sought to own their songs in perpetuity. The Bee Gees, the statement concluded, now owned the publishing rights to all their own songs dating back to 1967, with Stigwood still entitled to a modest sum but nothing like what he had been taking previously.

Stigwood shot back a rather tame response via an RSO statement. 'The press release issued by The Bee Gees is inconsistent with the terms of the settlement. Indeed, as was clearly understood, any settlement with The Bee Gees was conditional on a worldwide apology and without it no settlement would have been concluded.' The statement went on to describe the increase in The Bee Gees royalties as 'modest' and the settlement in terms of underpayment of recording and publishing royalties 'not material in the context of what they had earned'. There was no mention of the loss of the band's song publishing—the rights to which were worth tens of millions even at that time. That had been a major victory for the band, and Barry immediately began negotiating a new publishing deal with BMG for a new entity he formed, Gibb Brothers Music, which from now on controlled the publishing on all the songs written by himself, Robin, and Maurice from 1967 onward. He had no intention of appointing a new manager to replace Stigwood, and would now oversee the band's business affairs himself.

●

A new Bee Gees album, *Living Eyes*, was released by RSO in October 1981. It had been recorded at Middle Ear, with the band suggesting in the press they had cooked up a new sound, one that was an attempt to reintroduce the public to the 'the original Bee Gees'. Keen to distance themselves from their disco fame, Barry also kept the falsetto to a minimum.

The album was put together under great strain. On top of the antagonism between themselves and RSO, lurid details about Robin's private life were now being splashed all over the press. Accompanied by a private detective, he had broken into his own house in Surrey, convinced that Molly and her divorce attorney were having an affair and colluding to con him out of five million pounds. Molly went to the police. Robin said he had been forced to smash a window to gain entry because he did not have any keys. He told the *Daily Mirror* that he had found 'bombshell evidence' of the con and had passed the information on to the FBI and Scotland Yard. Molly said Robin's irrational behaviour was making life a misery for her and their two young children. There were reports he'd also been sending threatening letters to Molly as well as making threatening phone calls. She passed one such letter to the FBI in which Robin said he had hired a hit man to kill her. The press printed part of the letter, which read, 'I have taken out a contract. It is now a question of time.' The FBI wanted to speak to him.

During the process of recording the album, Barry had also fired Blue Weaver, Dennis Bryon, and Alan Kendall—the three musicians who had been crucial to the glorious 70s renaissance of The Bee Gees. Albhy Galuten had wanted to use only session men on the record. Bryon (who had recently asked Barry to be the best man at his wedding) and Weaver said they both received $150,000 severance payments. 'It was a recoupable advance on future earnings,' Bryon said. A bad atmosphere had permeated the whole project.

The album suffered from the backlash against disco and the band and sold fewer than 800,000 copies worldwide and failed to make the Top 40 in America or the UK. None of the singles taken from it fared better than the first, 'He's A Liar', which peaked at #30 in the US. The band heaped scorn on the lack of promotion and support offered up by

RSO. The label had now shed 80 percent of its employees, reducing its American staff from sixty to about twelve.

With RSO Records winding down, Stigwood hoped to continue the RSO film division. However, *The Fan*, a 1981 horror film staring Lauren Bacall, was a huge failure. It had cost almost nine million dollars to make and grossed only three million. Next, in 1982, he produced a sequel to *Grease*, *Grease 2*, with an eleven-million-dollar budget. Neither Travolta nor Newton-John had signed up for the movie, and it and the RSO-released soundtrack performed less well than expected. The film grossed only fifteen million dollars, and the soundtrack peaked at #71 on the US charts with the lead single, 'Back To School Again' by The Four Tops, also failing to break the Top 40. The film did however unearth a new star in Michelle Pfeiffer, proving Stigwood's appreciation for talent remained intact.

Stigwood's next project was another sequel, this time to *Saturday Night Fever*. He put twenty-two million dollars into *Staying Alive*, hiring *Rocky* star and writer Sylvester Stallone to write and direct the film. Norman Wexler was also hired to work on the script but would disown the movie upon seeing the final edit. Travolta resurrected the role of Tony Manero, now working tables in Manhattan while dreaming of making it as a dancer. 'I called it *Staying Awake*—it was ego gone mad,' said RSO Records boss Bill Oakes. 'It was shorter, five times more expensive, and not any good.'

Oakes put together the soundtrack for the movie. The Bee Gees supplied five new songs as their final obligation to RSO, with 'Stayin' Alive' used as the movie's theme tune. 'We gave 'em what we had and got out,' said Robin. 'It was a dreadful movie.' The film, released in 1983, confounded its critics—who were many—to gross sixty-five million dollars in America and almost ninety million worldwide, becoming one of the ten most successful films of the year. The lead single from the soundtrack album, The Bee Gees 'The Woman In You' was a modest success, reaching #24 in the US charts, while the soundtrack album reached #6 in the US and #14 in the UK, selling four and a half million copies worldwide.

It was the last significant release by RSO Records. The label closed its doors shortly thereafter, and its huge and rich back catalogue fell under the ownership of Polygram. Stigwood produced two more films before retiring and closing up all his operations. One was a forgettable comedy called *Young Lust*, while the other, an Australian war drama called *Gallipoli*, directed by Peter Weir and starring *Mad Max* star Mel Gibson, turned out be quite the opposite. It was a co-production with Rupert Murdoch, the pair having formed a film company to finance what was, at the time, the most expensive Australian movie ever made, at a cost of A$2.8 million. *Gallipoli* would be a major critical and commercial success, grossing twelve million dollars in Australia and almost six million in America.

Freddie Gershon recalled how, during the early 80s, he and Stigwood enjoyed a lifestyle of 'villas, jets, annual carnivals in Rio and Bahia, great yachts in the Caribbean sailing throughout the Mediterranean into North Africa, to the Pyramids to shoot locations with Mel Gibson, police escorts, private helicopters, hanging out backstage with Elton and Eric Clapton and Mae West'. Stigwood was, however, mostly to be found in Bermuda, having become close with Sir John Swan, the Premier of Bermuda from 1982 to 1995. 'He was a very good friend,' Swan said, 'not only to me but Bermuda as a whole.'

•

Barry moved his wife Linda and their three young children into a new luxury Miami mansion in Biscayne Bay. He also owned a thirty-six-hectare estate near London, part of a property portfolio that was said to be worth twenty million dollars. He continued to have success as a producer. In 1982, working again with Richardson and Galuten, he made an album at Middle Ear with soul veteran Dionne Warwick, one of the most successful singers in history. Her career had flagged in the 70s but been revitalised at Arista Records, where she'd been produced by Barry Manilow. Barry wrote all ten tracks on the Warwick album, six in collaboration with Maurice and Robin, three with Galuten. The standout was the lead single, 'Heartbreaker'. 'I cried my eyes out after we wrote it,' said Maurice. 'I drove home and thought, We should be doing this one.' Arista boss Clive Davis had wanted what Barry gave Streisand for Warwick—a slick, modern pop record. 'Heartbreaker' was a hit around the world, making the US Top 10 and reaching #2 in the UK. The album, also called *Heartbreaker*, sold three million copies worldwide and peaked at #3 in the UK. The Gibbs' distinctive voices were all over it.

Next came Kenny Rogers, the avuncular country & western star. He had recently signed to RCA Records, after a couple of misfiring albums on Liberty, and approached Barry about working with him on a new album. Again, much of the recording was done at Middle Ear, with the Barry, Richardson, and Galuten producing, but the project only came to life when Dolly Parton agreed to duet with Rogers on 'Islands In The Stream', a track written by Barry, Robin, and Maurice. Parton, a huge star on the country scene, had only recently broken through into the American mainstream following her starring role in 1980 smash hit film *9–5* and a #1 pop hit with the theme tune. Released as the album's lead single, 'Islands In The Stream' went to #1 in America, the country's best-selling single of 1983, selling over two million copies. It was also a hit around the world. 'She was the queen of country, he was the king,' said Maurice. The Rogers album, *Eyes That See In The Dark*, peaked at #6 in America, becoming his best-selling album of the decade.

Barry was rewarded for this hot streak when he signed a multimillion-dollar solo deal with MCA Records in 1983. His first album, *New Voyager*, was released in 1984. It had taken him nine months to record and was a giant flop, reaching only #72 in the US charts after a single, 'Shine Shine', faltered at #37 in the singles chart. Galuten had refused to work on the record, believing it a retrograde step. Barry recorded another solo album soon after, but it would never be released. He remained in demand as a producer and songwriter, however, agreeing to produce an album for superstar Diana Ross for RCA Records. Michael Jackson, now the world's biggest pop star following the release of his *Thriller* album—which had superseded *Fever* to become the best-selling record in history, spawning seven Top 10 singles—co-produced the album's title track and lead single, 'Eaten Alive'. He and Barry sang backing vocals on the song.

Jackson was now Godfather to one of Barry's children and would use Barry's Miami home as a hideout when he visited the city. 'He'd sit in the kitchen and watch the fans outside his hotel on TV, just giggling—Hee hee!,' Barry recalled. 'He lived upstairs for a while, right before his child-molestation trial. We never discussed the case. We would just sit around and write and get drunk. Michael liked wine—there were a few nights when he just went to sleep on the floor.'

The 'Eaten Alive' single was not a huge commercial success—surprisingly, considering who was involved in it—peaking at #77 in the American charts, but a second single from the Ross album, 'Chain Reaction', written by Barry, Maurice, and Robin, was. It went to #1 in the UK and Australia (peaking at #66 in the US) and helped the *Eaten Alive* album reach #11 in the UK, although its success in Europe was not matched in America, where it failed to break the Top 40. It would be Barry's final studio collaboration with Albhy Galuten.

There were rumours Barry was considering album projects with Neil Diamond and Julio Iglesias in 1986, but instead he decided to relaunch

The Bee Gees, signing a new record deal for the band with Warner Bros
Records. Robin, now thirty-six, was in reasonable shape. Like Barry, he
had attempted to get a solo career off the ground, signing to Polydor
in the UK, but his three solo albums had met with little acclaim or
success. His most recent had spawned a lone hit, 'Boys Do Fall In Love',
that peaked at #37 on the *Billboard* singles chart in 1985. His divorce
had been finalised—he'd grumbled in the press that the settlement had
cost him a million pounds and been sentenced to two weeks in jail
for breach of confidentiality but freed on appeal—and so had a long-
running custody battle that he claimed had prevented him from seeing
his children for six years and left him on the 'verge of madness'.

He had recently remarried. His new wife was Dwina Murphy,
twenty-two, whom he had met in the late 1970s. She was described
in the press as an 'erotic artist' who dabbled in art, books, acting, and
modelling. They had a young son together already and lived in an
imposing twelfth-century medieval mansion in Oxfordshire. It had a
heated swimming pool and tennis courts that would, bizarrely, soon be
converted in to a small-scale version of Stonehenge. Murphy had a long
interest in neo-druidism, a religion that promoted harmony with nature,
and was patroness of the druids. More interesting to the press was the
fact the couple talked about their sex lives candidly. Robin said Murphy
was bisexual and had a steady girlfriend. 'It turns me on to see her in bed
with other girls,' he said. 'I'm allowed to watch and join in as well.'

The Bee Gees told the press how thrilled they were to be back
together as a band to record their first album since *Living Eyes*.

'We work better as a team,' said Robin.

'We enjoy being The Bee Gees,' said Barry.

'When we get together and write, it's not like three individuals, it's
like one person in the room,' said Maurice.

Released in 1987, *E.S.P.* failed to trouble the American charts, and nor did any of its singles. Barry blamed the disco hangover for this lack of success in the country they had once ruled. 'We had material success but creatively nobody would take us seriously,' he said. 'The question was who was going to allow us to forget the *Fever* thing.'

The band's critical rehabilitation would begin in Europe. The album's lead single, 'You Win Again', written by Barry, Robin, and Maurice, caught fire, reaching #1 in the UK and across Europe, selling well over one million copies. Princess Diana called it her favourite single of the year. The *E.S.P* album would peak at #5 in the UK while reaching #1 in Germany, selling close to one and half million copies. The band was nominated for 'Best British Group' at the 1988 BRIT Awards and 'You Win Again' won them another Ivor Novello Award for 'Best Contemporary Song'. Despite this success, the old divisions and rancour quickly resurfaced. 'The band really began to fragment,' said Barry. 'Robin began to feel he should be singing more. "You Win Again" was just one too many hits with my voice. It stopped being three people all interested in one thing and became a "What about me?" syndrome.'

●

The sudden death of Andy Gibb in March 1988 forced The Bee Gees to revaluate.

Andy had just turned thirty. Soon after Stigwood dropped him, he had landed a prominent role as co-host of the popular Saturday-night American music show *Solid Gold*. He regularly sang on the show, performing covers of chart hits or duetting with star guests. He became more famous, however, due to a high-profile relationship with *Dallas* star Victoria Principal. She was eight years his senior, recently divorced, a former *Playboy* model with a party girl image and a string of famous boyfriends, including Frank Sinatra. Her role in the long-running, prime-time CBS series had made her one of the country's biggest TV stars, and she was shrewd, refusing to consent to CBS owning her non-*Dallas* endeavours.

Principal and Andy had become one of the hottest couples in Los Angeles, and there was endless drama for the tabloids to feed on, not least when Andy was rushed to hospital suffering from mysterious pains. They released a single, duetting on The Everly Brothers' track 'All I Have To Do Is Dream', which they performed together on *Solid Gold*. It peaked at #52 in America. They were always splitting up and getting back together. Principal said his behaviour was erratic and that he was becoming very, very thin—'Like a human skeleton,' he admitted. She threw him out in 1982. 'I told him he would have to choose between me and his problem,' she said, later saying that watching him destroy himself with drugs had been horrifying.

Andy suffered a very public nervous breakdown. According to his mum, Barbara, he was 'crying all day from the moment he woke'. 'I wanted to commit suicide,' he said. 'Nothing mattered after Victoria left.' He spent $1,000 a day on coke and stayed awake for two weeks, locked in his bedroom, failing to turn up for work on *Solid Gold*. He was fired, his reputation in tatters. There was a rumoured suicide attempt, and he ended up in psychiatric care in Santa Barbara. He came back to make the rounds of American chat shows, coming clean about his drug addiction and claiming rehabilitation—the usual 'too hell and back' stuff. He'd landed a last-chance starring role in the Tim Rice/Andrew Lloyd Webber musical *Joseph And The Amazing Technicolor Dreamcoat* on Broadway. 'Everyone's dream,' he said. But he was soon missing shows and was quickly fired. He spent the mid-80s peddling a schmaltzy nightclub act, picking up residencies in casinos and hotels in places such as Atlantic City, Lake Tahoe, and Las Vegas, as well as Sun City in South Africa. The act included Bee Gees covers and a Mills Brothers medley alongside his own hits. Sometimes he demanded drugs before he would go onstage.

In 1984, Andy was found unconscious in a New York hotel. In 1985, Barbara accompanied him during a stay at the Betty Ford Clinic in California, and he entered Alcoholics Anonymous. He found it difficult to accept he was no longer a star. He had, he said, at one time been making 'a couple of million a week'. Now he was broke, selling off jewellery to survive. In 1986 he earned under $10,000, and in 1987 he filed for bankruptcy. He had debts of over one million dollars and few assets.

Dennis Bryon, The Bee Gees' old drummer, was living with Andy in Los Angeles at the time, and had played drums with him on and off since 1984. Andy refused to come out of his room for gigs, he recalled, and there were 'unsavoury characters' at the house. 'After midnight, most nights, different women would sneak in and out through the basement,' he said. Twice in a month, Andy was rushed to hospital complaining of chest pains, convinced he was having a heart attack. Then, after a couple of days of detoxing in hospital, he'd come home and 'go at it again' said Bryon. After a prolonged period when Andy refused to leave his room or face anyone, Bryon kicked open the door. 'I didn't believe what I was seeing,' he said. 'Andy was sitting on his bed in his robe playing with a real Uzi. There was an almost empty bottle of vodka on the side table and rotting leftover food all over the place. His clothes were strewn everywhere, the room was complete disaster.'

'Get out,' Andy screamed.

He fired Bryon the next day. Three further spells in rehab followed. His family offered him an incentive to stay sober: if he did, he would be allowed to join The Bee Gees, and Barry would produce a new solo record. Andy moved back to Miami, recorded demos at Middle Ear, and lived on handouts. He appeared to be getting healthy, playing tennis with Barry and gaining his pilot's license.

Barry talked to Maurice and Robin about Andy joining The Bee Gees.

'Six months before his death, I campaigned to get him included,' he said. Barry said he was outvoted two-to-one, so instead he helped get Andy a solo deal with Island Records in the UK. Andy moved into a cottage on Robin's Oxfordshire estate, optimistic, he said, about making it 'big again'. But he was soon confessing to Robin the doubts that plagued him: did he have talent, or was he just trading on the family name?

Robin wondered if Andy was really cut out for the music business. Why didn't he pursue what he really wanted to do, which was to be a pilot? 'But he had this feeling he had to prove himself to us, which was a mistake,' Robin added.

Andy started to miss important appointments, refusing to leave the cottage or take telephone calls. 'His confidence was shot and he was afraid of the world and not succeeding,' said Robin. He has started drinking heavily again. 'He just went downhill so fast, he was in a terrible state of depression,' said Robin. He polished off bottle after bottle of vodka, and at one point fell and smashed his face against the wall, losing several teeth. 'I might as well be dead,' he told his mum. He argued with Maurice and Barry, who believed tough love was the answer. He was rushed to hospital with intense chest pains but discharged himself. A few weeks later, he felt the same pains and checked himself in to hospital again. He spent the night sedated and was found dead the next morning—the cause attributed to heart problems, exacerbated by cocaine use.

'It was the saddest, most desperate moment of my life,' said Barry. The inescapable fact for the Gibbs was that they had decided Andy's career for him. They had engineered his stardom. It had destroyed and now killed him.

The guilt was unbearable. Maurice hit the bottle. The press reported that Andy had been on a massive cocaine binge prior to his death, and that his mum had given him money for drugs. Father Hugh also began drinking heavily. 'He stopped living when Andy died,' said Barry. 'He used to hide behind his masculine persona. Mum was the backbone.' Hugh died four years later, aged seventy-six, and was buried next to Andy in LA. 'He willed it on himself in the end,' said Barry.

Two months after Andy's death, The Bee Gees performed live for the first time in almost a decade at Atlantic Records' fortieth-anniversary party at Madison Square Garden. They followed this with performances in the UK, at a charity gig at the Royal Albert Hall and at the celebrations for Nelson Mandela's seventieth birthday at Wembley Stadium. Andy's death, said Barry, had motivated them to grab life again. They finished a new album, *One*. The title track gave them their first US Top 10 hit in a decade, peaking at #7 in September 1989, selling 500,000 copies.

'I'm not about to accept that The Bee Gees popularity died with the disco craze in 1980,' said Barry, now forty-three. 'That music only represented two albums in our long career.' He explained how, for years, journalists had asked him how the group could carry on after 'the joke' of *Saturday Night Fever*. 'I want to see the Bee Gees where they are not made fun of; it may never happen but I am prepared for the fight,' he said, dismissing the band's image as 'disco wimps'. Of 'Stayin' Alive', he said, 'We'd like to dress it in a white suit and gold chains and set it on fire.'

The success of the 'One' single in America was disappointingly not replicated by the band's new album, which failed to make the American Top 40. Its highest chart position was in Germany, where it made #4, while it peaked at #29 in the UK. The band went back on tour, their first series of dates since the *Spirits* tour of 1979, and found they could still command sizeable crowds, playing 20,000-capacity venues in America, 50,000-capacity football stadiums in Germany, and sell-out concerts in Australia and Japan. In the UK, a concert at Wembley Arena was broadcast live on BBC Radio 1.

The bout of band activity continued with another new album in 1991, *High Civilization*, which sold 1.1 million worldwide. Although it was another flop in America—where they were still considered predominantly a disco-era act—the lead single, 'Secret Love', made #5 in the UK and #2 in Germany. The album concluded The Bee Gees' three-album commitment to Warners, and in a return to their roots the band signed a new deal with Polygram label Polydor, which repackaged the band's back catalogue.

Tales From The Brothers Gibb was an incredible seventy-plus song collection, spanning four decades, presented as a four-CD collection—one of the first ever 'boxed sets'. There was also a more affordable best-of album for Europe that peaked at #6 in the UK and sold over two million copies.

●

Personal problems continued to dog the band, however. Hugh died the day after what would have been Andy's birthday in 1992. Barry and Linda's fourth child was born prematurely and desperately ill. Their eldest son had started drinking and using heroin.

Robin's home was broken into, a forty-three-year-old stalker caught hiding in a wardrobe armed with camera, camcorder, rubber gloves, screwdriver, and Stanley knife. Robin and Dwina remained distant from the rest of the Gibb clan, pursuing druidism—she drove a Jaguar XJRS with the private number plate 'DRU1D'—and continuing to attract headlines. 'My wife cheats on me now,' Robin said, 'not with men. Yeah, she's gay. She's proud of it.'

Maurice's drinking was out of control. He'd been an alcoholic for fourteen years now. Life was often a haze, a blur. He admitted he was a nasty drunk, abusive, obnoxious, and belligerent. In 1991 he'd pulled a gun on his family at their seafront mansion in Miami's Biscayne Bay.

He'd been on a month-long brandy binge. 'The kids were scared to death,' his wife Yvonne said. His son was fifteen at the time. It was, Maurice said, a new 'rock bottom'. Afterwards he broke down, crying uncontrollably. 'I became that monster,' he said. He went into rehab and in 1992 told the BBC he was sober.

In 1993, the band delivered their first new album for Polydor, *Size Isn't Everything*, dedicating it to their father. Recording it had been testing, with fights between the brothers commonplace. They were largely divorced from one another now, living separate lives, able to operate only professionally. The album again flopped in America but sold 700,000 worldwide, and in the UK three singles from it all made the Top 30, with the most successful, 'For Whom The Bell Tolls', peaking at #3. A major revival beckoned in Europe, but a huge tour set for 1994 was postponed due to Barry's chronic arthritis and a newly diagnosed heart problem. There were also reports Maurice was back in rehab after being arrested for drink-driving. He would later admit that when he looked in the mirror all he saw was 'darkness'.

The band's rise in popularity in the UK continued apace, however. A new generation was introduced to their work when leading boy band Take That released a cover version of 'How Deep Is Your Love'. The single went to #1 in the UK and around Europe in 1996. The same year, the UK's second-biggest boy band, Boyzone, released a cover version of another Bee Gees song, 'Words', and that too went to #1 in the UK and around Europe. Even the country's hottest new rock'n'roll act, Oasis, were talking up The Bee Gees in the media, naming them as one of their favourite bands.

In February 1997, ahead of the release of a new album *Still Waters*, The Bee Gees re-emerged to perform a medley of their hits live at the BRIT Awards in London alongside Prince, Manic Street Preachers, and The Spice Girls. They were there to collect an award for 'Outstanding

Contribution To Music', which had been won by David Bowie the year previous. It was reported that 'To Love Somebody' had been played an astonishing four million times on the radio in the UK. The televised BRIT Awards brought the band squarely back into the mainstream and also rekindled their relationship with Stigwood, who was in the audience at the Earls Court Exhibition Centre for the ceremony. During the band's acceptance speech, Barry called him 'the greatest showman in world' and demanded, 'If you don't accept this alongside us tonight, we won't accept either. We love you.' Stigwood obliged. 'Be like The Bee Gees,' he said, 'and never give up.'

Stigwood was enjoying his own spectacular comeback and planning to launch a four-million-pound stage musical based on *Saturday Night Fever*. He persuaded the band to back the project that night. He was now based on the Isle of Wight, a sunny holiday island off the south coast of England, having given up on Bermuda in the early 90s, selling one of his yachts to John Paul Getty. He lived in opulence on the Isle of Man in the famous Barton Moor estate, once used by the Royal family. The historic Jacobean manor house had cost him £1.15m in late 1991, and he spent many years restoring the property and its extensive grounds.

After almost a decade of silence, he had re-emerged in 1993 to produce a new version of musical *Grease* on the London stage. The show took four million pounds in advance bookings and would run until 1999.

At the BRITs, he was basking in another successful comeback project, having produced a movie version of *Evita* starring Madonna. The film, released in December 1996, was a box-office smash, grossing $141 million worldwide. In January 1997 it had won multiple Golden Globe awards, including 'Best Film', 'Best Original Song', and 'Best Actress' for Madonna, and was nominated for five Oscars. Now, the sixty-four-year old Stigwood was frothing with ideas for the *Saturday Night Fever* musical, which was planned to open at the London Palladium in 1998.

The Bee Gees found Stigwood had lost none of his outlandish style—in London he stayed in a huge suite at the luxury five-star Claridge's in Mayfair and flew to and from the Isle of White by helicopter. The band were swept up in Stigwood's enthusiasm for the new musical, which would feature all the familiar songs plus Bee Gees hits such as 'Tragedy' and 'Nights On Broadway' that were not in the original movie. They agreed to Stigwood's request they write a new song for the show—a 'big ballad, if possible'. It was just like the old days.

The band's new album, *Still Waters*, released in March 1997, became their biggest hit in twenty years, selling five million copies worldwide, reaching #2 in the UK and Germany and #11 in America, where the band were also now finally being acknowledged for their catalogue of work and critically revaluated. In January they had won the 'International Artist Award' at the televised American Music Awards, and in May were inducted into the Rock and Roll Hall of Fame by Brian Wilson, a fan of their music, who called them 'Britain's first family of harmony', adding, 'Only Elvis Presley, The Beatles, Michael Jackson, Garth Brooks, and Paul McCartney have outsold The Bee Gees.' Maurice called the honour 'the pinnacle' of the band's career. The lead single from *Still Waters*, 'Alone', peaked at #28 in the US charts and was a hit throughout Europe, reaching #5 in the UK. The album spawned two more Top 20 UK singles. In America, rapper Wyclef Jean sampled 'Stayin' Alive' for a track called 'We Trying To Stay Alive' which went to #3 on the rap charts and made #13 in the UK.

'It seems that we've stopped being this camp joke and become genuine part of pop culture again,' said Barry. 'The media doesn't perceive us as being strange or silly any more. We feel we're into our third period of fame now.' Plans for a large scale American tour had to be abandoned, however, with Barry's arthritis to blame, an operation to fix degenerating discs in his spine having been unsuccessful. The pain was so bad, he said, that he struggled to walk, and he felt it might be impossible for him to ever tour again.

Instead, the band organised what they said would be their final ever concert: a pay-per-view gig televised by HBO at the 15,000-capacity MGM Grand Garden Arena in Las Vegas. The show featured thirty-two huge Gibb brother hits, including those made famous by Andy Gibb, Dolly Parton and Kenny Rogers, Diana Ross, and Barbra Streisand. There were guest-appearances by Céline Dion (singing a new song The Bee Gees had written for her, 'Immortality'), Frankie Valli, and Olivia Newton-John. A DVD of the gig, *One Night Only*, sold 1.7 million copies, while a live album of the concert sold five million copies, peaking at #4 in the UK. The band members were pictured on the cover recreating the famous Francesco Scavullo shot used on the cover of *Saturday Night Fever*.

Disco was also enjoying a critical resurgence; there was a 'new obsession with the 70s', said Barry. John Travolta, whose career had been on a long downward spiral, had recently been revitalised by hip director Quentin Tarantino, who cast him in his film *Pulp Fiction*. Tarantino spoke about his admiration for *Saturday Night Fever*. At Christie's in New York, the white three-piece polyester suit Travolta had worn in the film sold for $145,000, a price that smashed the previous record of $46,000 for Marilyn Monroe's dress from *There's No Business Like Showbusiness*. Today, the suit is valued at $200,000 and held in the world-famous Smithsonian Institution.

Two then-current films, *54* and *The Last Days Of Disco*, featured disco as their subject, while *Carlito's Way*, starring Al Pacino, had its lead character living above a disco and a disco soundtrack. Disco music was now being discussed as having had the same cultural resonance as punk. 'It's easy to say it's superfluous because it's disco,' said Nile Rodgers.

'These songs are powerful; they tell a story ... "More Than A Woman", "You Should Be Dancing", and "Disco Inferno", that's serious stuff. That's just as relevant and as valid—and I know people don't like to hear this stuff—as when the Sex Pistols or Pink Floyd or The Beatles are delivering a message. This is politically, socially relevant stuff, and it's just a reflection of the times.' For punk historian Jon Savage, 'the hedonism propagated by disco was more immediately subversive of established morality' than punk.

British boy band 911 released a cover version of 'More Than A Woman' that went to #2 in the UK, while manufactured pop act Steps went one better, taking their version of 'Tragedy' to #1. Madonna, Elton John, and George Michael all heaped praise on The Bee Gees. In America, in early 1998, a *Saturday Night Fever* reunion concert was a sell-out at New York's Madison Square Garden. The Bee Gees were persuaded onto the stage to perform their hits from the film alongside Yvonne Elliman, KC & The Sunshine Band, Tavares, Kool & The Gang, and The Trammps.

At the press launch for Stigwood's *Saturday Night Fever* musical in London, Barry said, 'The 70s are so popular again ... still part of everyone's hearts and minds.' Maurice called 'Stayin' Alive' the 'national anthem of the 70s'; it was a song, Robin added, that could instantly conjure an image in your mind.

Stigwood was full of praise for The Bee Gees. 'They will go down in history as one of the finest composers, lyricists and arrangers,' he said. 'They will be referred to as some kind of Mozart in today's history.' In adapting the film for the stage, he had made it suitable for all the family, with no foul language, drug use, or violence against women. The Gibbs had given him 'Immortality', recorded by Céline Dion, for the show. She was the biggest female star of the moment, having just scored two albums that sold in excess of thirty million copies each, while her 'My Heart Will Go On' was one of the best-selling singles of all time.

'Immortality' went to #5 in the UK—a useful piece of promotion for the new *Saturday Night Fever* West End show, which took four million pounds in advance bookings. At the opening night, in May 1998, The Bee Gees mixed with the Duchess of York and ABBA and saw the show receive a standing ovation. It would run for a further two years in London. At a cost of six and a half million dollars, the show transferred to Broadway in 1999, selling twenty million dollars of advance tickets and running for 501 shows.

Stigwood was showered with praise for the success of the musical. Sir Cameron Mackintosh—the man behind hit musicals such as *Miss Saigon*, *The Phantom Of The Opera*, *Les Misérables*, and *Cats*, and described as 'the most successful, influential and powerful theatrical producer in the world' by the *New York Times*—had started his career as an assistant stage manager on Stigwood's London production of *Hair* in the late 60s, and he and Stigwood had remained pals, investing in a racehorse together as part of syndicate that also included Lord Delfont and Andrew Lloyd Webber. Mackintosh said Stigwood was 'the first to understand how to take a musical and duplicate it around the world'. Sir Andrew Lloyd Webber, who had written *Cats* and *The Phantom* said, 'I get terribly annoyed when people say it was Cameron or me who invented the global approach to musicals. It wasn't. Robert taught us all how to do it.'

●

The Bee Gees reneged on the promise that the Las Vegas show would be their final ever concert and performed a series of One Night Only events during 1998 and 1999. The well-spaced shows suited Barry's health and were also hugely lucrative. It had recently been revealed the Gibbs were among the high-profile music names that the British government had investigated over non-payment of taxes. Barry and Maurice were asked to pay three million pounds as a settlement, while Robin was asked to pay a whopping eighteen million pounds. The One Night Only gigs attracted huge audiences around the world: 56,000 at Wembley Stadium, 72,000 at Sydney's Olympic Stadium, 42,000 in Buenos Aires, and 61,000 in Auckland.

A new album, *This Is Where I Came In*, was ready by 2001. It continued the revitalisation of The Bee Gees as band and brand, peaking at #16 in America and #6 in the UK and reaching the Top 10 in Canada and Germany. The album spawned a popular single, the title track, which reached #18 in the UK. Their work continued to provide inspiration to others. American girl group Destiny's Child took a version of the Barry and Robin song 'Emotion' (a hit for Samantha Sang in 1978) to #3 in the UK and #10 in America. One of the band's singers, Beyoncé Knowles, spoke about her love of The Bee Gees. Steps reached #2 in the UK with their second cover version of a Gibbs song, this time, 'Chain Reaction'.

At the end of 2001, another Bee Gees compilation album, *Their Greatest Hits: The Record*, was released, selling over three million copies worldwide, with almost a third of those sales in UK, where the album hit #5 in the charts. The brothers, who had been awarded CBEs in the New Year's Honours list, appeared to be the closest they had been for years. Barry said they were contented and had finally stopped hurting one another. In Miami, Robin said he had bought a home next door but one to Barry, who now lived in an even bigger, more extravagant mansion on Miami Beach's 'Millionaire Row' with a full-size basketball court and giant fountain out front. 'Maurice,' Robin said, 'lives just down the street'—three blocks away in a new home he'd bought for $7.1 million. In England, their houses were only fifty miles apart.

It was a surprise then when Barry said The Bee Gees were taking a break 'to find ourselves as individuals' with Robin going to work on a solo album and Barry writing new songs with his old friend Michael Jackson. There had been another major disagreement between the brothers, this time resulting from Barry's handling of the band's business affairs. He had severed ties with British lawyer Michael Eaton, who had represented the band for more than thirty years, and hired John Branca, a high-profile Hollywood music business lawyer, to represent the band. Barry hoped Branca would help him regain ownership of The Bee Gees' master recordings and allowed him to also begin negotiating a new publishing deal for the band's catalogue of songs. Branca had convinced Barry there was big money in syncing, in ring tones, computer games, movies, and TV. Maurice and Robin had rebelled and refused to work with Branca, saying they were happy to continue their relationship with Eaton.

Barry was angry; he had assured Branca he would be getting all three brothers. Although it was complicated, he decided to let Branca make a separate publishing deal for his share of the Bee Gees songs he'd written. The *New York Times* estimated the value of Barry's share of the band's song catalogue at sixty million dollars. Barry signed a new publishing deal with Warner/Chappell Music, while Maurice and Robin stayed with BMG. Barry continued to work with Branca in his attempts to regain ownership of The Bee Gees' master recordings, which had passed from RSO to Polygram. He said he was the only band member motivated to do so. 'That was disturbing and distressing, and that's one of the reasons we didn't get along very well in the end. Because I had to do this on my own.'

●

On January 12 2003, Maurice died. He was fifty-three. It happened unexpectedly and suddenly. Having collapsed at home, he'd been rushed to hospital where, after suffering a heart attack, doctors performed surgery on an intestinal blockage. They found part of his intestine to be gangrenous and also removed some of his stomach. It was believed he'd had an undiagnosed twisted intestine from birth. Maurice slipped into a coma and died. He was suffering from emphysema and heart disease, his body weakened by what he had put it through, chiefly a lifetime of hard drinking and smoking. Barry was too upset to attend the funeral held in Miami, where Robin spoke on behalf of the family. Barry paid his respects privately while accompanied by Michael Jackson. 'There were too many bad times and not enough good times,' he said. 'There was so much more to us, but we didn't see it. There was so much more life in us that we didn't attempt, so much neurosis that we could have avoided between us all because everyone wanted to be the individual star. And we never knew what we were.'

A month after Maurice's death, The Bee Gees were handed the 'Legend Award' at the televised Grammy Awards, held at Madison Square Garden in New York. The award had previously been given to stars such as Elton John and Michael Jackson. 'The Bee Gees will not stop here,' Barry said. '[We] will not disintegrate because we've lost Mo. It means we will go on and make another album.' Barry and Robin could find little common ground after that, however, and soon decided to 'retire' the band. They released a compilation album, *Number Ones*, in 2004, as a tribute to Maurice. It sold over a million copies, but a planned tribute concert to their brother was abandoned, with Barry and Robin disagreeing over details. 'The distance between us became more and more dramatic,' said Barry.

In 2005, Barry reunited with Barbra Streisand to produce *Guilty Too*, the cover photograph recreating their pose from the 1980 *Guilty* record. Barry had written all the songs on the album, chiefly in collaboration with his sons, Ashley and Stephen. He also provided backing vocals and duetted with Streisand on two tracks. *Guilty Too* made #5 in America and #3 in the UK, selling well around the world. Stigwood was moved to call Barry 'one of the great composers of all time'.

Barry's decision to work with Branca toward regaining ownership of the band's master recordings was vindicated when, in 2006, he signed an exclusive agreement with Warner Music subsidiary Rhino Entertainment for the band's entire catalogue from 1965 to 2001. He admitted that his decision to allow Branca to split the group's publishing had been a mistake, however: the result, he said, of a 'mid-life crisis'. He fixed this, and the Gibb Brothers Music publishing company was reassigned as a whole to Universal, which had recently acquired BMG. The brothers' song catalogue was said to be worth around $150 million, and was generating an annual income for Barry alone of $5 million. Even Robin could not keep track of the chart successes of their many songs: the band's own endless hits around the world and the scores of other hits from among the 2,500 acts who had recorded cover versions of the Gibb brother songs—'How Deep Is Your Love', for example, had been recorded more than 400 times! In the *Sunday Times* Rich List, both Robin and Barry were said to be worth £110 million.

They performed old Bee Gees songs together intermittently, chiefly for charity, but also for huge TV shows such as *American Idol* in 2007—the year Barry acted as a mentor on the show. There was talk of a comeback as The Bee Gees and a band biopic, directed by Steven Spielberg. Nothing happened. Robin tried to resurrect his solo career, but after an album of Christmas songs failed to chart, a new album of original songs lay unreleased. He continued with his charity efforts, performing live occasionally, hitting the headlines in 2008 with more revelations emerging about his private life. His thirty-three-year-old housekeeper, Claire Yang, had given birth to his daughter. It was claimed that his wife Dwina had converted to the Brahma Kumaris movement and was committed to sexual abstinence, and that Robin had been having an affair with Yang for the past eight years.

In 2010, Robin landed a role as mentor on the Australian version of *X Factor*, but the sixty-one-year-old was plagued by health problems. Suffering from abdominal pains, he had surgery on a blocked intestine, and after a series of further illnesses he was diagnosed with colon and liver cancer in 2011. He appeared drawn and thin and was deeply depressed. In an interview with the *NME* he said he wondered 'if all the tragedies my family has suffered is a karmic price we are paying for the fame and fortune we've had'. He added that he wanted to get back with Barry and make an album.

After undergoing chemotherapy, Robin's cancer went into remission. 'It's gone,' he told the press. 'They can't see it no more. I've done it.' He began planning an ambitious new project: a performance at the Royal Albert Hall of an orchestral score, *The Titanic Requiem*, which he had written in collaboration with his son, Robin-John. The Royal Philharmonic Orchestra had recorded the score, and the show was planned for April 2012, to commemorate the one hundredth anniversary of the sinking of the Titanic.

In March, a month before the show, Robin went to hospital for intestinal surgery, contracted pneumonia, and went into coma. Barry visited his bedside and sang him a song. The pair had not spoken for a year. 'We functioned musically but we never functioned in any other way,' Barry said. 'We were brothers but we weren't really friends.' All his life, Barry said, Robin had been desperate for hit records, always chasing the next big hit. When Robin emerged briefly from the coma, Barry told Robin he loved him and to stop worrying: their childhood dream had come true. Robin never left hospital. He died on May 20 of liver and kidney failure. He was sixty-two.

Roger Daltrey led the tributes. 'To me,' he said, 'singing is about moving people, and Robin's voice had something about it that could move me and, I'm sure, millions of others. It was almost like his heart was on the outside.' Robin had been an ardent New Labour supporter and close friend of former British Prime Minister Tony Blair, who had holidayed at Robin's Miami mansion. 'Robin was not only an exceptional and extraordinary musician and songwriter,' Blair said, 'he was a highly intelligent, interesting, and committed human being. He was a great friend with a wonderful open and fertile mind and a student of history and politics.'

Barry delivered the eulogy at Robin's funeral. 'Even right up to the end we found conflict with each other,' he said. 'If there's conflict in your lives—get rid of it … my greatest regret is that every brother I've lost was in a moment we were not getting on. I've lost all of my brothers without being friends with them.' He talked about the strong connection Robin had shared with Maurice. 'They were both beautiful,' he said, 'and now they're together. I think the greatest pain for Robin in the past ten years was losing his twin brother, and I think it did all kinds of things to him.'

●

In 2013, the *Saturday Night Fever* soundtrack album—which by then had sold approximately forty million copies worldwide, making it the seventh best-selling album of all time—was added to the National Recording Registry in the Library of Congress on the basis of its cultural significance. Barry, who was now a US citizen, set off on a sixteen-date Mythology world tour, named after a recent lavish four-disc boxed-set career overview of the Gibb brothers, with a disc each focusing on the work of one of the four brothers. Barry, now sixty-seven, had put together a band that included his son Stephen on guitar and Maurice's daughter Samantha, who sang onstage with him. The set list would cover the whole of the band's career, and appropriately the tour began in Australia, where he played to 25,000 at the Rod Laver Arena in Melbourne. The tour had a relaxed schedule, taking in arena shows in England in 2013 and six American dates in 2014, climaxing with a gig at the 17,500-capacity Hollywood Bowl in Los Angeles. Barry said he just wanted to keep his family's music alive. 'That's my job now,' he said. 'Before my brothers died, I wouldn't have thought of it that way. It's important that people remember these songs.'

Robert Stigwood died in January 2016, aged eighty-one. Although no official cause of death was given, he had been in poor health since a bungled hip operation in 2004. He had retreated to his Isle of Wight mansion following the success of the *Saturday Night Fever* musical and had seldom been seen since. 'When his wealth became so gargantuan, his success so tediously predictable, the ennui set in,' said Freddie Gershon. 'Sadly, it never left.'

In 2006, aged seventy-two, he'd sold the mansion (which sold again in 2009 for a reported nine million pounds) and moved to a smaller villa in the south of France. That same year he'd made a rare public appearance at the Ivor Novello Awards in London to see The Bee Gees handed the 'Academy Fellowship' award, a huge honour among songwriters and composers—only fifteen others, including Paul McCartney, Andrew Lloyd Webber, and Elton John, had been granted it during the academy's sixty-year history. In his acceptance speech Barry described Stigwood as 'the man who turned our whole industry upside down'.

In France, Stigwood refused all interviews and grew frail. The British news media frequently ranked him as one of the wealthiest people in showbusiness, with a fortune of approximately £200 million. In 2014, he'd set up the Robert Stigwood Fellowship Programme to support the development of artists and music-industry entrepreneurs in Adelaide and South Australia. Just prior to his death, he had been inducted into the South Australian Hall of Fame at a ceremony in Australia House in London. After a lengthy tribute, he was hoisted out of his wheelchair, walked unsteadily to the podium and gave a rambling acceptance speech, sharing the credit for his success with the 'wonderful people who helped me on my journey', naming Beryl Vertue as a 'real gem'.

His death was made public in a statement by Robin's son Spencer Gibb, to whom Stigwood was godfather. Spencer called Stigwood 'a creative genius' and the 'driving force behind The Bee Gees' career' and thanked him for his 'kindness to me over the years as well as his mentorship to my family'.

'He was the last, in my view, of the great, great showmen,' Sir Andrew Lloyd Webber told the BBC. 'His enthusiasm for music, and success in music, was unequalled.'

Pete Townshend wrote a touching eulogy, revealing he and Stigwood had been talking in recent years 'about a possible remake, maybe using animation' of *Tommy*. 'There is no question The Bee Gees were his master stroke,' he added, 'a complex band of brothers each immensely talented in his own way.'

'Robert changed the world and only for the better and he was certainly important to my career,' John Travolta said. 'His legacy lives on and he will forever be remembered.'

Barry issued a statement full of praise for the man he called 'an enigma'. In it, he said, 'All the success we had was because of Robert Stigwood.'

Six months later, in August 2016, Barbara Gibb died from natural causes at her home in Miami. She was aged ninety-five and had recently suffered a mild stroke. Affectionately known as 'the rock', she had always been the heart of the Gibb family, a strong, proud Mancunian woman. Whenever Barry had felt the grief at the loss of his brothers becoming overwhelming, he had sought comfort in her strength.

'I know it's worse for her than it is for me,' he said.

'I do my crying at night,' she had said. 'During the day you have to carry on. You have to be strong for the family.'

Concerns for his mother's health had forced Barry to withdraw from playing the Sunday afternoon legends slot at Glastonbury festival in June, unable to commit to delivering a full set. He did, however, make a surprise appearance at the festival climax to sing two tracks—'To Love Somebody' and 'Stayin' Alive'—with headliners Coldplay in front of eighty thousand people.

In October, he released a new solo album, only the second of his career. *In The Now* featured songs written with his sons Ashley and Stephen and made #2 in UK. It sold over half a million copies and was a hit in Australia and across Europe, peaking at #63 in America. It was well received critically, and the seventy-year-old appeared healthy and happy during promotional appearances.

He also continued to take care of business, and in December 2016 was able to announce he had signed The Bee Gees' back catalogue of master recordings to Universal's Capitol Records, a record label Barry said was 'associated with the greatest artists of all time', among them Frank Sinatra, The Beatles, and The Beach Boys. The long-term, worldwide agreement covered the band's entire catalogue—all twenty-two studio albums, plus various compilations, unreleased recordings, and several soundtracks, including *Saturday Night Fever*.

Capitol promised numerous sales and marketing campaigns aimed at breathing new life into the catalogue. *Variety* and *Billboard*, reporting on the deal, reeled off a few of the band's achievements: 220 million records sold, nine American #1s, fourteen other Top 10 hits, eight Grammy awards, five American Music Awards, a BRIT Award for 'Outstanding Contribution to Music' and a 'Legend Award' from the World Music Awards. They had also been inducted into the Rock and Roll Hall of

Fame, the Songwriters Hall of Fame, the Vocal Group Hall of Fame, and the Dance Music Hall of Fame. Capitol Music Group chairman and CEO Steve Barnett called the catalogue 'one of the most esteemed and important bodies of work in the history of recorded music'. The newly knighted Universal Music Group chairman and CEO Lucian Grainge, often named as the most powerful man in the music industry, said, 'There are few artists in history who have created a body of work so successful, diverse and timeless as Barry, Robin, and Maurice.'

'The whole family is overwhelmed by this new agreement,' Barry said, adding how he wished his brothers were here to share the good news with them. 'I will never forget my brothers,' he said. 'They will always be a part of everything I do.'

NOTES AND SOURCES

The text in this book is based on extensive research, interviews and published accounts. Any reconstructed dialogue does not represent the exact words used by the characters at the time but captures the flavour of the discussions. The occasional conversion of historic cash figures into their current worth was done via thisismoney. co.uk and, for the dollar, measuringworth.com.

The author interviewed Nik Cohn at length for Andrew Loog Oldham's memoirs *Stoned* and *2Stoned* and subsequently organised for a Christmas story written by Cohn to be published in a UK magazine. Pete Townshend and Chris Hutchins (RSO employee and, briefly, Robin Gibb's manager) were also originally interviewed for *Stoned* and *2Stoned*. Interviews with Tu Sweet ('The True Story Of Saturday Night', 2015] and Pete Townshend ('On Pinball Wizard—Pt. 1', 2005) are available on YouTube.

Although not a comprehensive list, the following newspaper and magazine articles were particularly useful: 'Tribal Rites Of The New Saturday Night', *New York*, June 1976; 'Nik Cohn's Fever Dream', *New York Times*, December 2011; 'Fever Pitch', *Vanity Fair*, August 2013; 'Mr Saturday Night', *Independent*, May 1998; 'The Heart of Saturday Night', *Mojo*, May 2007; 'Saturday Night's Big Bang', *New York*, December 1997; 'The Legend Of Saturday Night', *Nerve*, 2005; 'Disco's Saturday Night Fiction', *Observer*, June 2016; 'Saturday Night Fever: The Life', *New York Times*, June 1996; 'How Can You Mend A Broken Group?', *Rolling Stone*, July 1977; 'Barry Gibb: The Last Brother', *Rolling Stone*, July 2014; 'The Night Disco Died', *Chicago Tribune*, July 2016; 'Fever Pitch', *Guardian*, September 1994.

A variety of other magazines and newspapers were used as source material. These included *Billboard*, the *Evening Standard*, *Playboy*, *Crawdaddy*, *NME*, *Melody Maker*, the *LA Times*, the *Daily Mirror*, *Sounds*, *Village Voice*, *The Wire*, *Time*, *Newsweek*, *Entertainment Weekly*, the *Daily Express*, *LIFE*, *People*, *Creem*, and *Variety*. An interview with Robert Stigwood by Simon Fanshawe published in 2006 (simonfanshawe.com) was also useful.

The author comprehensively researched all the available music, videos, TV appearances, TV specials, films, and documentaries relating to The Bee Gees and *Saturday Night Fever*. The following books were invaluable regarding research into disco as a musical genre: *Stayin' Alive: The 1970s And The Last Days Of The Working Class* by Jefferson Cowie (The New Press, 2010); *Hot Stuff: Disco And The Remaking of American Culture* by Alice Echols (WW Norton, 2010); *The Last Party: Studio 54, Disco, And The Culture of the Night* by Anthony Haden-Guest (William Morrow, 1997); *Saturday Night Fever Forever: The Story Of Disco* by Alan Jones and Jussi Kantonen (Mainstream, 1999); *Turn The Beat Around: The Secret History Of Disco* by Peter Shapiro (Faber & Faber, 2009); and *Love Saves The Day: A History Of American Dance Music Culture, 1970–1979* by Tim Lawrence (Duke University Press, 2004). The books by Haden-Guest and Shapiro carried useful quotes relating to The Bee Gees from Freddie Gershon and Nile Rodgers respectively.

Further general background colour was provided by the following books: *Eric Clapton: The Autobiography* (Century, 2007); *King Of Cool: John Travolta* by Wesley Clarkson (John Blake, 2005); *Ball The Wall: Nik Cohn In The Age Of Rock* (Picador, 1989); *Cats On A Chandelier: The Andrew Lloyd Webber Story* by Michael Coveney (Hutchinson, 1999); *Sweetie Baby Cookie Honey* by Freddie Gershon (HarperCollins, 1988); *Party Animals: A Hollywood Tale Of Sex, Drugs And Rock 'N' Roll Starring The Fabulous Allan Carr* by Robert Hofler (Da Capo, 2010);

Lulu: I Don't Want To Fight (Sphere, 2010); *Black Vinyl White Powder* by Simon Napier-Bell (Ebury, 2001); *Behind The Smile: My Autobiography* by Paul Nicholas (Andre Deutsch, 1999); *Stoned* by Andrew Loog Oldham (Vintage, 2001); *Moguls: Inside The Business Of Show Business* by Michael Pye (Holt, Rinehart and Winston, 1990); *Oh, What A Circus: The Autobiography* by Tim Rice (Hodder & Stoughton, 1999); and *Motherless Child: The Definitive Biography Of Eric Clapton* by Paul Scott (Headline, 2005). The chapter on Stigwood in the Pye book was particularly rewarding.

Regarding previous books on The Bee Gees, the author read them all: *Tragedy: The Ballad Of The Bee Gees* by Jeff Apter (Jawbone, 2016); *You Should Be Dancing: My Life With The Bee Gees* by Dennis Bryon (ECW, 2015); *Tales Of The Brothers Gibb: The Ultimate Biography Of The Bee Gees* by Melinda Bilyeu, Hector Cook, and Andrew Mon Hughes (Omnibus, 2001); *Bee Gees, The Authorized Biography* by Barry, Robin, and Maurice Gibb with David Leaf (Octopus, 1979); *The Bee Gees: The Biography* by David Meyer (Da Capo, 2013); *The Bee Gees* by Larry Pryce (Panther, 1979); *Bee Gees: The Day-By-Day Story, 1945–1972* by Andrew Sandoval (RetroFuture, 2012); *Rock 'n Pop Stars: The Bee Gees* by Craig Schumacher (Creative Education, 1979); *Treasures Of The Bee Gees* by Brian Southall (Carlton, 2011); *The Bee Gees* by Kim Stevens (Scholastic, 1978); and *The Incredible Bee Gees* by Dick Tatham (Futurama, 1979). The Bryon book and interviews with Blue Weaver and Albhy Galuten in the Bilyeu, Cook, and Mon Hughes book were especially illuminating.

The author would like to thank Kevin Pocklington at Jenny Brown Associates, Tom Seabrook at Jawbone, and Andrew Oldham for introducing him to Nik Cohn and Robert Stigwood.

INDEX